METROLAB
RESEARCH | DEVELOPMENT | SERVICE

I0807434

Metropolitan Design as a New Discipline

Roland Krebs
Stefan Mayr
Cédric Ramière
Claudia Staubmann
(eds.)

jovis

DIALOGUE

LOCAL ACTION

Metropolitan Areas Worldwide

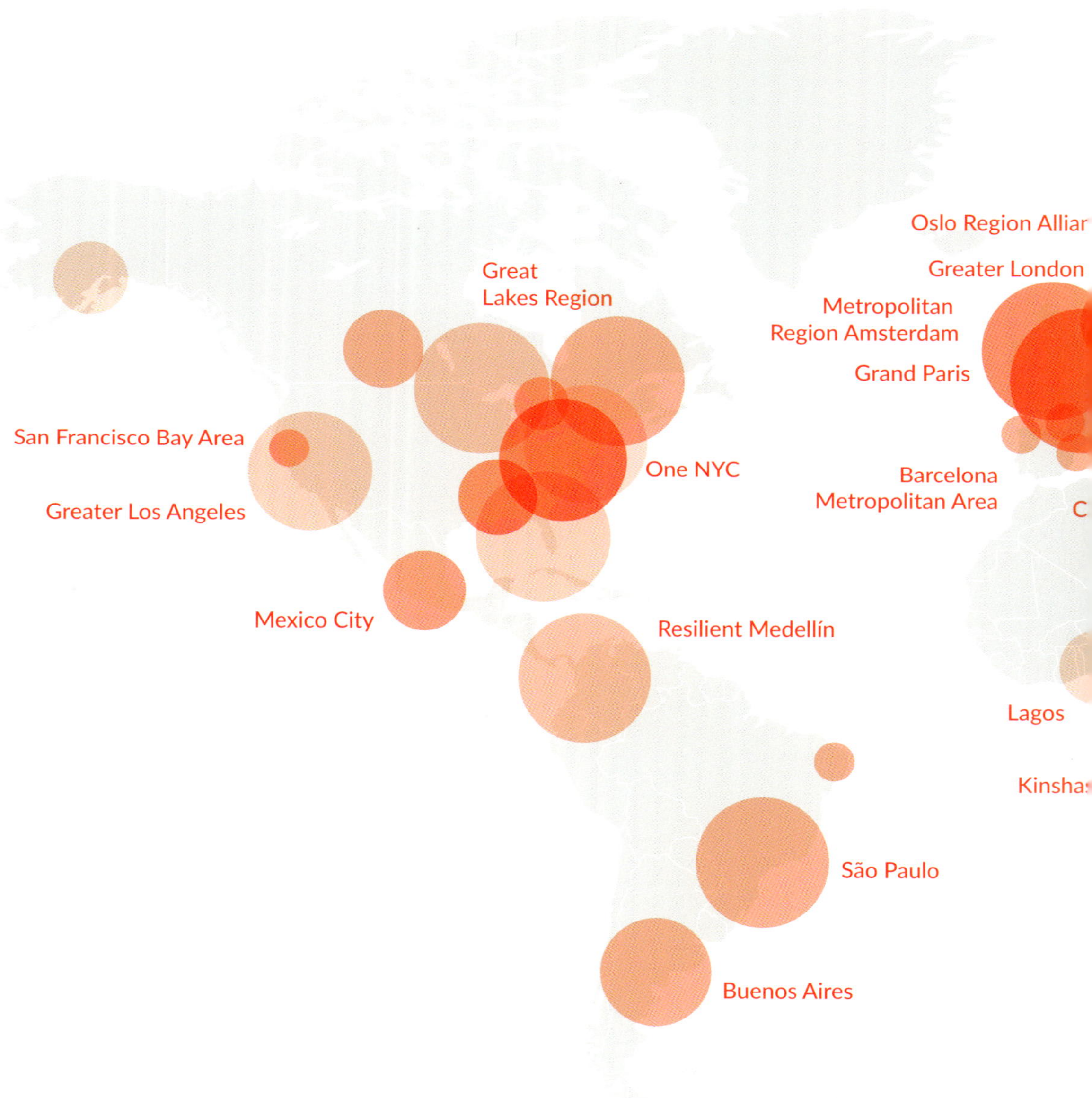

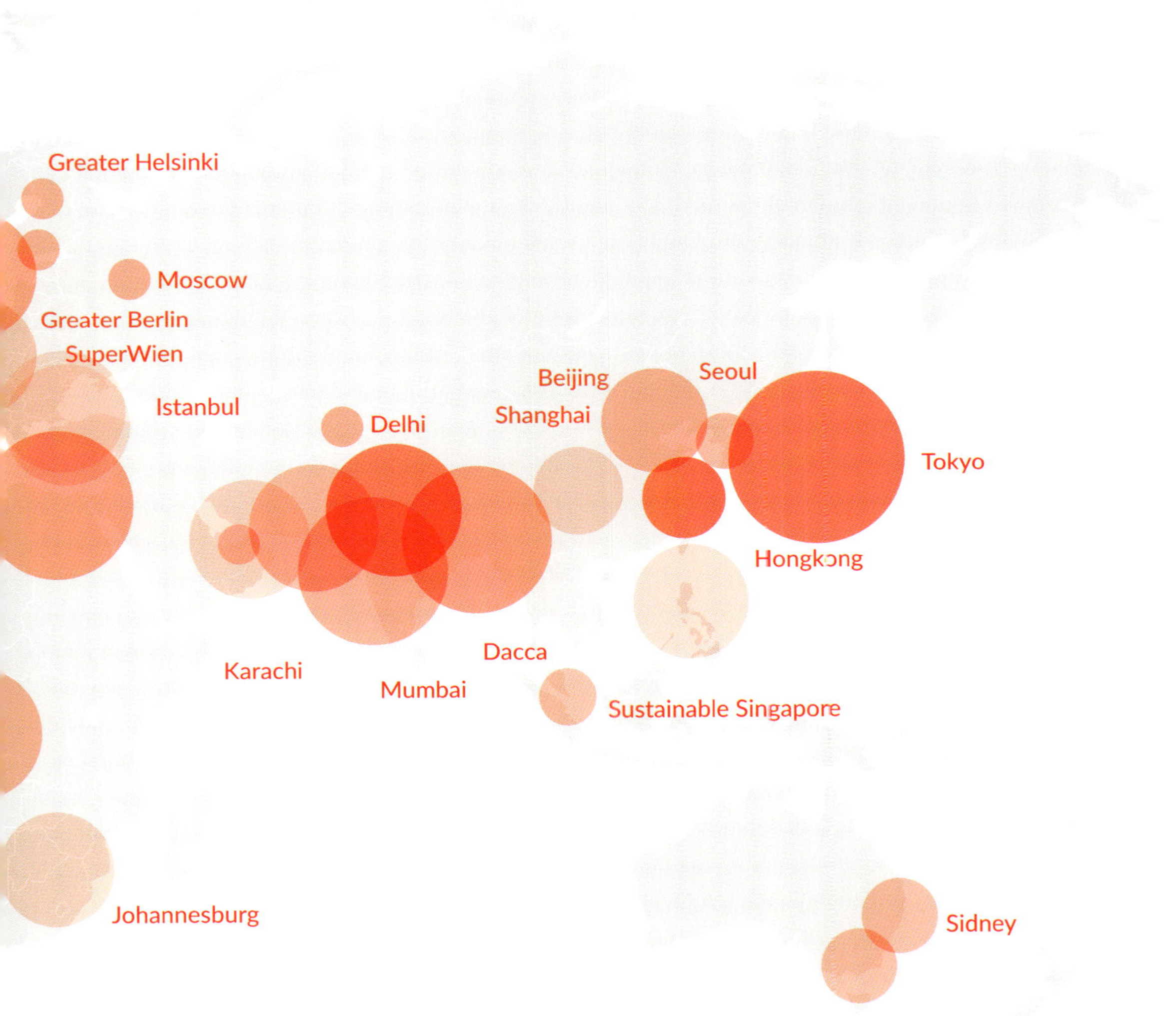
Greater Helsinki
Moscow
Greater Berlin
SuperWien
Istanbul
Delhi
Beijing
Shanghai
Seoul
Tokyo
Hongkong
Karachi
Mumbai
Dacca
Sustainable Singapore
Johannesburg
Sidney

FASCINATION

THE CENTURY OF METROPOLITAN PLANNING

Cities and urban agglomerations are not only inhabited by more than 60% of the world's population and are expected to continue to grow, but consume over two-thirds of the world's energy and produce more than 70% of global carbon dioxide emissions (United Nations 2020). At the same time, according to the current *Intergovernmental Panel on Climate Change (IPCC)* report, the continuous trend of urbanization *“also offers a critical opportunity in the near-term, to advance climate resilient development”*. The adaptability of urban areas can substantially increase by *“[i]ntegrated, inclusive planning and investment in everyday decision-making about urban infrastructure, including social, ecological and grey/ physical infrastructures”* (IPCC 2022:33).

Against the backdrop of this huge responsibility of urban areas in combating the climate crisis and its consequences, the demand of integrated and long-term spatial development across sectors and levels becomes evident. However, metropolitan planning is often not yet sufficiently integrated into contemporary planning practice and culture.

Triggered by suburbanization trends and the unquestioned belief in continuous growth over the last decades, many planning mistakes have been made that can only be revised to a limited extend today, such as the enormous amount of soil sealing through uncoordinated settlement development, or the dominance of individual car traffic through missing investments in public transport infrastructure. This miscellaneous spatial development not only has negative impacts on the climate, but also on our society, an uncoordinated response to growth pressures in urban areas often goes hand in hand with rising social inequalities.
In order to better align spatial development strategies and corresponding implementation measures across administrative borders, there is a need to strengthen the city-regional and metropolitan governance and planning discipline, following a place-based, multi-level and participatory approach.
As an important first step, awareness must me raised about pressing challenges that can only be solved on metropolitan scale, as the core city strongly depends on its surrounding municipalities and vice versa. The expansion and maintenance of a functioning mobility system that does not rely on fossil fuels, the preservation of natural free spaces, wetlands and agricultural lands, the development of compact settlements with vibrant mixed-use centers, the comprehensive provision of social infrastructure, as well as the transformation of the energy system to renewables, are just a few examples to show the relevance of integrated planning on a city-regional scale.

MOBILITY AS THE BACKBONE OF METROPOLITAN DEVELOPMENT

Increasing economic, social and infrastructural linkages between cities and its surrounding areas go hand in hand with a rise in commuter traffic, which can rarely be handled entirely by public transport and, thus, is often connected to a high demand of resources, traffic noise, pollutants and CO2 emissions. In order to reduce the overload of the transport system and to allow quick and resource-efficient commmuting in the metropolitan area, a strong collaboration across administrative boundaries is necessary. Only a joint strategy with coordinated measures from the local to the metropolitan scale is able to manage traffic flows environmentally and climate compatible, through a shift of the modal split in the direction of environmentally friendly and active forms of mobility, as well as reduction of total traffic. Furthermore, defining functional areas according to the intensity of mobility movements (e.g. commuter flows) is a big chance to reduce inequality within a city region and achieve a territorial rebalance. Accordingly, cross-border thinking and planning is key to developing a well-integrated transportation network and therefore an interconnected metropolitan area of proximity.

DRIVING URBAN TRANSFORMATION ALONG MOBILITY LINKS

A network of well-connected multi-modal mobility hubs should serve as a backbone for spatial development of the metropolitan area. Concentrating settlement development around mobility hubs provides the ultimate opportunity to develop multifunctional centers with a high standard of living, strengthening the polycentric network of the metropolitan region, and enabling the shift of individual car-use to public transport and active forms of mobility. Thus, mobility development always serves as a driver of settlement development (and vice versa), which means that these two dynamics must always be thought of together, so land use can be reduced, public transport strengthened and road infrastructure relieved, and a city region of short distances created. The *Grand Paris Express*, Europe's largest infrastructure project, establishing a network of multi-modal hubs as the backbone for settlement development, is one of the first examples of European metropolitan regions showing that cross-border cooperation is key to drive urban transformation along mobility links (see article by Alexandre Di Cocco).

NEW TECHNOLOGIES CAN ONLY PAVE THE WAY TO MOBILITY TRANSITION

As the range of mobility options is becoming more and more differentiated, the high potential of multi-modal, shared and connected mobility is becoming increasingly clear. Although new technologies, such as shared mobility offers through platforms, or automated and electric vehicles, can pave the way to a more resource-efficient mobility system, these technological innovations need to be managed in a coordinated way, in order to make use of its potentials. Not only new technologies, but above all the stronger integration of different forms of mobility make it possible to develop adapted solutions for different spatial situations and social needs. In this regard, the smooth connection of different micro-public-transport-systems in order to cope with the "first-" and "last-mile" is one of the main challenges. Moreover, in order to make sure that users can easily plan, book and pay for their journeys with multiple types of mobility services, a common platform that offers a joint digital channel is also needed on the city-regional scale.

TRANSFORMING THE STREETSCAPE

Transforming mobility systems means transforming spaces not only on the regional but also on the local level. As mobility-on-demand urban transportation systems, such as multi-modal hubs, strongly relate to their surrounding public space, its design has the potential to promote active forms of mobility and to ensure easy accessibility to the multi-modal offers. The implementation of new mobility services should therefore go hand in hand with rethinking the streetscape on a neighborhood scale.

RADIAL ROADS AS MULTI-MODAL MOBILITY CORRIDORS

Radial streets that connect the core city with its outskirts, as well as to other cities, are distinctive and shaping elements of metropolitan areas that have already undergone a variety of transformations over the past decades. Today, they mostly are perceived as monofunctional roads whose only function is creating a connection from A to B, which are usually overloaded by car traffic at peak times. Instead of adding additional lanes—in the belief that this will reduce congestion—these roads should be redefined as multi-modal corridors, strongly integrated into a broader mobility network. Radial roads have perfect conditions to be converted into bicycle highways or to be used as public bus routes. By transforming the streetscape and adding new functions to the public space, radial roads can become vivid and climate-fit spaces that promote active forms of mobility.

First approaches are made in European metropolitan areas, showing the high transformative potential of radial roads as metropolitan development corridors. In the *Barcelona Metropolitan Area (AMB)*, the Metropolitan Avenues are being transformed into a sustainable mobility network, accompanied by a broad participa- tion process (see articles by Javier Ortigosa and Judith Recio Heredia). ►

SETTING INCENTIVES TO CHANGE MOBILITY BEHAVIOUR

Transforming our mobility system and rethinking mobility infrastructure is strongly linked to processes of social change, making awareness building to an important component of a transition towards an ecologically just city region. It has been shown that people are particularly open to change in situations of transition, e.g. in regard to using alternative modes of mobility when moving to a newly developed housing area. Therefore, especially in urban development areas, there is a great opportunity to make changes in mobility behavior appealing, for example by offering a pool of cars and cargo-bikes for residents. One way or another, using shared and active forms of mobility is a matter of values, not just the infrastructure provided as a hardware. Thus, in addition to setting the right incentives, such as new multi-modal offers or policies, awareness building is an important component of mobility change. Understanding and further developing use-based approaches will be the first step in expanding the range of environmentally friendly and sustainable services according to demand and steering them in the right direction—towards an ecologically just city.

CREATING A POLYCENTRIC NETWORK WITH MIXED-USE PATTERNS

Based on the suburbanization trend since the 1970ies, many growing cities have been influenced by the phenomenon of uncoordinated extension of housing, commercial and industrial areas beyond administrative borders. Urban sprawl is connected to a massive use of land and energy, a lack of urbanity and social life and can lead to social segregation. As the high consumption of land and sealing of soils has become a threat to the ecology and climate, the consequent development of compact settlement structures with mixed-use centers needs to be forced, and the general consumption of soil need so be significantly reduced. The increasing trend of multi-local and mobile lifestyles through digitalization, also has impacts on the built environment and needs to be considered on the city regional scale. While more flexible forms of working through home office regulations offer the possibility to strengthen centralities and offer decentralised office spaces for residents, the rise of online retail, on the other hand, entails risks of dying centers.
As cities and local governments have significant authority over land-use policies and regulations, the possibilities for managing settlement development and distributing uses at metropolitan level is quite limited. That is precisely why there is need to identify and make use of alternative ways to better coordinate growth across administrative borders. In addition to formal inter-municipal financing instruments, regional associations with certain powers for decisions and funding that promote the joint coordination of land policies as well as informal instruments such as strategy papers enable coordinated and balanced territorial development.

DEFINING QUALITATIVE GROWTH CRITERIA

In order to prevent further urban sprawl in city regions and to make an impact on local land-use and building regulations, the definition of overarching criteria for urban planning and building culture, such as specifying a minimum density is necessary. Such quality criteria can unfold their effect in, among others, the development of new or redevelopment of existing housing areas. A quantitative increase of building density needs to go hand in hand with a qualitative densification—including an intensification of social and technical infrastructure, creation of additional (co-)working places and cultural and leisure facilities, in order to prevent monofunctional settlement development and safeguard services of general interest. The creation of new centralities with mixed-use or recreational patterns, with commercial and non-commercial use add value to segregated "non-places" and convert them into "places".

TRANSLATE METROPOLITAN STRATEGIES INTO PLACE-BASED SOLUTIONS

An effective instrument to concentrate urban growth on selected centers and to coordinate urban growth across administrative borders is to organize metropolitan planning competitions based on pre-defined spatial focus areas. The innovative housing program 50 000 *Naturally Accessible Homes* initiated by Bordeaux Métropole in France (see article by Jérome Gôze) demonstrates that a coordinated approach can be more effective in combating urban sprawl by quality densification than if spatial units act individually. Taking into account specific local requirements in terms of density, diversity, accessibility, environmental and climatic conditions, tailored responses could successfully be developed in different urban situations. Transforming focus areas into place-based projects enables compact, socially, and economically mixed centers within the polycentric network of the metropolis.

OVERCOMING INTER-MUNICIPAL COMPETITION THROUGH INTEGRATIVE PLANNING INSTRUMENTS

The competition between municipalities can be seen as one of the main hindrances for a coordinated growth on metropolitan scale. For tax and financial reasons, neighbouring communities often compete with each other to attract new residential and commercial development. Therefore, in order to proactively balance metropolitan growth, strong integrative planning instruments are needed. For example, the inter-municipal mobilization of financial resources serves as an instrument to jointly respond to challenges related to uncoordinated urban growth, including spatial and social fragmentation frequently leading to unequal living conditions. A shared budget allows for the integrated and targeted development of the metropolitan area to be driven by different political stakeholders meeting at eye level. Moreover, compensation mechanisms that balance profits and costs between urban centers and surrounding, structurally weak municipalities, such as an inter-municipal financial equalization have proven to be an effective instrument to support more sustainable spatial development.

CO-CREATING INCLUSIVE NEIGHBORHOODS

One of the main challenges of urban growth is integrating expansion areas into the built city. At the metropolitan level it is hard to organize participation because the actions are decided and implemented on the local, municipal level. Therefore, it is important to a good relationship between stakeholders and the local groups.

To create more inclusive and just neighborhoods, it is necessary to also involve those groups who are not seen or heard at first glance as well as those who do not live there yet. As institutionalized participation is limited in its reach, new, more engaging formats should be integrated into day to day and formal planning processes to overcome these hurdles. The advantages of co-creative approaches, such as urban Living Labs and local Think-Tanks, lie in their experimental character, the opening of new perspectives and the productive handling of failure, whereby the process itself becomes the actual result. The openness of such dialogue-oriented formats enables ►

the exchange and cooperation of stakeholders across encrusted structures and, thus, also stimulates collective learning processes and knowledge spillovers. Further, the possibility of co-creation also strengthens the identification of the participating actors with the common metropolitan area and enables to spot more short-term and soft actions.

TOWARDS CARBON-NEUTRAL CITY REGIONS

Due to strong urban-rural linkages in terms of ecology, climate, and energy, the metropolitan area is the appropriate framework for developing and effectively implementing climate change mitigation and adaptation strategies. In addition to the urgently required energy transition away from fossil fuels and towards renewable energy sources, our lifestyles need to become more sustainable, regarding the way we live, consume and move, in order to reach the target of carbon-neutral city regions.

RETHINKING COMMON WAYS OF PRODUCTION AND CONSUMPTION

When discussing how to create resilient urban agglomerations, the question of common ways of production and consumption comes into focus, in addition to rethinking usual ways how we live and move within urban areas. Accordingly, the concept of the circular economy, which aims to close material and energy loops through durable design, maintenance, repair, reuse, remanufacturing, refurbishment and recycling, supports the idea of the sharing economy and is an important component of our future carbon- and climate-neutral economy. While the circular economy concept is already partly practiced in civic society led initiatives and on smaller scales, such as in energy cooperatives or urban agriculture projects, and should be taken to the next level. Experiments at the neighborhood level need to be scaled up to the metropolitan level where, for example, recycling building materials can bring about real change. However, since almost every transformation requires energy and generates a certain amount of waste, the concept of the circular economy cannot stand alone.

THE ROLE OF LAND MANAGEMENT TO SUPPORT SELF-SUFFICIENCY AND PROTECT BIODIVERSITY

Metropolitan areas must activate and strengthen their own potentials and focus on existing resources in terms of energy efficiency, renewable energy systems and local and sustainable food production. However, this transformation towards a self-sufficient metropolitan area is only possible if there are appropriate spatial concepts for it. To establish a largely independent energy supply, it is necessary, for example, to provide land for the expansion of renewable energy infrastructure. Urban agriculture and innovative forms of (vertical) farming also require space to grow food in a sustainable way within the city region. Therefore, local land resources should be identified and qualified - not only in the interest of self-sufficiency, but also of biodiversity.

Thus, the protection of functioning ecosystems and their integration into urban development concepts and strategies, is a major challenge and places high demands on land management. As there is no specific agency for dedicating land for biodiversity (as there is for securing affordable housing, for example), new planning instruments are needed. In view of increasing land consumption, soil sealing and urban sprawl, urban development and planning are strongly challenged to ensure and strengthen the diversity and quality of open spaces and green and blue infrastructures that contribute to the ecological balance of the living environment. In addition to strategically planned green networks, innovative strategies are needed to create and protect fertile soils that serve as arable land.

TRANSFORMATION STARTS IN OUR MINDS

There needs to be a fundamental rethinking of the way we live and work together, which implies a general change in values in our social and economic system. Since unsustainable lifestyles are deeply embedded in economic, social and cultural practices (e.g. intensive use of motorized transport, or occupying too much living space per person), these need to be renegotiated with the help of awareness raising. In order to prevent that action is taken only when the pressure of suffering (e.g. due to the increase of heat islands) becomes too high, it is enormously important to empower the local population. Accordingly, one of the key challenges is to contribute to problem-solving competence by raising general awareness of problematic urban transformation processes. Finally, creating resilient urban landscapes requires not only a variety of measures through climate-sensitive planning (adaptation to climate change, preservation of biodiversity or reuse of existing resources), but also the involvement of people and their local creativity and knowledge. The real hotspots of transformation are our minds.

METROPOLITAN GOVERNANCE AS PREREQUISITE FOR SUSTAINABLE DEVELOPMENT

Whether economic or settlement development, landscape and nature conservation or major infrastructural concerns - a multitude of interests requires a supra-local perspective that acknowledges the metropolitan area as a functional unit. For example, water management, energy transition, shifting transportation to more sustainable modes, or even small-scale climate adaptation strategies address extensive functional interconnections and spatial relations and thus require intensive cooperation. However, metropolitan regions are somehow a "black whole" of governance.

THE METROPOLITAN DILEMMA

A lot of research has been carried out to analyze different forms of cooperation in functional urban areas, indicating that the level of strong (institutionalized) collaborations in functional urban areas is very low. In only one third of metropolitan areas in the EU, some kind of metropolitan cooperation can be identified, which, however, either do not have strong enough functions to achieve effective impact, or do not cover the whole functional area. Thus, inter-municipal cooperation structures often do not display existing functional relations between the core city and its surrounding municipalities. (OECD Metropolitan Governance Survey 2014)

One effective way to achieve functional expansion or territorial adjustment are conscious policies, backed by the national level. Ideally, the central government sets a legal framework that clarifies a vertical chain of responsibilities and gives power to metropolitan agencies for decisions and funding. Countries such as France or Poland show that incentives, such as tax benefits, can be provided at the national level to motivate administratively separated entities such as municipalities to cooperate with each other. EU funding initiatives are also increasingly helpful in this regard.

Only if the lack of metropolitan governance is addressed in ongoing discussions can persistent political structures be loosened, and systemic obstacles overcome to pursue shared visions and strategies. This benefits not only the integration of different spatial areas (cooperation among neighboring municipalities, urban and peri-urban areas), but also the integration of and dialogue between different government levels. ▸

FINDING THE RIGHT BALANCE

By distinguishing the forms of cooperation in city regions between institutional and procedural forms of cooperation, a great diversity becomes clear. On the one hand, French metropolitan regions, as well as the Barcelona Metropolitan Area, Greater Manchester, or the Stuttgart Region can be defined as institutional forms of cooperation, as they are firmly demarcated areas and are formally authorized with competences. On the other hand, procedural forms of cooperation are characterized by informal coordination of activities in flexible spatial contexts (Metropolitan Research Institute Budapest 2018). Such approaches are followed by the *Metropolitanraum Zurich* as a private association and the network organization *Metropoolregio Amsterdam*, for example.

There is no patent recipe when it comes to the question of the “right” form of cooperation on metropolitan level. As institutionalized cooperation is not suitable in all cases, but rather informal cooperation structures, it has to be decided for each respective metropolitan area which degree of institutionalization is the right one.

ADVANTAGES AND DISADVANTAGES OF INFORMAL, PROJECT-BASED FORMS OF COOPERATION

In many cases, an institutionalized form of cooperation on metropolitan level is (at least on the short term) not possible, due to political, legal or spatial configurations. However, some examples already have shown that a certain degree of informality of processes and the formation of project-based collaborations can be very fruitful.

Even in metropolitan areas with lacking competences on city-regional scale and without any “strategic frame”, successful projects across administrative borders can be initiated, contributing to a more sustainable spatial development in the city region. One of the main advantages of informal forms of cooperation is that project-based work is much easier if it is done in cooperation with actors who are willing to participate in a project and who trust each other, instead of actors who are forced to cooperate by law. If the membership and participation in a metropolitan association, for example, is voluntary, greater political will is expected and less persuasion needs to be done than in formalized and institutionalized structures.

Another advantage of informal, project-based forms of cooperation is that spatial delineation can be adopted regarding the topic and purpose of the respective project (transport infrastructure, green space development, etc.). If new spatial units come into focus of spatial development for a certain amount of time, the structural flexibility as a central characteristic of strategic planning, in regard to the spatial and temporal dimension, becomes evident. However, while informal, small-scale institutionalized networks often increase credibility and trust among stakeholders, much also depends on the commitment of individuals, such as individual mayors or parties. Another challenge of informal, project-based cooperation is connected to funding. While in institutionalized forms of cooperation, municipalities involved must make a financial contribution and a common budget is available to implement projects, informal collaboration are dependent on (external) resources, such as EU or national funding.

SEEKING AN INTEGRATED APPROACH

A good coordination of planning and design is key in dealing with multilevel governance structures. Integrated Action Plans help develop strategic place-based solutions with an integrated and multisectoral planning approach. The integration of the economic, social, and environmental dimension in the planning is complex, however it is necessary to joint up solutions on all levels and minimize the effects of negative externalities.

In general, the metropolitan level is an excellent area of action for coordination and cooperation between different teams of municipal offices an align dimensions like environment, economy mobility, culture, and social aspects. Small scale projects are excellent to test and embed project ideas on a local level and to satisfy residents' needs to connect with those above-mentioned dimensions of sustainability.

FUNDING METROPOLITAN PROJECTS

In general, for small municipalities it is hard to finance projects with metropolitan impact due to their limited budget. Therefore, it is unlikely that they implement metropolitan projects. A solution could be to shop good ideas to regional and national government and to gradually start acting in steps with small projects instead of waiting for big infrastructural projects to come.

BUILDING COOPERATION WITH POSITIVE TOPICS

Thus, cross-border cooperation is easier and more likely to lead to successes, when rather "soft" and positive topics are addressed, such as recreational spaces and green space development. When it comes to issues that could lead to restrictions on local scale, or initiate conflicts with residents, such as compact settlement development, it is much harder to initiate joint projects across municipal borders. Although, with rater "easy" projects, such as a regional park development, collaborations on metropolitan scale can be "tested", and can serve as an impetus to then initiate more complex and challenging projects.

The right balance must be found between the pragmatic, formalized approach of city administrations and informal, co-creative forms of cooperation. "Form follows function" is becoming an important principle when it comes to finding the right degree of institutionalization.

THE ROLE OF INTERMEDIARIES

As morphological, functional and legal definitions of metropolitan areas often do not coincide, neutral and independent advisory services are needed to help identify the actual needs of metropolitan development areas and to equalize the uneven distribution of power relations, for example between the core city and the surrounding municipalities. Intermediaries further enable the collaboration of the different fields of planning, decision-making and assist in balancing public and private Interests. ▪

The metropolitan region is not only a topic for planners and politicians

Interview with **Thomas Madreiter**—City of Vienna

MetroLab: As planning director in Vienna, you have to cope with a multitude of different scales on a daily basis. What is your personal and professional connection to the metropolitan area of Vienna?

Thomas Madreiter: On a personal level, I appreciate very much, living in a city of millions, that is embedded in a regional structure, ranging from very rural areas to urban and highly urbanized areas, such as Bratislava or, of course, the urbanized areas south of Vienna. I find that insanely interesting, personally. Professionally, I am also responsible for the spatial aspects of regional development as head of urban planning in Vienna, a city that has long and consciously cultivated a broader approach, that does not stop at administrative borders.

When referring to the metropolis, what is in your opinion an appropriate definition of "metropolis"? What defines it as a planning area?

By using the term "planning area" you quickly end up with diplomatic questions, namely who actually plans what? Therefore, I prefer the term "consideration area". For me, a metropolis is characterized by a certain concentration of population and high level of interconnectedness, interaction and exchange. It is important to find a term for the common living space in which everyone can find themselves, because language can also have an exclusionary effect and immediately evokes images in the mind. Therefore, a differentiated, but still common identity that works internally and externally has to be found.

"A differentiated, but still common identity that works internally and externally has to be found"

What do you regard as the most formative challenges that metropolitan regions must now address?

On the one hand, there is a trend towards urbanization, which, despite rumors to the contrary, I believe continues unabated even after Covid-19. In this respect, there is always friction between urban and rural areas in a metropolitan region, which I believe always includes and must include rural spaces.

There is a strong need to discuss images of urbanity. We have to talk about the frictions and then find solutions for them.

As an approach, I very much like a quote from Konrad Paul Liessmann, who said that urbanity is primarily something that arises first and foremost in the mind and cannot necessarily be measured or counted, for example in the form of infrastructure facilities. This raises the question of whether there is such a thing as a mindset in a metropolitan region, how this mindset can be developed, and how high-quality sustainable structures and opportunities can be created in the metropolitan area, so that there are no isolated sub-areas.

“There is a strong need to discuss images of urbanity. We have to talk about the frictions and then find solutions for them”

You just highlighted the importance of a common image of the metropolitan area. In our work at *MetroLab* we strongly agree that a common vision is fundamental for strengthening the metropolitan scale. How can such images be created in which all units can find themselves? Do you have any particular tools in mind to start the discourse on metropolitan planning?

In a discourse it is like everywhere in life, you have to tackle it. Of course, there are methods and processes that can trigger such a figurative impetus and regional planners have an operational function, but at the end of the day it is a socio-political question. What boundaries do set in our minds? Where do we differentiate between us and them? These are the questions that need to be addressed and negotiated.

The creation of the *CENTROPE* region, for example, was an attempt to stimulate the discourse on the regional level which succeeded in some ways, but failed in others. On a smaller scale, it is the *PGO* and the *Stadt-Umland-Management* that advocate the regional scale. More innovative instruments, such as launching a competition for the development of the metropolitan region, are also worth considering, to generate new images and start the discourse. It is essential that the discourse goes beyond the professional community and includes civil society actors from the very beginning. If the mobility network is only discussed with traffic planners, the discourse will be ineffective in socio-political terms.

“The discourse on metropolitan planning must go beyond the professional community and also include civil society actors from the very beginning”

We need to address fundamental questions such as: Who are we? Who do we want to be? What kind of spatial-functional environment do we want to live in? How do we want to interact with each other? How do we want to use, improve, and optimize opportunities? This discourse can only be conducted using participatory and co-creative methods. As a primarily top-down structured process of a political administrative systems inevitably reaches certain limits, a sensible balance of top-down leadership and civil society impulses is needed. ▸

Particularly challenging for the Vienna metropolitan region are the very different size ratios. The city of Vienna dominates in purely quantitative terms with its approximately 2 million inhabitants. This requires a specific intelligence in order not to fall into methods or patterns that are then actually dominating. From the urban perspective, that means letting go to some extent and letting others have their say and enduring that, which is often difficult.

What do you see as the indispensable actors, instruments and structures needed for successful communication and cooperation across administrative boundaries?

In order to give the metropolitan region socio-political relevance, you have to ask yourself what the mental map of your environment looks like. Where do you go on weekends? Where does your mental map break off? How does public transport work, do you need 17 different maps or does it work as a network? The metropolitan region is not just a topic for planners and politicians. Promising initiatives and impulses must be set, but cooperation cannot be forced. As we know, people often assume that others are similar to themselves. But this is a serious mistake. Responsibilities, administrative structures, procedures, and processes that look similar often are not.

Against the backdrop of the multiple crises, we are currently facing as a society and in relation to the question of how interregional cooperation could be targeted, do you see the climate crisis in particular as a window of opportunity to kick-start collaboration?

"I believe that the climate crisis is giving rise to new questions and a new duality of rural and dense regions. The question is, how do they deal with each other?"

The climate crisis is a major window of opportunity. It is now a matter of making use of the crisis structure we are facing. For this purpose, appropriate dialog and participatory formats must be developed. It is important to set impulses that will be noticed and adequately taken up and it is up to the people to decide what kind of impulses these might be.
I believe that the climate crisis is giving rise to new questions and a new duality of rural and dense regions. The question is, how do they deal with each other?

The question of how we will live together in the future also relates to the topic of moving between and within administrative borders. How will we move around the metropolis in the future?

On the one hand, I think the quality of the mobility system will have to improve. People in the metropolitan region will always be mobile. The difference is whether I am mobile because I want to be, or whether I am forced to drive 17 kilometers to get to school, the supermarket or the pub. The region has to become small-scale-regional again and strive for so-called decentralized concentration. We need a new form or a new positive interpretation of urbanity. This does not mean that everyone has to end up living in 2-million-strong agglomerations, but that concentrated, more-dense forms of building have to be found, depending on the scale and size of the site. For me, this is an absolute key to success - for climatic reasons, for cost reasons, for many reasons.

Finally, what is your personal vision for the Vienna Metropolitan Region in the future? What can Vienna learn from other metropolises? How would you also like the metropolitan region to look in the future?

"Challenges regarding energy supply, mobility, recreation or food production cannot be solved singularly by contiguous local authorities. We have to evolve structurally and methodically to achieve a good balance of interests"

Not only do I like to run, I also like to ride my bike. And every cyclist knows that stability and standing still are not the same thing, but that stability is gained through movement. In order to keep the region stable enough that it still looks similar to today in the future, it has to become very mobile and agile. That means finding new formats to solve challenges together and negotiate them together. Challenges regarding energy supply, mobility, recreation or food production cannot be solved singularly by contiguous local authorities. We have to evolve structurally and methodically to achieve a good balance of interests. According to my vision, the region will ultimately not look much different than it does today because I love this region, enjoy spending my free time within the and hope that it will manage to retain its qualities. ▪

Metropolitan planning must take an integrated approach

Interview with **Joan Caba**—Àrea Metropolitana de Barcelona (AMB)

MetroLab: You were born and raised in the Barcelona Metropolitan Area and are also professionally responsible for its development. What do you see as the new role of metropolitan areas? How do you steer development at the *Àrea Metropolitana de Barcelona (AMB)*?

Joan Caba: A metropolitan area is for me defined by its interactions. People move within the metropolitan area to satisfy their needs such as work, education, shopping, leisure and culture, without considering the administrative borders they cross.
To get around, you need mobility infrastructure, which is why mobility is the backbone of metropolitan development. At *AMB*, we are developing a metropolitan masterplan that creates a network of metropolitan avenues and metropolitan streets, that serve as channels for public transportation and active mobility, connecting municipalities (see article by Javier Ortigosa). Similar projects are being discussed and implemented in Porto, Helsinki, Paris, Lyon, Brussels, Hamburg and many other European cities and metropolises. Transforming these avenues also means activating and unleashing new development and new regeneration for these areas to create new centralities, with housing, places to work, services and social infrastructure. Unlike the planning paradigms of the 1960s and 1970s, which were based on specialized zoning connected basically by private mobility, we need to create a human-scale metropolitan area. A polycentric network of mixed-use centralities, well integrated and connected by public transport and active mobility is the hardware of a human-scale metropolis. In the case of *AMB*, we are fostering a polycentric metropolis by defining new well connected metropolitan centralities that will complement the existing urban areas triggering integral regeneration and, on the other hand, will reduce the distances towards the human-scale metropolis. Public transport and active forms of mobility are key in achieving this goal.

"Unlike the planning paradigms of the 1960s and 1970s, which were based on specialized zoning connected basically by private mobility, we need to create a human-scale metropolitan area"

In the context of sustainability transformation, multi-level governance structures as well as inter-municipal cooperation mechanisms are necessary to create intra-regional synergies. How can these be achieved? How can the right stakeholders be identified and combined to ensure successful collaboration?

"Metropolitan authorities or agencies are the perfect facilitator who could bring all the stakeholders together to initiate a planning process"

Most challenges that cities and metropolises are facing, like climate change adaptation, housing, mobility, public facilities and open spaces, are not possible to be tackled by individual projects that try to solve one problem. The scale, the scope and the complexity are not right. In my opinion, to succeed we need an integrated metropolitan approach where the plan tries to solve as many problems as possible with a realistic implementation and without causing other problems elsewhere. This logical approach involves lots of challenges in terms of administrative borders, interdepartmental collaborations, multilevel governance, etc. Establishing innovative processes that bring together the civil society and all the administrative units involved—the various municipalities, the regional government and sometimes even the central government—is perhaps the best way to meet these major challenges.

The first step to create an integrated plan is to define the governance of the process. It must be clarified who needs to be involved and how decision-making will proceed throughout the process. This means defining what everyone's role is in the process, who will ultimately make the decision and who will be responsible for implementing the actions co-decided by everyone.

The second step is a joint diagnosis of the challenges and problems. Most of the time, different actors have different interpretations of the same situation and therefore pursue different goals. For example, for a municipality, the national road might be a barrier and a no-go area with lots of externalities, and should even be eliminated. For the regional government the same road might be a bottleneck to enter the main city that should be enlarged to meet the demand for cars. By looking at the problem in an integrated and collaborative way, both sides can understand and realise that the diagnosis is more complex and innovative and integrated solutions are needed. When the diagnosis is shared, joint actions and strategies are also easier to implement. This takes time, but it ensures that the result is much better than a top-down approach.

Metropolitan authorities or agencies have inter-municipal collaboration and multi-level governance in their DNA as they are constantly dealing with these cross-border issues. Therefore, they are the perfect facilitator who can bring all the stakeholders together to initiate a planning process.

What potential do you ascribe to co-creative approaches in the planning process? How are citizens involved on a metropolitan scale?

Co-creation requires the involvement of local citizens. For us, as a metropolitan body, it is very difficult to involve the citizens because we do not engage with them in our daily work. Therefore, it is almost impossible for us to know who are the main actors that we need to involve in the process, who can involve other citizens and NGOs, or who can better communicate the specific needs of the area. So we work closely with the municipalities that know the area best. ▸

A good examples of metropolitan co-creation plans are the integrated action plans developed in the *URBACT RiConnect* Network. *RiConnect* is a network of 8 metropolises which aim is to rethink, transform and integrate mobility infrastructures in order to reconnect people, neighbourhoods, cities and natural spaces.

Avinguda des Vallès is the *AMB* integrated plan with the objective of transforming the national roads into metropolitan avenues (see article by Judith Recio Heredia). In order to realise a common diagnosis, everyone should have the same comparative analysis for the area and share the same language. When you work with citizens, technicians and representatives, the language is different. It is important to collect objective data, such as how many cars use this street per day, and then to compare it to other spatial contexts that are similar in size and profile to be able to interpret the information. Finally, discussing best-practice examples and new images of what the area could look like makes it easier to move beyond the day-to-day problems and say: change is possible, we can start dreaming. And, if you arrive at this point, everything is possible.

What is your role as metropolitan authority in steering sustainable metropolitan development?

"We don't have to keep reinventing the wheel. We can use the knowledge we have gained in one area and transfer it to another"

One of our main competences is to support municipalities in urban planning, especially the smaller ones, which have few technical staff. We try to apply the same methodology: first, build a comprehensive understanding of the territory, second develop a multidisciplinary and collective diagnosis and then, concretion of proposals with alternatives. With this methodology, any project, independently of their scale, have a metropolitan perspective with a place-based solution and with some take-aways for similar problems. Therefore, even though, the local-specific context of another project may be different, the methodology or the inputs to arrive at a plan can be similar, and we don't have to keep reinventing the wheel. We can use the knowledge we have gained in one area and transfer it to another.

Mobility certainly plays a major role in creating resilient metropolitan areas. What else are aspects of a climate-friendly metropolis? How do you make sure an integrated approach is followed?

"In the end, we need to create resilient metropolitan areas, which secure water, energy, and food supplies and are ramped up against natural disaster"

The consequences of the climate crisis are already very visible today. We specially notice this in the Mediterranean climate with high temperature waves that set a new record every year, big floods and fires. But it is also visible everywhere. In the end, we need to create resilient metropolitan areas, which secure water, energy, and food supplies and are ramped up against natural disasters. The territory and the opportunities are limited, all these aspects are interrelated, so an integrated approach that tries to solve as many problems as possible without generating new ones seems reasonable. And, to do so, all the relevant stakeholders should be part of the process. There are no shortcuts.

I would like to highlight that it is important to not only invest in built-up areas, but also in open spaces. We need to find nature-based solutions to contain natural disasters, secure short distance supply, protect existing open spaces and create new ones.

Further, metropolitan areas are and should be places of welcome and opportunities for a better future. Also, cities are the most efficient environment in energy consumption and wealth generation and, in consequence, a perfect tool to fight against climate change. The responsibility of welcoming new people in most cases means providing new housing, new jobs and new services without growing in extension. The main challenge here is to allocate this growth in existing areas with not only maintaining the standard of life of the neighbours already living there, but also as an opportunity to create more, safer and better public spaces, social infrastructure, climate-friendly and high-quality public transport, affordable housing as well as educational and job opportunities, among others. To sum up, a more sustainable, equitable and attractive metropolis for all.

Why is the metropolitan scale of special importance in combatting the climate crisis?

"Metropolitan areas are large enough to develop and plan high-impact strategies, but also small enough to implement them"

The metropolitan scale is probably the most effective scale to fight climate change, because metropolitan areas are large enough to develop and plan high-impact strategies, but also small enough to implement them. As mediators, they can provide a link between the regional/national/European legislation, which sets the major direction, and the local level. For the implementation of climate targets, we need the local level to find integrated and place-based solutions in close cooperation with local stakeholders and residents. It is everyone's responsibility to prefer in front of your house trees than car parks spaces. ▪

Mapping: understanding metropolitan phenomena
Filming: setting space in motion
Stakeholder Mapping: making power relations visible
Data Mining: collecting quantitative and qualitative data
Explorative Walks: collective exploration of the area
Visionary Maps: reinterpreting the metropolitan area
VISUAL MANIFESTATION OF THE CREATIVE VISION
Travelling Exhibition: making the vision tangible
Art Installations: making visions real
Photographing: depicting multiple realities
Movie Night: stimulating discussions about emerging topics
Design Studio: testing the metropolitan vision

Forum Discussion:
bringing different perspectives on the table
(Online) Survey:
obtaining the perspective of local experts
Pitch Night:
a catalyst for new ideas
Walkshop:
collective identification of intervention areas
International Lectures:
learning from international perspectives
Urban Living Labs:
shaping places together
LOCAL ACTION PLAN
METROPOLITAN STRATEGY
Case Studies Discussion:
stimulate the imagination
Expert Interviews:
drawing on expert knowledge
Online Exhibition:
creating an online presentation platform
Wanted:
Open Calls:
encouraging community-led development

CO-CREATION TOOLBOX

FROM CREATIVE VISION TO LOCAL ACTION

As a metropolitan Think Tank and consulting service for the integrated development of metropolitan areas and city regions, the *MetroLab* introduces participative, integrative and creative-artistic elements to develop innovative metropolitan strategies as well as place-based solutions. Based on a co-creative and dialogue-oriented planning and design approach it fosters not only placemaking interventions, but also the transfer of cutting-edge knowledge in creative urban planning and administration. Facing the immensity of contemporary urban challenges, the *MetroLab* has developed an elaborated collection of diverse tools for metropolitan planning and design. The toolbox is an integral part of the *MetroLab* approach and is used in the frame of several projects. The tools can be adapted to the specific needs of city regions, districts and municipalities, making them applicable to different urban areas.

We live in an age of fast-growing cities, which constantly have to prove their ability to innovate and adapt to changing conditions. Pressing issues of urbanization such as climate change mitigation, the handling of uncontrolled settlement growth, increasing competitive pressure, demographic change, or the adaption to new mobility patterns do not stop at the (administrative) city boundaries and direct the focus to the metropolitan level. Not only the development of (built) infrastructure ("hardware") needs to be considered from a cross-border, metropolitan perspective, but also its uses and functions ("software") as well as governance and management ("orgware"). The need of an intensified cooperation across administrative borders and better coordination among all levels of governance becomes evident.
In this context, a number of questions arise that we as urban planners, researchers, city administrators and civil society have to face: What might the increasingly functionally integrated metropolitan landscape and its new spatial patterns look like? How will this shape our consumer behaviour and leisure activities, and how will we move within the metropolitan area? What future vision of urbanity and metroopolitan life we want to build on to integrate pressing social and spatial developments in a sustainable way?

THE "SUPERWIEN METROPOLE" AS AN IDEA GENERATOR...

These thoughts have inspired us to a former project, that resulted in sketching a new vision for the metropolitan area of Vienna, which we refer to as *SuperWien*: the Vienna-Bratislava-Wiener Neustadt area. In the publication of the same name, an impressive re-branding of the area was created by reinterpreting well-known urban narratives through atypical images (Mayr & Ramière 2018). In this way, *SuperWien* becomes a radical idea generator for planners, municipalities and their residents, who are presented with a new conception of their common space.
The intention of creating a provocative new image that left many questions unanswered was to stimulate a discussion about metropolitan development across administrative borders and beyond encrusted institutional structures and planning approaches. Thus, the *SuperWien Metropole* was seen as a common starting point for the Vienna – Bratislava region, from which interdisciplinary and cross-sectoral connections are spun onwards and a broader process of integrated metropolitan development is envisioned.

... LEADING TO A COMMON NARRATIVE?

In response to such a provocative idea for the metropolitan area, a common vision and narrative for the whole functional area serves as an important driver for cross-border cooperation and interregional collaboration. Creating a common sense about the future development on the larger scale is the prerequisite to drive joint projects forward and to face metropolitan challenges such as coordinating land use and transportation projects across municipal boundaries. In order that all stakeholders, political decision-makers as well as citizens can co-create it and find themselves in it, the definition of an inclusive metropolitan narrative should be framed as an open process.

THE FOUNDATION OF METROLAB

The question on how to stimulate and moderate such an open process between different decision makers of different levels and the civil society, was the initial starting point of *MetroLab*. Based on the lack of cooperation beyond administrative borders, the *MetroLab* points to the crucial importance of the metropolitan dimension and the need for creative governance that bring together a variety of stakeholders and fosters cooperation. The *MetroLab* advocates for a new type of metropolitan planning, which as a discipline of practice promotes a co-creative and dialogue-oriented urban planning and design approach. The ongoing global trend of metropolisation is seen as a driver for innovation and opportunity to strengthen the development and management of metropolitan areas and to understand this process as a concious design task.

INITIATING AN INTERNATIONAL DIALOGUE

As many efforts already have been taken in different urban contexts that give answers to complex challenges of metropolitanization and make aware of the importance of cross-sectoral and multi-level cooperation, an international exchange between metropolitan areas and city regions is seen as very fruitful. Especially when it comes to the question on how to manage integrated development processes across administrative borders, or which planning tools are suitable to translate an overall and abstract strategic vision into place-based solutions, there is high demand to learn from each other. In order to make existing knowledge more visible and create an exchange of experiences, the *MetroLab* launched an *International Dialogue on Metropolitan Planning* as a first step to build up an international metropolitan platform. As a series of public events, so called *MetroLab Forums* (see Chapter *DIALOGUE*), each of which is devoted to a specific topic of metropolitan planning and development, a varied program of interactive and discursive formats was offered. Taking up the approach of trans-local learning, an exchange of knowledge on best practices and instruments of metropolitan planning and development took place by means of international lectures. Whether and to what extent the various approaches and innovative tools presented can be transferred to the Viennese context of city-regional development was then discussed in panels with local experts.

PROVIDING AN OPEN-SOURCE ACTION GUIDE FOR METROPOLITAN PLANNING

Following the consensus that a stronger focus on dialogue-oriented and co-creative planning instruments is necessary to find a common metropolitan narrative, to translate overarching objectives into local action and to coordinate between different levels of scale, *MetroLab* created an open-source toolbox for metropolitan planning with the intension to share these experiences and make them accessible to other urban planners, researchers, local authorities and civil society. In exchange with an interdisciplinary network of metropolitan areas, the toolbox is expected to continue further as a continiuously expandable pool of knowledge. To better understand and manage complex planning processes at different scales and between multiple stakeholder groups, the *MetroLab* designed a generalized and simplified process that can serve as reference point, athough the planning and development process of a metropolitan area always depends on the respective spatial context and planning culture:

1. Creative Vision Building
2. Metropolitan Dialogue
3. Local Action

However, the sequence of these phases should not be understood as a linear process, as changes at the local level can influence overarching strategies and vice versa.

Designing a process

The *MetroLab Toolbox* is built on a generalized planning process derived from experience gained in various planning projects in metropolitan areas. Although the planning process of a metropolitan area needs to be adapted to the respective spatial contexts and planning culture, there are three main phases that should, based on the co-creative approach of *MetroLab*, always be followed:

In the first phase, the Creative Vision Building, a broad analysis of the governance structures, the history of the area, as well as a data collection and analysis is conducted. Based on the results, a creative vision for the metropolitan area is designed that creates a new image of the area, initiating a discussion.

During the second phase, the Metropolitan Dialogue, the vision is being discussed with a variety of stakeholders from the private and public sector, as a basis to develop a metropolitan strategy, including emerging topics and development goals. In the Local Action phase, several target areas within the metropolitan area will be defined. In close cooperation with responsible administrative bodies as well as the local community, first (temporary) interventions are implemented, and local action plans are developed.

As a preparatory step of each planning process, the specific situation and initial point of the respective metropolitan area needs to be screened in order to create a tailor-made toolbox for development. In some cases, the first phase might already be well advanced, as a comprehensive analysis of the metropolitan area has been conducted recently, but an overall vision and image (as outcome of phase 1) is missing. In other cases, you have to start at zero, as previous development visions and strategies are concentrated on the city level only and did not consider the cross-border, metropolitan level. In general, the sequence of these phases should not be understood as a linear process, although the outcomes of each phase are an important basis to enter the next phase. As there are strong interrelations between the phases, especially phases 2 and 3 can occasionally overlap.

1 CREATIVE VISION BUILDING

Creative Vision Building aims to understand and recontextualise metropolitan phenomena. It creates the basis to develop cross-border strategies and a new image and identity for the metropolitan area. The outcome of this first phase is the visionary representation of the functional urban area through various forms and media such as art installations, printed media, exhibitions etc. To enable a new reading of the space a set of research, analysis and presentation tools supporting the collection, interpretation and visualisation of data can be applied.

2 METROPOLITAN DIALOGUE

Taking the Creative Vision as a starting point, the aim of the metropolitan dialogue phase is to collectively discuss and (re-)process the comprehensive metropolitan strategy. By initiating a dialogue between decision-makers, planning authorities, city administration, urban researchers and designers as well as external (international) experts, a creative knowledge exchange is established. In the long term, this platform can continue to exist as a wider cross-sectoral and interdisciplinary network.

3 LOCAL ACTION

Translating metropolitan strategies into Local Action is the goal of the third phase. In addition to the stakeholder involvement during the Metropolitan Dialogue (second phase), it is aiming to strongly engage the local community to co-creatively develop local action plans. This should not only stimulate the implementation of first temporary interventions, but also give long-term perspectives. This results in identifying with the overall metropolitan vision and at the same time contributes to local empowerment and capacity building.

Tools for metropolitan planning

The multifunctional *MetroLab Toolbox* for integrated metropolitan development consists of research and analysis tools, presentation tools as well as interactive and dialogue-oriented tools. Accordingly, the different types of tools are used for various purposes: researching and analysing, presenting as well as stimulating dialogue and co-creating Metropolitan Visions, Strategies and Actions.

RESEARCH & ANALYSIS TOOLS

These types of tools aim at analysing the spatial structure, as well as the economic, demographic, ecological development of the metropolitan area. They are mainly used in phase 1, as a basis to prepare the creative vision, but can also be useful at a later point in the process. Some of the tools can be defined as more conventional research tools, such as collecting and processing quantitative data (statistics, geoinformation). Others might seem rather unusual at the first glance, but are important to get a comprehensive picture of the metropolis. Especially perceptual tools, such as observing, walking, as well as questioning tools are necessary to get a sense of place.

PRESENTATION TOOLS

Aiming at presenting (interim) results to the public, these types of tools can be used in all phases, mainly as a transition to the next phase. The presentation tools have a visual and artistic character as their purpose is to spread a certain image of the metropolitan area that attracts attention. Popular methods of presentation are, among others, maps, movies, books, as well as exhibitions.

STIMULATING DIALOGUE TOOLS

These kinds of tools are mainly used during phases 2 and 3—Metropolitan Dialogue and Local Action—and have the purpose to initiate discussions. In contrast to presentation tools, they not only give information about a certain topic, but also actively involve different stakeholder groups in the process. Some of these tools include more conventional workshop methods that are well known, but still can be very effective. Mostly, they are combined with presentation tools that serve as a basis for discussion.

CO-CREATION TOOLS

These types of tools are similar to dialogue tools, however, they are more interactive and have a stronger implementation character. They are mainly applied in the Local Action phase, as they rather can be used for a specific case study on the local level. Aiming at involving the local community and other stakeholder groups, they have a participatory character.

process design phase

1 CREATIVE VISION BUILDING → 2 METROPOLITAN DIALOG

tools & outcomes

- Data Mining: collecting quantitative and qualitative data
- Mapping: understanding metropolitan phenomena
- Photographing: depicting multiple realities
- Filming: setting space in motion
- Stakeholder Mapping: making power relations visible
- Explorative Walks: collective exploration of the area
- Visionary Maps: Reinterpreting the metropolitan area

→ OUTCOME #1: VISUAL MANIFESTATION OF THE CREATIVE VISION →

- Art Installations: making visions real
- Travelling Exhibition: making the vision tangible and setting it in motion
- Online Exhibition: creating an online presentation platform
- (Online) Survey: obtaining the perspective of local experts

type of tool

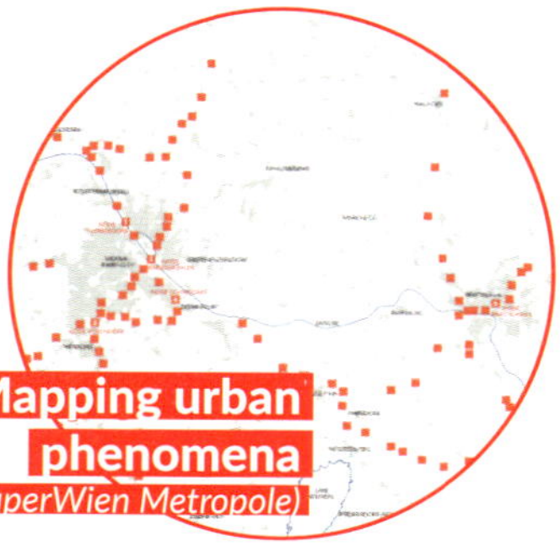

Mapping urban phenomena
(SuperWien Metropole)

Art Installations
(Tirol City)

3 LOCA_ACTION

- Expert Interviews: drawing on expert knowledge
- Movie Night: stimulating discussions on emerging topics
- International Lectures: learning from international approaches
- Forum Discussion: bringing different perspectives on the table
- Design Studio: testing the metropolitan vision

→ **OUTCOME #2: METROPOLITAN STRATEGY** →

- Walkshop: collective identification of intervention areas
- Case Studies Discussion: stimulate the imagination
- Urban Living Labs: shaping places together
- Pitch Night: a catalyst for new ideas
- Open Calls: encouraging community-led development

→ **OUTCOME #3: LOCAL ACTION PLAN**

Forum Discussion
(MetroLab)

Walkshop
(MetroLab)

Urbal Living Lab
(PlaceCity Floridsdorf)

PHASE 1 CREATIVE VISION BUILDING

Creative Vision Building as the first phase aims to understand and recontextualise metropolitan phenomena and creates the basis to develop cross-border strategies as well as a new image and identity for the metropolitan area. First of all, to gain profound knowledge of the spatial, social, cultural, economical and ecological conditions on a local scale, it is recommended to conduct empirical field research and to closely observe and question place-specific dynamics and create a sense of place. In addition to regular (desk) research (researching existing development strategies, policies and the history of the metropolitan area as well as doing a governance analysis), this approach, which serves to fully immerse into the specific area of investigation, is followed by the assessment of the data collected in the process (documents, notes, observations, informal conversations, etc.). This data is then reinterpreted and presented using visual tools (maps, photos, videos and films), helping to establish a new image of the space. Finally, the outcome of this first process design phase is the visionary representation of the functional urban area through various media such as art installations, exhibitions, printed or digital media.

⟶ OUTCOME: visual manifestation of the creative vision

TOOLS COLLECTION

» Data Mining: collecting quantitative and qualitative data
» Mapping: understanding metropolitan phenomena
» Photographing: depicting multiple realities
» Filming: setting space in motion
» Stakeholder Mapping: making power relations visible
» Explorative Walks: collective exploration of the metropolitan area
» Visionary Maps: reinterpreting the metropolitan area

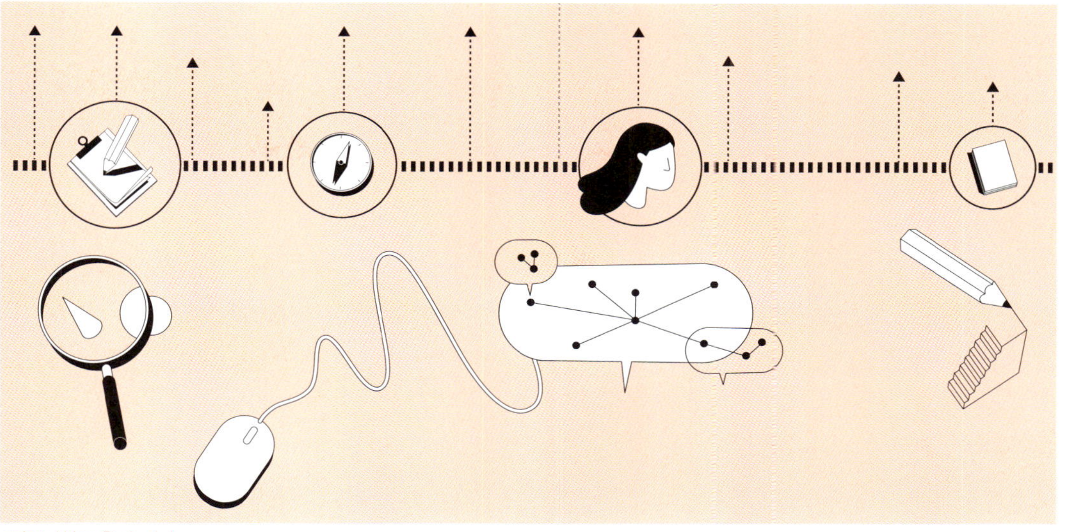

project: Urban Design Lab

DATA MINING

COLLECTING QUANTITATIVE AND QUALITATIVE DATA

1 CREATIVE VISION BUILDING

RESEARCHING AND ANALYSING

WHY

- collect sectoral and local-specific data
- identify pressing challenges and opportunities of development
- gain a holistic overview and understand specific locational charactersitics

WHAT

As a starting point of the Creative Vision Building Process, basic data needs to be collected in order to obtain an adequate overview and understanding of spatial phenomena. This includes the preparation and basic research on development strategies, policies and the historical background of the metropolitan area as well as the collection of socio-demographic and socio-economic data. The data collection forms the basis for further processing and interpretation of the data and identification of development trends. Data mining as a research and analysis tool helps to identify development challenges and opportunities and is therefore an inevitable step in approaching a metropolitan area.

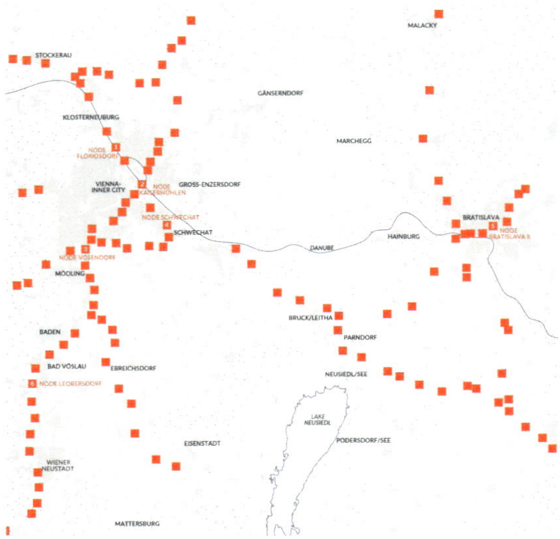

project: SuperWien Metropole

MAPPING

UNDERSTANDING METROPOLITAN PHENOMENA

1 CREATIVE VISION BUILDING

RESEARCHING AND ANALYSING

WHY

- reveal unknown spatial phenomena
- uncover multi-layered spatial relationships
- draw attention on existing functional connections within the metropolitan area

Special tip!
Switch on all your senses - not only the visible, but also sounds or smells can be mapped. Also, the tool only unfolds its full potential when it is used collectively, e.g. in the context of a collaborative mapping session.

WHAT

Mapping as a researching and analysing tool can be applied in different ways. As the simplest version, mapping is conducted analog in combination with explorative walks, equipped with printed base maps and various stickers, colored pencils, etc. Also, mental maps can be suitable for starting a mapping process and questioning one's own biased perspectives and fixed images of space. As cognitive maps they are oriented towards a relational concept of space linking perception, spatial representation and behaviour in space. However, analog mapping activities are limited to spatial sections and need to be complemented by digital mapping in order to become an overview of the whole metropolitan area. Thus, in addition to generating multi-sensory qualitative data, geo-based quantitative data should be collected and analysed. Depending on available resources, a GIS database could be built up, containing information about various thematic layers, such as green spaces, agricultural land, nature reserves, mobility axes, population density, waternetwork, etc. In the framework of an "layered analysis" different thematic layers are merged into one overall map, which will make cross-border spatial phenomena and functional connections visible.

project: SuperWien Metropole

PHOTOGRAPHING

DEPICTING MULTIPLE REALITIES

1 CREATIVE VISION BUILDING

RESEARCHING AND ANALYSING

WHY

» reflect on and show different facets of the metropolitan area
» documenting different spatial contexts at eye level
» creating an image of one specific or multiple reality/ies

Special tip!
In combination with questioning tools, visual images can also be used to elicit comments and thus stimulate a reflection process. This is demonstrated by the method of photo elicitation.

WHAT

Although photographing spatial phenomena is a very simple tool it is essential for the analysis of space. By looking through the lense of a camera, one will perceive the space differently and new, previously unnoticed facets of the environment will become visible. Especially in combination with mapping activities, photography serves as an indispensable means of documentation. By conducting and evaluating thematic photo walks within the metropolitan area, new contexts are recognized. Moreover, photographs can serve as a basis for (artistic) montages or exhibitions in the later process. Instead of orthophotos and maps, they create an image of reality at eye level that is easily understandable and yet leaves room for interpretation. In addition to the classic snapshot, photography has the potential to make (problematic) spatial transformation processes comprehensible, especially when used repeatedly.

film: Montparnasse Vibrations

FILMING
SETTING SPACE IN MOTION

1 CREATIVE VISION BUILDING

RESEARCHING AND ANALYSING

WHY

- reflect on and highlight different facets of the metropolitan area
- documenting different spatial contexts at eye level
- creating an image of one specific or multiple reality/ies

WHAT

If filming is applied as an analysis and research tool, it can serve as observation of everyday life in specific places within the metropolitan area. By filming, for example, a transportation node over a longer period of time, behavioral patterns of different user groups as well as spatial transformations are made visible and can be analysed. Similar to the Photographing tool, new spatial phenomena will become visible by perceiving the reality through a lense. Movies can also serve as a means of presentation of the metropolitan vision in the later process, serving as an artistic and entertaining medium that can initiate discussion in the form of art installations.

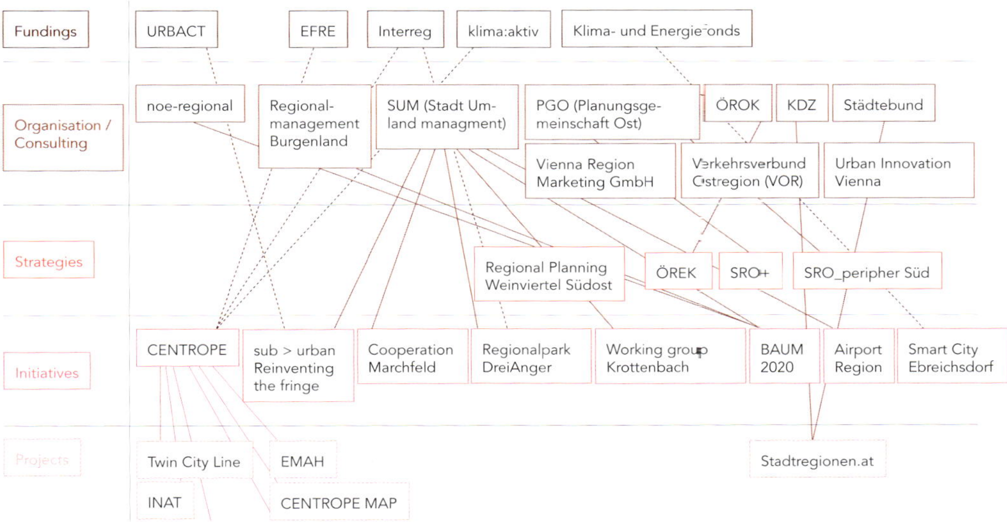

in the frame of MetroLab

STAKEHOLDER MAPPING

MAKING POWER RELATIONS VISIBLE

1 CREATIVE VISION BUILDING

RESEARCHING AND ANALYSING

WHY

» understand and visualise power relations/hierarchies between individual stakeholder groups/institutions
» get an overview and an idea of how to navigate within the network of stakeholders
» important basis to create a metropolitan platform/network

WHAT

Creating a stakeholder map is an important step towards understanding the (power) relations between individual institutions or people. The mapping process requires to create a list of the most important actors that shape the metropolitan area that represent the public, private and academic sector as well as the civil society. Once these diverse and multidisciplinary stakeholders (Universities, cities and regional governments, municipalities, public agencies, NGO's etc.) are categorized in thematic groups (e.g. education and culture, public administration, economy etc.) their relations should be visualized, which can take different forms. The Stakeholder Map gives a first indication of essential members to be involved in building the Metropolitan Dialogue Platform. This platform, which will accompany the planning process throughout its entire duration and will remain active even afterwards, involves the most important actors who have a stake in the development of the project. The Stakeholder Map can moreover be used as a basis for discussion e.g. in interviews. A suitable map requires in-depth research, but the tool can be very helpful especially at the beginning of the planning process and can significantly improve the outcome.

MetroLab Walkshop

EXPLORATIVE WALKS
COLLECTIVE EXPLORATION OF THE AREA

CREATIVE VISION BUILIDNG

RESEARCHING/ ANALYSING

STIMULATING DIALOGUE

WHY

- explore specific / unusual places within the metropolitan area by walking
- compare existing maps with reality
- invite (local) experts to tell stories about the space

Special tip!
Explorative Walks are more effective by combining them with other research and analysis tools, such as mapping and photographing.

WHAT

Together with members of the municipal and/or regional authority, representatives of the local communities and various other stakeholders, the metropolitan area is explored through walking tours. Accompanied by external experts on specific topics, such as mobility, urban agriculture, or housing, current challenges and potentials are being explored and discussed. In addition, local experts that know the respective area very well, such as residents or local entrepreneurs, should be invited to talk about the history and potential future development of their neighborhood. Therefore, during these walks we learn about spaces and their stories, historical background, urban morphology, social and cultural significance, and many other hidden aspects that may emerge. In order to get a broader understanding of the metropolitan area, its functional relations and contrasts, several walks should be organized in different territories with different thematic focuses. The routes of the walks need to be well chosen and prepared - depending on the size and fitness of the participants, so that they can stay active and receptive throughout the entire experience.

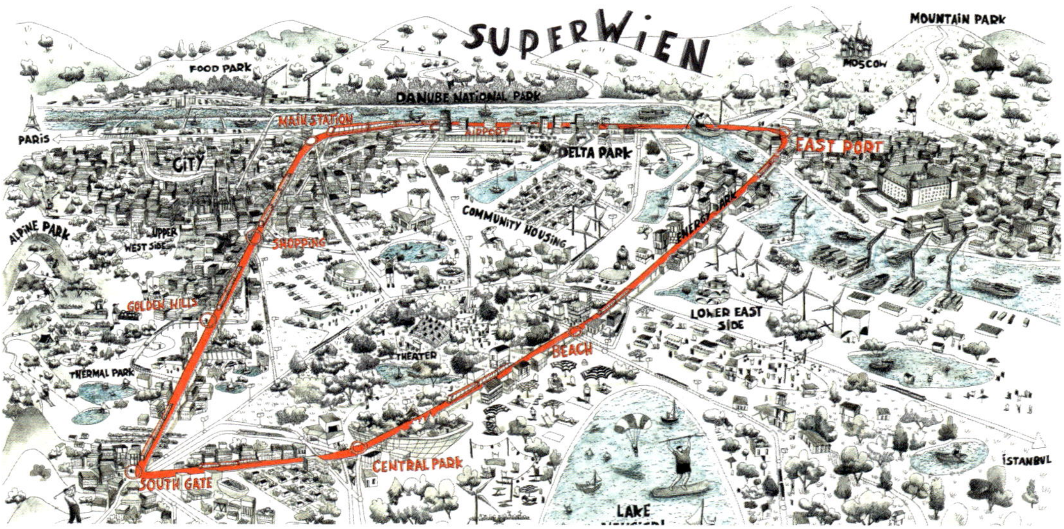

project: SuperWien Metropole

VISIONARY MAPS

REINTERPRETING THE METROPOLITAN AREA

1 CREATIVE VISION BUILIDNG | STIMULATING DIALOGUE | PRESENTING

WHY

- creating a new image and identity of the metropolitan area
- reinterpreting and recontextualizing qualitative and quantitative data
- maps can be displayed with the help of illustrations, collages, etc.
- as provocative image, it initiates discussion and functions as starting point of a metropolitan dialogue (Phase 2)

WHAT

As an outcome of the Creative Vision Building (phase 1) and basis for the Metropolitan Dialogue (phase 2), one strong image is produced giving the metropolitan area a new identity and communicating the main idea of its future development. Instead of creating a picture that considers as much as qualitative and quantitative data as possible and aims to predict the most likely future, only specific aspects of the metropolitan area are visualized in order to produce a new image that has the power to attract attention and initiate a debate. By reinterpreting and recontextualizing urban phenomena and functional relations within the metropolitan area the future development is consciously steered into a certain direction. The hiding of existing boundaries and formation of new spatial units is a very effective method to make cross-border relations visible. The most common media to present this future image of the metropolitan area are maps, which, however, can take over various forms, depending on their style and degree of abstraction. A city map has the potential to show the metropolitan area as one continuous territory and highlights only specific characteristics. A metro map, on the other hand, focuses on the linkages and connections between the places within the metropolitan area without giving more information about them.

PHASE 2 METROPOLITAN DIALOGUE

The new creative vision of the metropolitan region is supported by exhibitions, lectures and debates which are organised as part of a multifaceted discussion format. For example, the *International Dialogue on Metropolitan Planning* launched by *MetroLab* consists of four topic-specific *MetroLab* Forums and takes the creative vision of *SuperWien Metropole* as a starting point to open up the conversation. The comprehensive metropolitan vision is collectively discussed and (re)processed in cooperation with decision-makers, planning authorities, city administration, urban researchers and designers. Moreover, (international) experts are strongly involved in the process (by giving international lectures, expert interviews etc.) and contribute their specific knowledge about concepts of metropolitan planning. Interactive and discursive tools enable a creative knowledge exchange between different stakeholder groups and, in the long term, create the basis to form a broader, cross-sectoral and interdisciplinary network.

⟶ OUTCOME: a metropolitan strategy that includes case-specific emerging topics and is based on the new image of the metropolitan area (Phase 1)

TOOLS COLLECTION

» Art Installations: making visions real
» Traveling Exhibition: making the vision tangible and setting it in motion
» Online Exhibition: creating an online presentation platform
» (Online) Survey: obtaining the perspective of local experts
» Expert Interviews: drawing on expert knowledge
» Movie Night: stimulating discussions on emerging topics
» International Lectures: learning from international approaches
» Forum Discussion: bringing different perspectives on the table
» Design Studio: testing the metropolitan vision

project: TirolCity

ART INSTALLATIONS

MAKING VISIONS REAL

2 METROPOLITAN DIALOGUE | PRESENTING | STIMULATING DIALOGUE

WHY

- generate high attention by being visible in public space and address a new target audience
- communicate the vision in an artistic/creative setting
- initiate a debate about the future of the metropolitan area

Special tip! Provocation is a proven means of attracting attention.

WHAT

Art installations are used as an umbrella term for various kinds of creative presentation formats that are rather unconventional for urban development processes. The general idea is that the metropolitan vision is presented to the public by using, for example, audiovisual installations, open air exhibitions, performances, flash mobs, or even entire theater plays. In this way, certain issues and topics of the metropolitan vision are addressed indirectly; sometimes also quite directly. Applying such creative and rather surprising presentation formats, a wider audience is being reached that normally does not deal with urban development issues and would not take part in urban planning processes. Art installations most commonly are organized as temporary installations or interventions in public space and should be created in cooperation with professional artists

in the frame of MetroLab

TRAVELLING EXHIBITION

MAKING THE VISION TANGIBLE AND SETTING IT IN MOTION

2 METROPOLITAN DIALOGUE — PRESENTING — STIMULATING DIALOGUE

WHY

- be visible in public space and arouse interest of the public
- spread information, present vision to broad audience
- initiate a debate about the future of the metropolitan area

Special tip!
It is advised to support the exhibition by organising a side-programme that includes activities such as debate sessions or walkshops.

WHAT

Similar to art installations, public traveling exhibitions are a suitable tool to spread information in a creative way and arouse interest of the public. They are an ideal presentation tool to communicate a vision as well as to stimulate, or even provoke, the audience with it. The curators need to decide what content they want to focus on and whether their main aim is to only spread condensed information or also to collect information by integrating interactive features such as QR-codes that lead to a survey. In order to reach a greater audience, it is particularly useful to organise the public exhibition as a travelling exhibition that moves within the metropolitan area. To do so, the different stops should be chosen wisely and the main actors responsible for the different locations should be contacted at an early stage so that they can help prepare and promote the exhibition. To make its handling as easy as possible, exhibition content can be shown e.g. through a temporary and easily movable installation (panels/building fences etc.) or by more permanent structures such as a wooden construction.

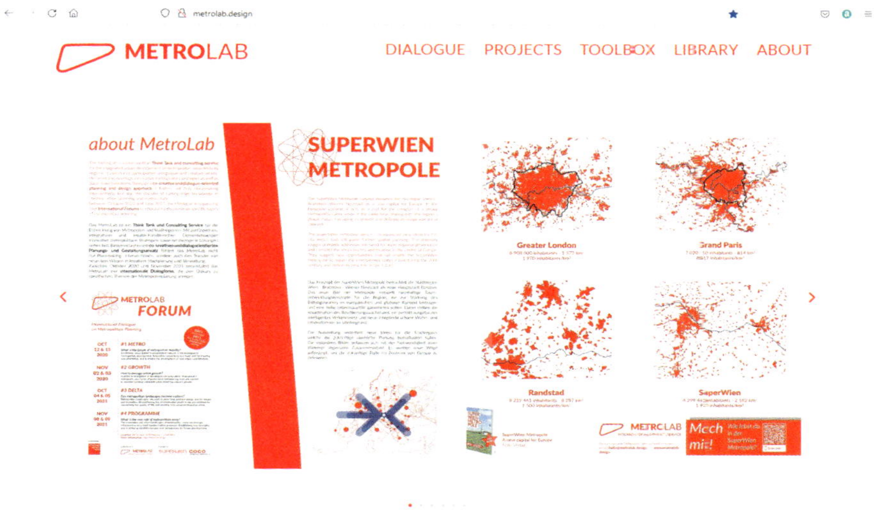

ONLINE EXHIBITION

CREATING AN ONLINE PRESENTATION PLATFORM

2 METROPOLITAN DIALOGUE — PRESENTING — STIMULATING DIALOGUE

WHY

- be accessible for a broad audience over a longer period of time
- easy to implement and access, in contrast to physical exhibitions
- can form part of an online archive

WHAT

If the public exhibition cannot take place as intended or should be made accessible to a broader audience over a longer period of time, an online exhibition might be a great alternative tool to convey and spread information in a creative way and to arouse interest of the public. In any case, online exhibitions can be a good addition to public exhibitions by which an even broader audience is reached. Specific topics related to the metropolis can be displayed and highlighted in the exhibition. In order to not only spread information, but also to get input by the audience, the online exhibition can be combined with an interactive online survey based on the topics of the exhibition and exploring public opinion on them. Online exhibitions can also be supported by organising a side programme such as a virtual presentation or a guided tour through the exhibition by the curators.

How do you live in the SuperWien Metropolis?

Dear residents of the city region Vienna-Wr.Neustadt-Bratislava! We would be delighted if you could take a few minutes of your time and tell us in the following questions how your life in the SuperWien city region is shaping up and what visions you have for this common living space!

in the frame of MetroLab

(ONLINE) SURVEY

OBTAINING THE PERSPECTIVE OF LOCAL EXPERTS

2 METROPOLITAN DIALOGUE

RESEARCHING AND ANALYSING

WHY

» easy to implement and access
» information can be collected and interpreted quickly
» generate a "mood picture" of certain stakeholder groups

WHAT

The main target group of (online) surveys are people who live and/or work within the metropolitan area and, thus, are daily users of its infrastructure and services. With the help of (online) surveys, their perceptions, needs and visions of the common living space can be retrieved, so the valuable information can then be incorporated into the development of a strategy. Online surveys in particular are very quick to implement and spread, inexpensive and easy to access. However, they need to be prepared carefully so that the collected information can be used for the creation of the strategy. Moreover, not all target groups can be reached through this digital medium. For the case the travelling exhibition contains a QR-code leading to the online survey, it is even more important to support the people at the exhibition site in filling it out. In addition, a printed survey should be provided for those who do not have access to a smart phone or computer.

in the frame of MetroLab

EXPERT INTERVIEWS

DRAWING ON EXPERT KNOWLEDGE

2 METROPOLITAN DIALOGUE

RESEARCHING AND ANALYSING

WHY

- collect and compare different perspectives on specific topics
- extend the stakeholder network
- expanding the knowledge horizon

Special tip.
Potential interview partners can be identified very well on the basis of the stakeholder map that has been created.

WHAT

Interviews deliver a broad overview of various aspects of the urban environment and everyday urban life. Therefore, they help to provide a deep insight into the physical and social constitution of the metropolitan area. To prepare each interview, a comprehensive questionnaire—based on collected existing material—is developed. This questionnaire should be topic specific, semi-structured and adjusted for different groups of stakeholders. The interview partners will be asked about the main problems in a specific thematic area of metropolitan development and their fears, but also about their hopes and the potential of the respective metropolitan area. The results of the interviews are an important source of information and the basis for the analysis and interpretation of challenges, needs and potentialities of the respective development area. By systemizing emerging topics as the main findings of the interviews, a quick overview of the most relevant issues for metropolitan development can be gained. Those emerging topics can be used as a basis to organize Forum Discussions and define a Metropolitan Strategy.

project: PlaceCity Floridsdorf

MOVIE NIGHT

STIMULATING DISCUSSIONS ON EMERGING TOPICS

2 METROPOLITAN DIALOGUE | PRESENTING | STIMULATING DIALOGUE

WHY

- get in contact with local community and initiate discussion
- share different perspectives / visions about certain topics
- target knowledge transfer

WHAT

Movie nights are a great creative and at the same time entertaining and low-threshold means of conveying different perspectives on a certain topic and initiating a discussion about it. It works best in combination with other tools such as a symposium including International Lectures and Forum Discussions on the same topic. Screening a movie is not only a great incentive for people to attend an event, but also a good conversation starter when followed by a moderated discussion. When a physical event is not possible, a movie night, including a discussion can also be organized online. The movie must be chosen with care so it perfectly fits the topic of the event. It is also very important to actively promote the event through different communication channels and platforms.

in the frame of MetroLab

INTERNATIONAL LECTURES

LEARNING FROM INTERNATIONAL APPROACHES

2 METROPOLITAN DIALOGUE

STIMULATING DIALOGUE

WHY

» broaden your knowledge horizon and learn from international good practice examples on metropolitan development
» get inspired by innovative tools and approaches for metropolitan planning and design
» reflect on the potential applicability of international approaches to the local context

WHAT

Through lectures of international experts from various fields (e.g. mobility and infrastructure development, housing etc.) who share their experiences on existing challenges and new approaches to different metropolitan areas, collective learning processes can be triggered. The knowledge exchange about good practice examples from different spatial contexts offers the opportunity to reflect on the development of one's own metropolitan area and to gain insights into already well-established processes. While international examples should always be considered against the background of their specific spatial and institutional setting, they can provide valuable inspirational input such as proven tools and approaches to handle various challenges of metropolitan areas for own projects. International Lectures should be combined with other tools, such as a Forum Discussion, to initiate a common debate and reflection between local planning representatives and the international speakers. They can be organised as physical events or online, whereby it is recommended to keep them short and precise to capture the full attention of the audience. The speakers need to be requested early enough and some guiding questions should be provided.

in the frame of MetroLab

FORUM DISCUSSION

BRINGING DIFFERENT PERSPECTIVES ON THE TABLE

2 METROPOLITAN DIALOGUE

STIMULATING DIALOGUE

WHY

» create an interdisciplinary knowledge exchange on specific topics of metropolitan development
» illuminate cross-sectional topics of supra-local importance from different angles
» different perspectives can contribute to close the theory-practice gap
» jointly reflect on the potential applicability of international approaches to the local context

WHAT

The Forum Discussion is a suitable tool to close an event, following International Lectures or other presentations. In addition to discussing current metropolitan developments (e.g. in mobility or housing), the panelists/(local) experts are for example invited to reflect on international approaches and projects, presented in the previously held presentations. Generally, a main topic and guiding question should be defined and used as the basis to choose the panelists. The stakeholder map can also be helpful here. When organizing a Forum Discussion, it's important to bear in mind that different stakeholder groups are represented on the panel, including the private sector, public administration, civil society and academia, among others. Regardless of the particular topic of discussion, different perspectives should be brought to the debate, which should be led by a moderator who is well informed about the topic and takes an impartial position. In order to open up the debate, the audience should also be invited to bring in their perspectives by asking questions to the panelists. Finally, a Forum Discussion can be organized as a physical event, as well as online.

MetroLab in Collaboration with TU Wien

DESIGN STUDIO

TESTING THE METROPOLITAN VISION

2 METROPOLITAN DIALOGUE — RESEARCHING/ ANALYSING — STIMULATING DIALOGUE

WHY

» break down the overarching vision and apply it to a local context
» making the vision more tangible through concrete design proposa s
» bringing in fresh ideas and new approaches

WHAT

The metropolitan vision, serving as a (provocative) future image of the te·rito·y and basis for developing a strategy, should be broken down exemplarily in order to make it mo·e tangible. In order to test its applicability to the local context, one specific sub are and/or a cross-cutting topic that is of high relevance for urban development, should be addressed in depth. In the framework of a Design Studio, different scenarios of urban development as well as concrete design solutions are developed that can be incorporated into the metropolitan strategy. A Design Studio can be organized as a student course or summer school, in cooperation with an academic institution. Thus, the students can play an active part in the strategy development by bringing in their fresh ideas and creative approaches.

PHASE 3
LOCAL ACTION

Translating metropolitan strategies into local action is the goal of the third phase. In addition to the stakeholders involved during the Metropolitan Dialogue (second phase), it is aiming to strongly engage the local community to co-creatively develop Local Action Plans together with planners and designers. In order to test and further develop long-term solutions, the implementation of first temporary interventions (in public space, ground floor zones etc.) is stimulated. Thus, by using interactive and discursive tools the overall metropolitan vision and strategy are brought to a realistic and feasible level in cooperation with the responsible planning officers at different levels and are evaluated by the local community. The Local Action Plans therefore elaborate and specify ideas for the local planning level which results in identifying with the overall regional and metropolitan vision. At the same time, the local community is being empowered by jointly co-creating their living environment in an Urban Living Lab setting.

⟶ OUTCOME: local action plan including (temporary) activation

TOOLS COLLECTION

» Walkshop: collective identification of intervention areas
» Case Studies Discussion: stimulate the imagination
» Urban Living Labs: shaping places together
» Pitch Night: a catalyst for new ideas
» Open Calls: encouraging community-led development

in the frame of MetroLab

WALKSHOP

COLLECTIVE IDENTIFICATION OF INTERVENTION AREAS

3 LOCAL ACTION | STIMULATING DIALOGUE | CO-CREATION

WHY

- understand everyday life and get closer to the community
- learn about the historical background, urban morphology, and social and cultural significance of a space
- identify potential areas of intervention

WHAT

In contrast to Explorative Walks, this tool focuses on one specific spatial territory within the metropolitan area that is in focus of development. The results of conducting this type of walkshop should be used as a basis to develop a Local Action Plan. By combining a walk with a workshop as a more interactive format, the participants learn more about spaces and their historical background, urban morphology, social and cultural significance, and other hidden aspects that may emerge. The group walks through the daily life of the neighborhood, which allows for a shared understanding of the workings and nature of the place. Both tangible and intangible values of the planning area are explored and immediately mapped by the participants. Possible mapping topics can be problem areas, but also potential intervention areas, landmarks, economic activities, building heights, etc. In addition, maps can also express very personal impressions, feelings, thoughts and qualitative information of the participants. This information on the physical-material but also immaterial nature of the environment will help to understand the complexity of the place and to get closer to the local communities which will be relevant for the longer-term planning process.

in the frame of MetroLab

CASE STUDIES DISCUSSION

STIMULATE THE IMAGINATION

3 LOCAL ACTION | STIMULATING DIALOGUE | CO-CREATION

WHY

- critical reflection of the planning area
- generate new ideas and solutions as basis for development of urban scenarios
- awake imagination of local community

WHAT

Experience has shown that exposing stakeholders to examples of successful projects from other cities can help to awaken their imagination as regards projects in their own neighborhood. A set of 15-20 "good practice" examples, selected and visualized by the planning team, is presented to the stakeholders in an exhibition setting. Participants have time to study the posters, either in groups or alone, and ask questions if needed. They are encouraged to think about similarities between the presented cases and the respective case in their own city, and find answers to specific questions, such as what are the strengths and weaknesses of the projects shown, if the solution is suitable or if it could be adjusted to fit into the planning area. Participants are asked to put their answers on Post-its and pin them onto the posers. A concluding group discussion on the results can help to generate new ideas but also to critically reflect on the transferability and suitability of certain concepts for the selected planning area. A case study discussion might be a useful basis for the collective development of urban scenarios in the next stage.

project: PlaceCity Floridsdorf

URBAN LIVING LABS

SHAPING PLACES TOGETHER

3 LOCAL ACTION STIMULATING DIALOGUE CO-CREATION

WHY

- provide a forum for urban innovation and improve urban interventions by prototyping
- integrate citizens as users and co-creators
- high level of stakeholder participation, co-creation, co-production, learning-loops and experimental approaches

WHAT

Urban Living Labs (ULLs) have proven to be a successful tool in many cities worldwide and, thus, should be at the center of each co-creation process on a local scale. Setting up an Urban Living Lab means being on site for a longer period of time and, in co-creation with different stakeholders, analysing and exploring the neighborhood, as well as testing prototypes. In this sense, ULLs provide a forum for innovation, applied to the development of new products, systems, services and processes in an urban area. The process of exploring and prototyping should always be launched by the joint identification of challenges and needs from the perspective of the local community (local residents as well as entrepreneurs, the public sector and academia). The exploratory phase should be followed by an experimentation phase that includes the joint development of a prototype of the proposed solution, as well as testing it. Based on several feedback loops, the final, permanent version can then be built. By being on site and testing the prototype in a real-time setting, the acceptance of the permanent intervention by the local community is expected to be higher than usual. This is also due to the use of working methods that integrate people into the entire development process as users and co-creators to explore, examine, test and evaluate new ideas, processes, systems, concepts and creative solutions in complex and everyday contexts.

project: PlaceCity Flordisdorf

PITCH NIGHT

A CATALYST FOR NEW IDEAS

3 LOCAL ACTION | STIMULATING DIALOGUE | CO-CREATION

WHY

- get a wide range of positions on the same topic
- stimulate a discussion

WHAT

A pitch night is usually an evening event at which 5 to 10 different speakers present their position or perspective on a specific topic in short "pitches", which should last no longer than 5 minutes each. This results in a wide range of positions on one and the same topic, but all of them taking a clear stance on sustainable and liveable transformations in cities and urban areas. A Pitch Night can be applied to very narrow, clear topics or to very open questions. However, it also is a great tool to give planners the opportunity to showcase projects that they have already realised or are about to implement. It offers not only a nice opportunity for citizens to get information in an informal atmosphere, but also for urban planners to receive feedback on their ideas.

project: PlaceCity Flordisdorf

OPEN CALL

ENCOURAGING COMMUNITY-LED DEVELOPMENT

3 LOCAL ACTION | STIMULATING DIALOGUE | CO-CREATION

WHY

- collect various ideas and (financially) support their implementation
- empower the local community to become actively involved in the metropolitan development
- identify and activate placemakers (potential future) users of specific places within the planning area

WHAT

Unlike conventional calls for tenders in the field of architecture or urban planning, Open Calls are targeted at everyone who is interested in proposing ideas and implementing their own projects in the metropolis, independent of their background or profession. Open Calls should focus on selected subareas (e.g. mobility nodes) and have a specific purpose, such as finding ideas to programme or redesign public spaces. Based on some criteria (e.g. main objectives, scale and costs of the project, target group), people can submit their visionary ideas and a jury decides which ones fulfill the criteria best. Through the openness of the calls, a wide variety of actors are invited to participate in shaping the metropolis through their projects and to experience it together. Therefore, it is advised to advertise them broadly to guarantee a diverse and high number of participants. In contrast to conventional planning competitions that ask for a specific design solution for a respective area, Open Calls aim to collect project ideas that can be implemented by the submitters themselves. Financial support should be provided by the organisers to assist the implementation. By using Open Calls to temporarily or permanently program the (public) spaces , it's an ideal tool to identify and activate placemakers and potential future users of specific places.

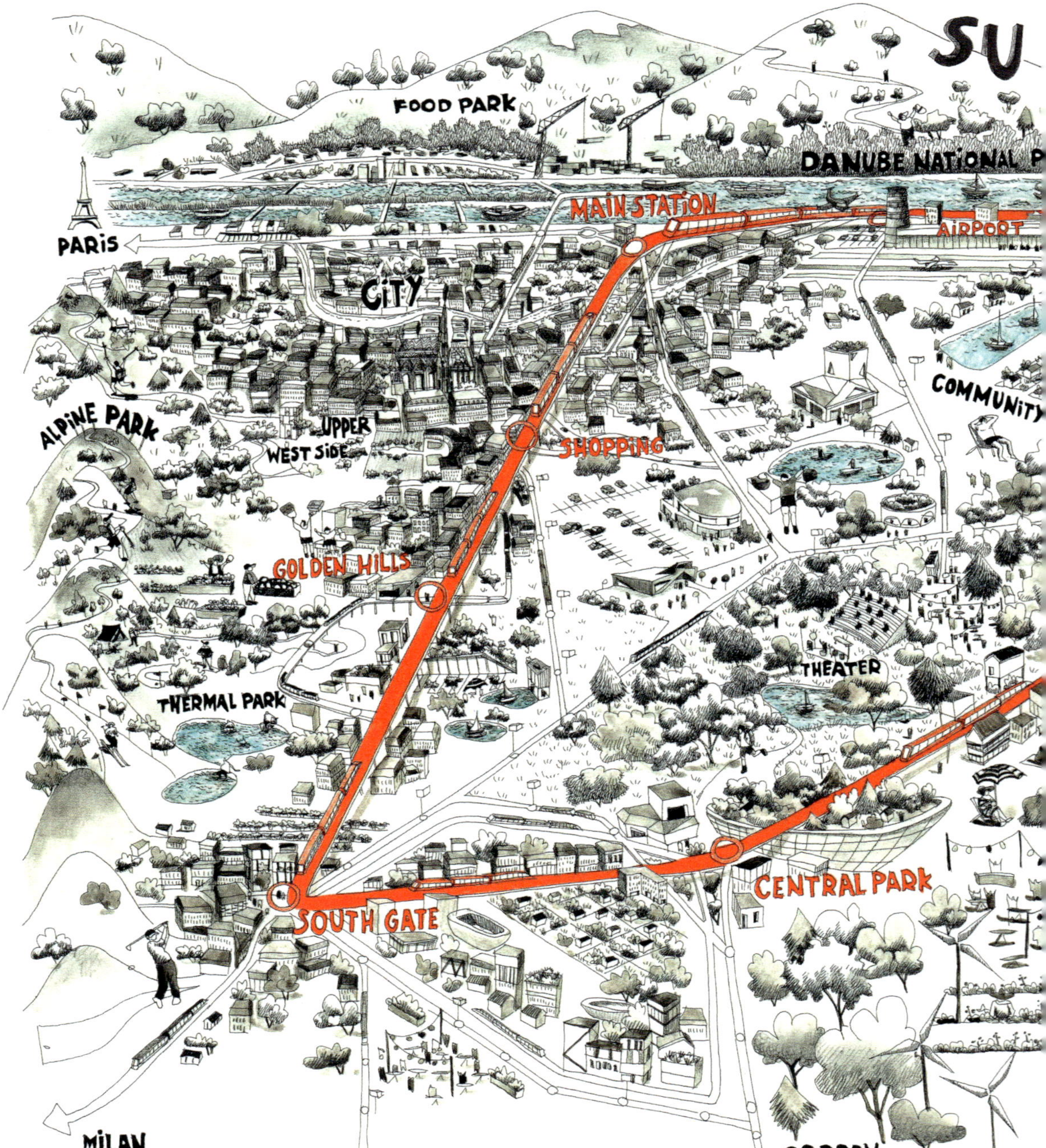
SU
FOOD PARK
DANUBE NATIONAL P
MAIN STATION
AIRPORT
PARIS
CITY
COMMUNITY
ALPINE PARK
UPPER WEST SIDE
SHOPPING
GOLDEN HILLS
THEATER
THERMAL PARK
CENTRAL PARK
SOUTH GATE
MILAN
SOPRON

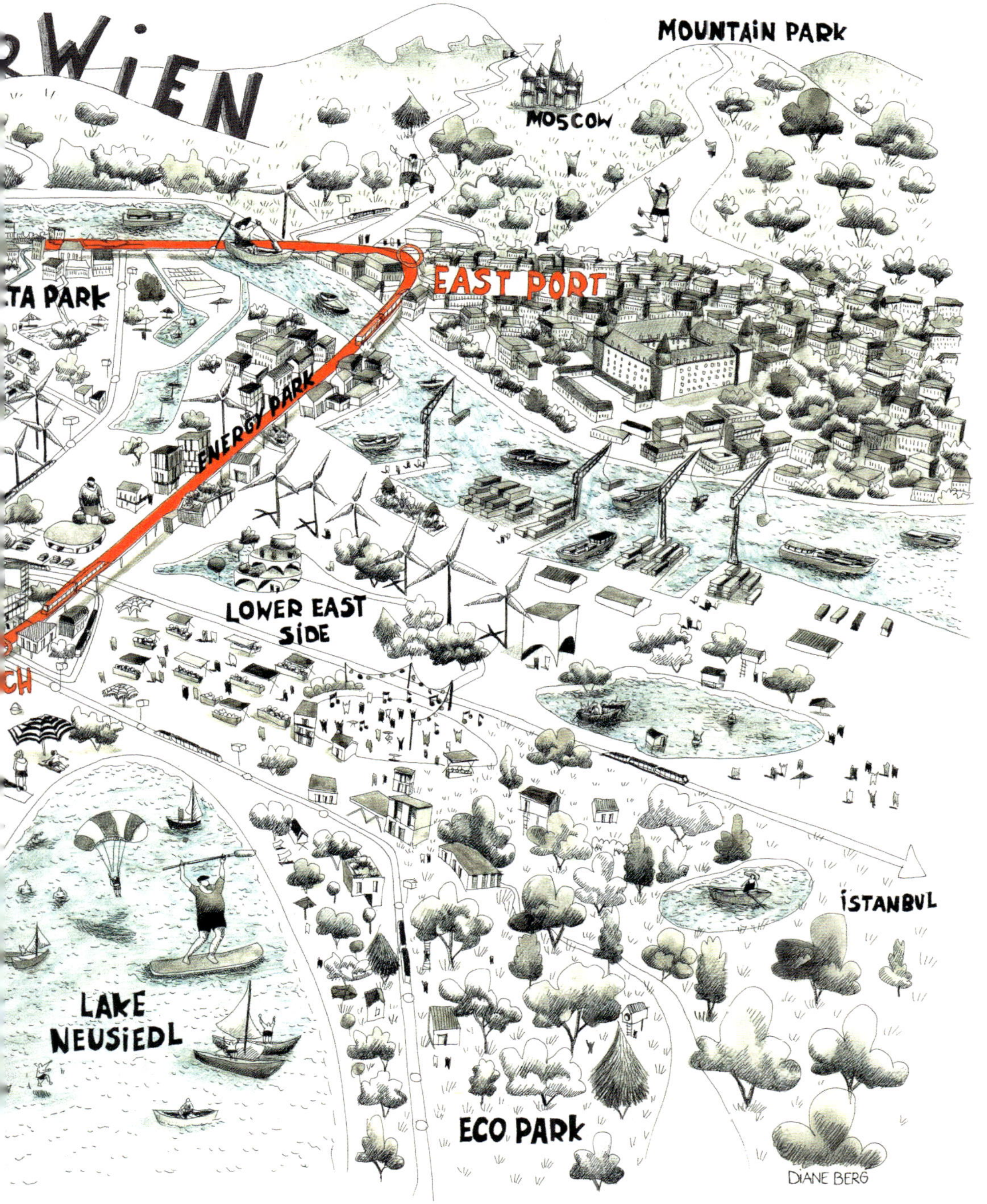
RWIEN
MOUNTAIN PARK
MOSCOW
TA PARK
EAST PORT
ENERGY PARK
LOWER EAST SIDE
CH
ISTANBUL
LAKE NEUSIEDL
ECO PARK
DIANE BERG

VISION BUILDING

CREATING NEW IMAGES

As functional regions often break with existing administrative delineations, there is not only a high demand for coherent spatial development, but also for the creation of a shared development perspective that then can drive co-ordinated spatial development on a larger scale. By understanding and recontextualizing metropolitan phenomena, creative images and a new reading of the space are created, that have the potential to break encrusted (administrative) structures and encourage thinking outside the box.

The discussion on future development paths should be framed as an open process. On the one hand, to ensure that all stakeholders, political decision-makers as well as citizens can co-create it and find themselves in it. On the other hand, because the discourse itself can convey a novel idea of regional togetherness, which can be identity-forming. Visionary images therefore act as an idea generator for further discussion and knowledge-production processes. A strong vision of the future is the basis for overcoming factors that hinder integrated development and for launching integrative projects across administrative borders.

Visions shape perception and can thus bring about change

A conversation between **Wolfgang Andexlinger**—City of Innsbruck, **Elke Mittmann**—École d'Architecture Strasbourg, **Janin Walter**—urban strategist and artist, and **MetroLab**

MetroLab: As *MetroLab* we reinterpret well-known urban narratives through new images with the intention of stimulating a discussion on metropolitan development. In this context, we understand the term "Metropole" as a generator of ideas that triggers images in the mind and initiates discourse. What is your understanding of vision-building?

Wolfgang Andexlinger: I would distinguish between two levels of vision-building. At the level of exploration, the instrument of vision-building is very valuable in providing a thought-provoking impulse and to stimulate the discussion on future development paths. The focus is thereby not on the actual spatial impact of the visionary image, but on the comparison of images of the future in order to sound out a viable direction for development. In my opinion, vision-building in the metropolitan region is precisely about this finding process. Once the framework and objectives are set, vision-building is about developing actual projects. This can, of course, be done cooperatively by seeking discourse with several teams of planners and other actors.

"I would distinguish between two levels of vision-building: exploration of future development paths and the development of actual projects"

Elke Mittmann: Vision-building can take many different forms. In the end something may be built, but a vision can also be an idea behind a new form of urbanity, i.e. how do you live within the metropolitan area? How do you define yourself as a citizen in a broader context? In my experience, vision-building is not only about the built environment, it is foremost about the intangible.

W.A.: Mental visions, I would think, are often much stronger than those captured in pictures, but at the same time leave more room for maneuver. Visualized images are rather perceived as reality and feel final. Therefore, I think it is very important to consciously communicate and point out that visionary images do not necessarily show a possible reality.

Janin Walter: Visions, namely the idea of what future space could look like, are an instrument of the traditional planning discipline. In the past, visions were developed solely in the planning office and then presented to the residents, and planners were often faced opposition. In integrated planning, it is assumed that locals know their living environment and needs best. The main questions are how the visioning process should be structured and who should be involved in the process. Usually, workshops are held to gather opinions and then translate them into a vision, which is iteratively fed back to the actors and translated into plans and models. In cultural planning, I take this a step further and break down the visions to a 1:1 scale in order to create a bodily experience and to open up the dialogue.

E.M.: We turned to the instrument of visioning out of lack of alternatives during the *IBA Stadtumbau* (Urban Renewal) in Saxony-Anhalt between 2002 and 2010, in which we sought answers to the population decline in eastern Germany. Traditional planning tools were not applicable in the face of shrinkage because they are exclusively designed for urban growth. The cities' task was to think of urban development not only from a technocratic or material perspective, but from an interdisciplinary angle. During this process, the cities were accompanied by the IBA office in order to jointly ask themselves which site-specific characteristics could be drawn upon that also had the potential to mobilize a large part of the local population. In addition to the moderation work, we applied participatory instruments and did a lot of public relations work to not only create a vision, but also to put it up for discussion. Civil society plays a crucial role in vision-building, because only when visionary images have horizontal backing among the population will they also be shared. Visions cannot be carried by one person alone, as vision-building is always related to an identification process.

"Civil society plays a crucial role in vision-building, because only when visionary images have horizontal backing among the population will they also be shared."

MetroLab: What do you see as the potentials and challenges in the integrated development of visionary images? What effect do vision statements have on the different groups of actors?

W.A.: In general, a high level of moderation competence is necessary in the participation of civil society. It must be made clear who holds which role in the participatory process and that not every element that is mentioned can be implemented. Nevertheless, I believe that a haptic-visual presentation is much more accessible than a theoretical one. Visionary images serve very well as a communication tool to represent complex issues in space. ▸

J.W.: Through collective vision-building, the actors and their bonds are strengthened and changes can be triggered at a local level, which planners or politicians can no longer control, but have to let go of. At the same time, the empowerment of actors through collective vision-building is also reflected externally and groups and neighborhoods at various scales are perceived in a more integrated way. Thus, vision-building has an internal and external identity-creating effect.

"Vision-building has an internally and externally identity-creating effect."

E.M.: Vision-buildings means highlighting unique features that can strengthen social cohesion through their identity-forming effect on actors. At the same time, shared visions mobilize different actors, apart from the planning discipline, and thus create a new form of planning culture that is rooted in the perception of a democratic living space. A democratic planning culture that creates the tools to open the dialogue, has the power to re-program spaces and create new, shared images.

W.A.: In my opinion, it is particularly important to have a discussion in advance about what should be achieved by vision-building: mobilization of actors, rejection of projects or scenarios, attention for a certain topic etc. After all, images tell stories and therefore trigger emotions. If, for example, visionary images are used to draw a positive picture of the future, in the best case many people will commit to a development path, which gives it more assertiveness. At the same time, there are also many disastrous images of the future, especially in connection to the climate crisis, which have a deterrent but also mobilizing effect.

"Exaggerations channel ideas and sharpen the picture by focusing on specific issues and reducing them to their essential elements."

J.W.: I also work with negative visions for strategic reasons, to sound out tendencies when actors have very different ideas of development. Exaggerations, which also stem from art, channel ideas and sharpen the picture by focusing on specific issues and reducing them to their essential elements. These are provocative, of course, but they can be used to explore different development directions.

E.M.: In general, with procedural planning, the end is usually unclear, which is of course interesting from different points of view, but politically hard to sell.

MetroLab: Recontextualizing and reinterpreting spatial phenomena at the metropolitan scale opens up new perspectives that have the potential to overcome administrative boundaries and sectoral responsibilities. We see a common development vision as a prerequisite for a comprehensive strategy with tangible objectives and fields of action, indicating spatial and thematic focus areas. In your opinion, what can visions do for the spatial perception of the metropolitan region?

J.W.: In my opinion, metropolitan strategies also require 1:1 implementation according to cultural planning. Ultimately, even at a large scale, strategies are implemented at the local level.

W.A.: I think the potential of visions on a regional and metropolitan level lies in their potential to break up administrative borders. If administrative borders are not shown in the picture, they also recede into the background mentally, just as administrative borders are often only recognizable at the place-name signs in reality. In people's lives, political borders mostly have less meaning than in the administrative sense. The same is true for sectoral responsibilities. Through visioning, administrative complexity loses importance because it is about the matter at hand. The focus is placed on what could be created if people work together on something.

"Through visioning, administrative complexity loses importance because it is about the matter at hand. The focus is placed on what could be created if people work together on something"

"Visions also create and sharpen perception and accordingly also have the potential to bring about change."

E.M.: Visions also create and sharpen perception and accordingly also have the potential to bring about change. This does not happen overnight, but visions have the power to change the perception of one's own city, one's own environment. ▪

TRAVELLING EXHIBITON

BRATISLAVA

GALERIE PERSPECTIVE, PARIS

LIESING

METROLAB FORUM #1 METRO

INTERNATIONAL LECTURES
Javier Ortigosa, Àrea Metropolitana de Barcelona
Floridea Di Ciommo, cambiaMO changing mobility
Alexandre Di Cocco, Société du Grand Paris
Michaël Leymarie, ADP Ingénierie

METROPOLITAN WALKSHOP
Gerald Franz, Urban Innovation Vienna
Max Mutz wohnbund:consult
Vincent Neumayer, Wiener Linien GmbH

MOVIE NIGHT
Marlene Rutzendorfer, Curator & Moderator
Michaël Leymarie/Cédric Ramière, Filmmakers
Timo Novotny, Filmmaker

FORUM DISCUSSION
Gregory Telepak, City of Vienna
Mathias Mitteregger, TU Wien
Vincent Neumayer, Wiener Linien GmbH
Stefan Mayr, MetroLab

MÖDLING
Josef Hameter, raum und plan
Hannes Koza, Mayor Vösendorf
Michaela Haidvogel, Vize-Mayor Maria Enzersdorf
Werner Deringer, Roland Geiwitsch & Nikolaus Ibesich, Municipal Cunstruction Department Mödling
Chris Schmitzer, Municipal Council Brunn am Gebirge
Silvia Drechsler, Vice-Mayor Mödling

RÖMERLAND CARNUNTUM
Inna Mlada, City Councilor Schwechat
Christian Berger, NÖ.Regional
Gabriele Preisinger, Cornelia Fischer & Sandra Karanitsch-Ackerl, Regional Management Römerland Carnuntum
Nikola Selakovic, Future Council Römerland Carnuntum
Hartmut Dumke, TU Wien
Daniel Youssef, TU Wien
Marianne Penker, BOKU

GERASDORF BEI WIEN
Robert Bachinger, City Councilor Gerasdorf
Benjamin Scepka, Municipal Council Gerasdorf
Christina Stockinger, City of Vienna
Renate Zuckerstätter, SUM North

DESIGN STUDIO DELTA

Stefan Mayr, MetroLab
Cédric Ramiere, MetroLab
Nela Kadic, TU Wien
Marcel Catalin Bumb, student
Vanessa Minhuey Espinoza, student
Felix Alexander Neudeck, student
Sara Borjanovic, student
Angelica Pedrotti, student
Ilia Verzakov, student
Jumi Radde, student
Theresa Steiner, student
Julius Bartz, student
Eketarina Mihaylova, student
Michal Vitcovic, student
Amanda Immler, student
Paulína Slivková, student
Katharina Stell, student

METROLAB FORUM #3 DELTA

FORUM DISCUSSION
Christina Stockinger, City of Vienna
Anna Detzlhofer , DnD Landschaftsplanung
Helga Kromp-Kolb, Climate Change Centre Austria
Herbert Bartik, Urban Innovation Vienna

METROPOLITAN WALKSHOP
Christina Stockinger, City of Vienna
Renate Zuckerstätter, SUM North

MOVIE NIGHT
Marlene Rutzendorfer, Curator & Moderator
Oliver Ressler, Filmmaker
Viktoria Bayer/Michael Reindel, Filmmakers

INTERNATIONAL LECTURES
Pia Kronberger-Nabielek, PBL Netherlands
Siri Frech, Raum+Strategie, Neuland gewinnen e.V.
Daniela Patti, Eutropian Research & Action
Hélène Coussedière, BASE Landscape Agency
Paraskevi Tarani, RiConnect, Major Development Agency Thessaloniki

METROTALK WORKSHOPS
Philipp Loidolt-Shen, Azolla Ecosystems
Vanessa Giolai & Daniel Löschenbrand, Urban Food Atlas
Christoph Fink, Metropolitan Cooking

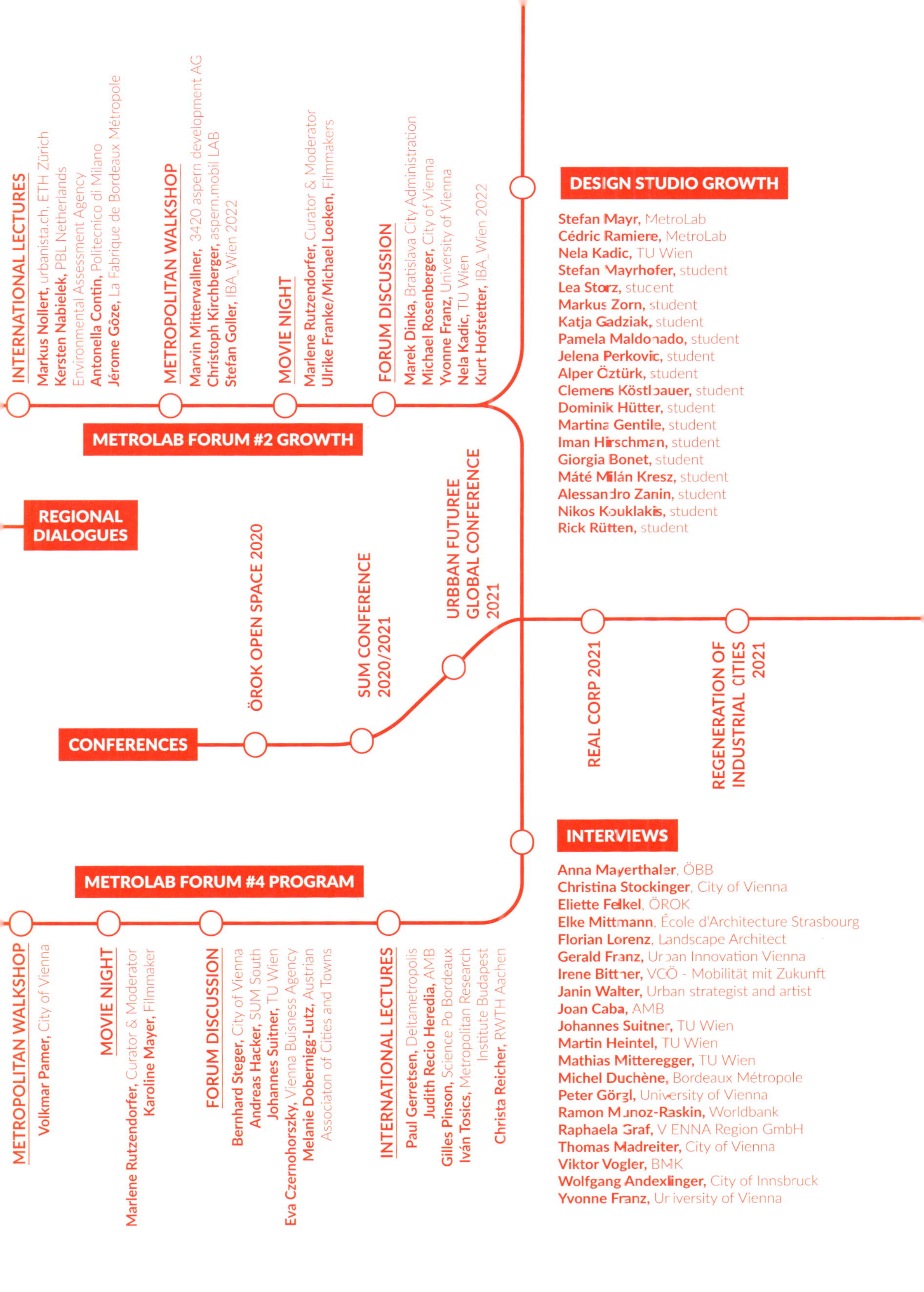
INTERNATIONAL LECTURES
Markus Nollert, urbanista.ch, ETH Zürich
Kersten Nabielek, PBL Netherlands Environmental Assessment Agency
Antonella Contin, Politecnico di Milano
Jérome Gôze, La Fabrique de Bordeaux Métropole
METROPOLITAN WALKSHOP
Marvin Mitterwallner, 3420 aspern development AG
Christoph Kirchberger, aspern.mobil LAB
Stefan Goller, IBA_Wien 2022
MOVIE NIGHT
Marlene Rutzendorfer, Curator & Moderator
Ulrike Franke/Michael Loeken, Filmmakers
FORUM DISCUSSION
Marek Dinka, Bratislava City Administration
Michael Rosenberger, City of Vienna
Yvonne Franz, University of Vienna
Nela Kadic, TU Wien
Kurt Hofstetter, IBA_Wien 2022
METROLAB FORUM #2 GROWTH
DESIGN STUDIO GROWTH
Stefan Mayr, MetroLab
Cédric Ramiere, MetroLab
Nela Kadic, TU Wien
Stefan Mayrhofer, student
Lea Storz, student
Markus Zorn, student
Katja Gadziak, student
Pamela Maldonado, student
Jelena Perkovic, student
Alper Öztürk, student
Clemens Köstlbauer, student
Dominik Hütter, student
Martina Gentile, student
Iman Hirschman, student
Giorgia Bonet, student
Máté Milán Kresz, student
Alessandro Zanin, student
Nikos Kouklakis, student
Rick Rütten, student
REGIONAL DIALOGUES
CONFERENCES
ÖROK OPEN SPACE 2020
SUM CONFERENCE 2020/2021
URBBAN FUTUREE GLOBAL CONFERENCE 2021
REAL CORP 2021
REGENERATION OF INDUSTRIAL CITIES 2021
INTERVIEWS
Anna Mayerthaler, ÖBB
Christina Stockinger, City of Vienna
Eliette Felkel, ÖROK
Elke Mittmann, École d'Architecture Strasbourg
Florian Lorenz, Landscape Architect
Gerald Franz, Urban Innovation Vienna
Irene Bittner, VCÖ - Mobilität mit Zukunft
Janin Walter, Urban strategist and artist
Joan Caba, AMB
Johannes Suitner, TU Wien
Martin Heintel, TU Wien
Mathias Mitteregger, TU Wien
Michel Duchène, Bordeaux Métropole
Peter Görgl, University of Vienna
Ramon Munoz-Raskin, Worldbank
Raphaela Graf, VIENNA Region GmbH
Thomas Madreiter, City of Vienna
Viktor Vogler, BMK
Wolfgang Andexlinger, City of Innsbruck
Yvonne Franz, University of Vienna
METROLAB FORUM #4 PROGRAM
METROPOLITAN WALKSHOP
Volkmar Pamer, City of Vienna
MOVIE NIGHT
Marlene Rutzendorfer, Curator & Moderator
Karoline Mayer, Filmmaker
FORUM DISCUSSION
Bernhard Steger, City of Vienna
Andreas Hacker, SUM South
Johannes Suitner, TU Wien
Eva Czernohorszky, Vienna Buisness Agency
Melanie Dobernigg-Lutz, Austrian Associaton of Cities and Towns
INTERNATIONAL LECTURES
Paul Gerretsen, Deltametropolis
Judith Recio Heredia, AMB
Gilles Pinson, Science Po Bordeaux
Iván Tosics, Metropolitan Research Institute Budapest
Christa Reicher, RWTH Aachen

DIALOGUE

INITIATING A CREATIVE KNOWLEDGE TRANSFER

Designing a city region that is open to metropolitan development means creating an open dialogue first, which implies finding the right format that supports the mutual exchange of knowledge on many levels. Since the *MetroLab* does not only develop large-scale metropolitan visions but also aims to foster place-based approaches, not only planning officials and experts participated actively in the process, but civil society and local residents. By the co-creation of metropolitan environments, *MetroLab* understands the involvement and cooperation of as many heterogeneous stakeholders as possible to jointly create knowledge, policies and tools, and to find and implement place-based solutions. In doing so, the metropolitan scale is reflected to translate creative visions into sustainable local action.

Co-production as an even more intense form of cooperation *"[...] aims at making engagement matter to both sides, by having the technically trained maker and the life-experienced dweller generate the plans in the first place; open urban forms [...] can serve as orienting points for doing so"* (Sennett 2018: 244).

METROLAB

FORUM

International Dialogue on Metropolitan Planning

DAY 1
Movie Night
DAY 2
Metropolitan Walks
International Lectures

OCT 12 & 13 2020	**#1 METRO** *What is the future of metropolitan mobility?* A coherent, cross-border transportation network is the backbone of metropolitan development. Innovative connectivity is a major tool for creating new centralities and to enable the development of new urban-rural lifestyles.
NOV 02 & 03 2020	**#2 GROWTH** *How to manage urban growth?* In order to strengthen or reconfigure the polycentric structure of a metropolis, new forms of governance and planning tools are needed to maintain existing standards while fostering compact growth.
OCT 04 & 05 2021	**#3 DELTA** *Can metropolitan landscapes become resilient?* Metropolitan landscapes are used to grow food, produce energy and for leisure and recreation. Strengthening the environmental assets is the precondition for maintaining the quality of life and creating crisis-proof metropolitan areas.
NOV 08 & 09 2021	**#4 PROGRAM** *What is the new role of metropolitan areas?* The economies and urban landscapes of metropolitan areas are strongly influenced by structural transformation processes. Establishing new synergies and re-defining governance structures creates new perspectives for future development.

Flyer International Dialogue on Metropolitan Planning

As a first step to stimulate the co-creative process, actors in a format that allowed for a multi-voiced dialogue in the city region were brought together: the *International Dialogue on Metropolitan Planning*. During a two-day program the *MetroLab Forum* offered the opportunity to listen to exciting lectures by international experts, participate in walkshops and watch and discuss selected movies. Taking up the approach of translocal learning, planning challenges and approaches of different metropolitan regions were discussed and innovative tools for metropolitan planning and design were shared and tested. The four-part dialogue series kicked-off in fall 2020 with the first two *MetroLab Forums* on mobility and growth. They were followed by two more forums on the importance of resilient urban landscapes and the new role and identity of city regions in 2021.

Forum Discussion
MetroLab Forum #3 DELTA

Opening of the *MetroLab Forum #3 DELTA*

International Lectures at the *MetroLab Forum #1 METRO*

International Lectures at the *MetroLab Forum #1 METRO*

Forum Discussion at the *MetroLab Forum #4 PROGRAM*

Opening of the *MetroLab Forum #1 METRO*

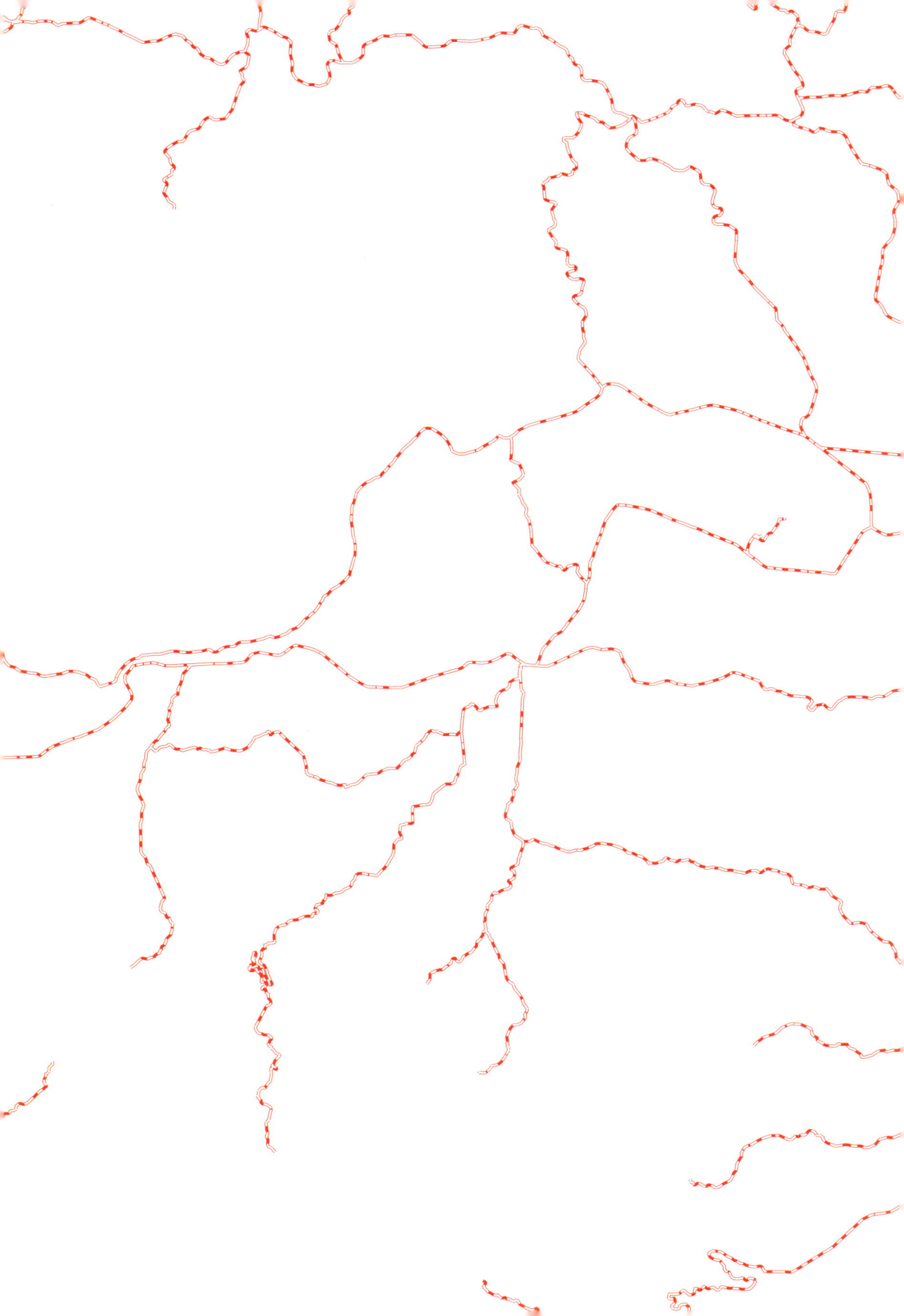

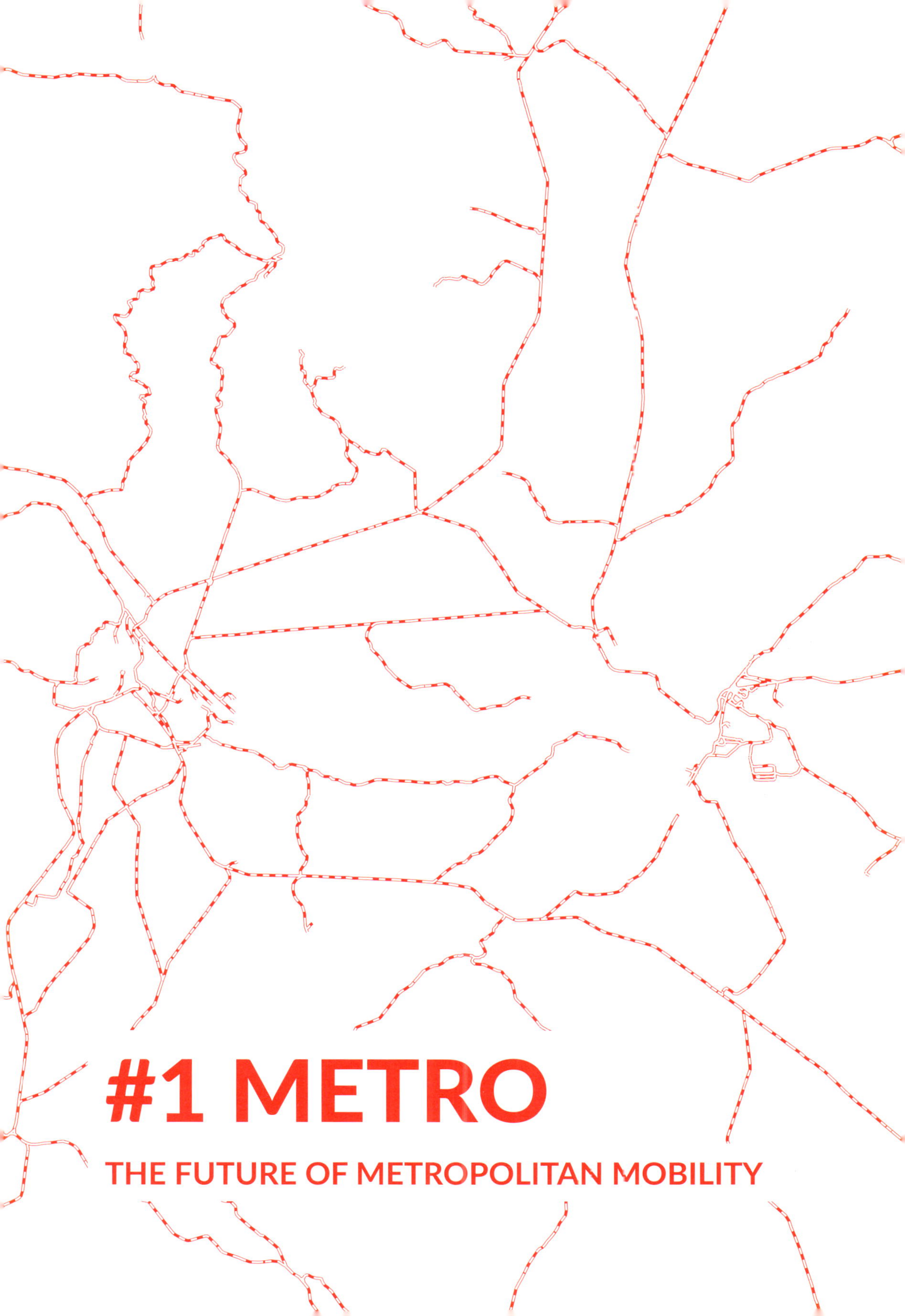

#1 METRO

THE FUTURE OF METROPOLITAN MOBILITY

Flyer MetroLab Forum #1 METRO

What is the future of metropolitan mobility?

A coherent, cross-border transportation network is the backbone of metropolitan development. In the future, our mobility systems not only will have to meet multi-modal, but also multi-optional demands. From the interlocking of different forms of mobility, to a smooth transition from walking or cycling to bus, train or car, the discussion is moving towards the general requirements of a successful interconnection of metropolitan areas. Discussing the future of metropolitan mobility means not only questioning existing mobility policy instruments and measures, but also encouraging sustainable and inclusive mobility as well as a territorial rebalance. By learning from other metropolitan areas such as Grand Paris, Barcelona and Madrid, a multi-perspective view is taken on when talking about the planning and management of public transport systems in the Vienna Metropolis. Also, light is shed on how far mobility is an essential tool for creating new centralities and enables the development of new urban-rural lifestyles.

UNDERSTANDING MOBILITY

Multi-modal hubs driving shared mobilty

Metropolitan Walkshop through Simmering

In mobility development, multi-modalit has become an indispensable buzzword, to which great importance is attached, especially regarding the expansion of environmentally friendly modes of transport. But what is the actual potential of networked and multimodal mobility and how can such new mobility concepts be integrated into district planning? The two mobility experts Vincent Neumayer and Gerald Franz have helped us to shed light on the subject.

On the way through Simmering, Vienna's 11th district, Vincent Neumayer, project manager at the department for multi-modal mobility management at *Wiener Linien*, introduced a group of twenty people to the first of Vienna's *WienMobil* stations. Developing and leading mobility projects in the field of new mobility services and screening relevant mobility trends is part of his daily business working for the most significant public transport provider in Vienna.

By sharing his vast knowledge about the services provided by this station, consisting of an e-carsharing station, several rental bicycles, a cargo rental bike and a bicycle storage box, the audience was given a wide-ranging insight into how a multi-modal mobility solution can manifest itself in the urban public space.

THE WIENMOBIL STATION AS A MULTI-MODAL HUB

The project, which was developed as one of several integrated smart city solutions for Simmering in the realm of *Smarter Together*, an urban regeneration initiative supported by the EU and implemented in the three cities of Vienna, Lyon and Munich, laid the foundation for the expansion of the *WienMobil* stations within the city. While the most recently opened stations are located in inner-city districts, the station under consideration is situated in a less central, but strategically important place. Positioned right next to the metro terminus of the U3, it serves to overcome the so-called "last mile" between the places of work or residence and the nearest public transport station, an important feature of the climate-friendly city.

> *"The objective in the city of Vienna is to achieve a share of less than twenty percent of trips done by cars by 2025."*
> *Vincent Neumayer*

Since potential users are mainly locals, the station serves as an important transfer point (e.g. from bike to metro or local buses) to reach specific destinations connecting the neighborhood with its wider surroundings.

Especially on weekends, the new mobility services are extensively used for recreational purposes.

As Neumayer points out, this small multimodal hub has great potential to drive shared mobility. It contributes to reduce motorised private transport by enabling a smooth transition from one mobility mode to the other without the need to own a vehicle at all. According to him, *"the objective in the City of Vienna is to achieve a share of less than twenty percent of trips done by cars by 2025."* Therefore, apart from boosting public transport ►

it is essential to support cycling, walking and shared modes of transportation even though shared mobility cannot currently be identified in the modal split surveys.

MULTI-MODAL AND SHARING MOBILITY AS A GAME CHANGER

According to Gerald Franz, Senior Expert for Mobility Management at the *Energy Center at Urban Innovation Vienna*, in order to further implement environmentally friendly mobility solutions in the fast-growing city, we need to be aware of two different starting points. While transforming mobility systems and services in dense city centers turns out to be quite a challenge, new urban development areas are more flexible to adapt to new demands. *"Public transport comes first,"* when it is a question of how places of work and residence are connected, he says. But nevertheless, additionally, other measures are also needed to support people in using alternative modes of transport instead of relying on a private car. Here too, multi-modal and sharing mobility (carsharing implemented in housing, better cycling facilities and bike service stations etc.) are the key to support sustainability in transport development. *"What we see when we implement these measures is that you really have to take people by the hand and clearly explain the new offers"*, Franz explains. He also points out that a problem which remains partly unsolved is how to deal with the large number of parking spaces in the city. If we really want the cityscape to change in this respect, much effort will be needed to deconstruct these places and put them to a new use, he emphasizes.

> *"What we see when we implement these measures is that you really have to take people by the hand and clearly explain the new offers."*
> *Gerald Franz*

He feels that there is a particular need to raise awareness regarding the necessary change in our mobility behavior. Only if there is a change in value is there a change in mobility, he argues. This becomes visible in newly emerging neighborhoods where the chance that new multi-modal and eco-friendly offers will be well received is quite high because newly arrived inhabitants are reached at a time when they can still rethink and change their mobility habits. Thus, it is more important than ever to also promote innovative alternatives to fossil mobility in residential construction, already existing and newly built. ▪

Scan to watch the video documentation of the Metropolitan Walkshop!

Vincent Neumayer
Project Manager, Multi-Modal Mobility Management, *Wiener Linien GmbH*

Michaël Leymarie
Urban Planning Expert in Mobility and Transportation Infrastructure, *ADP Ingénierie*, Paris

Gerald Franz
Senior Expert at *Energy Center, Urban Innovation Vienna*

If we stop imagining a bright future, we might as well not do it at all

Interview with **Anna Mayerthaler**—ÖBB (Austrian Federal Railways)

MetroLab: In the book *SuperWien Metropole. A New Capital for Europe*, in which provocative visionary images for the metropolitan area of Vienna are presented, we question existing boundaries on several levels. If we look at the Vienna city region, the question arises as to how far it extends from a transport planning perspective? What is the significance of borders for the city region?

Anna Mayerthaler: If we look at the accessibility of the public transport network, everything that can be reached within 20 to 25 minutes must almost be considered part of it, because in this area the work interdependencies and commuting relationships are still extremely strong. For planning, it is essential to ask about functional and not necessarily administrative boundaries. But when it comes to implementation, one unfortunately often ends up back at the politicians and the administrative units.

The *ÖBB 360°* program has made headlines for its pilot project in Korneuburg, a municipality in Lower Austria close to Vienna's city limits. There, new mobility services (car-sharing cars, e-scooters, e-bikes) are offered as a complement to public transport, thus enabling an environmentally friendly way to cover the "first" and "last" mile. What was the initial intention of the *ÖBB 360°* program?

"Companies are also increasingly acknowledging that it is no longer state of the art to simply hand over a company car to everyone from mid-management upwards."

The *ÖBB* deliberately wanted to promote the innovation sector in mobility development through the program. We then approached integrated mobility and noted in dialogue with the municipalities that there is a great need among the mayors to offer alternatives to motorised private transport for their residents. Often a change in thinking has already taken place in this regard and they realise that by offering alternative mobility concepts, for example, fewer parking spaces need to be built in residential buildings and the supermarket in the periphery may no longer need as many parking spaces in the future.

In addition, the bicycle infrastructure planning might also have to be adapted if services that require a certain infrastructure are launched within 6 months [Note: this was the case with the Korneuburg pilot project, for example].
Ultimately, it can be seen that the implementation of such projects relies very much on the commitment of individual decision-makers who identify integrated mobility as an important issue, while others still think very mono-modally. Companies are also increasingly acknowledging that it is no longer state of the art to simply hand over a company car to everyone from mid-management upwards, but that it is about sensitising people to use other means of transport and sharing modes and to create incentives, for example by providing a job bike instead of a company car or introducing a mobility budget.

What exactly is meant by "integrated" mobility?

"Integrated" means, that the mobility service matches the person's needs. In other words, mobility offers are integrated into the needs on the one hand and into systems such as *Mobility as a Service (MaaS)* on the other, and are therefore easy to use, access and book. There are many Mobility as a Service platforms and many want to gain a foothold in this platform business and offer mobility. Mostly, however, it is not a well-functioning IT solution that is needed, but the mobility solution on the ground. We intend, also in the interest of a public company, to cover these services of general interest and to provide mobility where it is needed. And we no longer have to do all of this with the classic tools. It doesn't always have to be a regular bus, that 50-seater that drives around empty once an hour.

How do you see the future potential of integrated mobility solutions?

Sharing cars, e-scooters and e-bikes are currently well accepted. Active mobility was also one of the profiteers of the pandemic—cycling in particular is now booming very much at the individual level. At the moment, it is rather difficult with our core business, public transport, as we have made a loss of 90% especially in long-distance transport in 2020. That also had a massive financial impact on us. But I think that will change again. We will not completely stop travelling and I am convinced that public transport is the only logical answer to the challenges of the climate crisis. It is the backbone of our transport system and if we don't rely on it, we have lost. Then, the pandemic is the least of our problems. ▸

"[...] I am convinced that public transport is the only logical answer to the challenges of the climate crisis."

With the *SuperWien Metropole* we have taken a look into the future and proposed a *SuperRing* structure that is not only an important hub of a Europe-wide intercity transport system, but also facilitates commuting within the city region (Vienna - Wr. Neustadt - Bratislava) with train connections upgraded to metros. In your opinion, what is the contribution of such visions, or utopias in general?

One has to think a lot with the help of utopias. If we stop imagining a bright future, then we might as well not do it at all. We should express and capture a lot more crazy ideas so that people can actually envision them. Whether it's the superblocks in Barcelona or the highways along the Seine in Paris to green up the riverbank and make it usable again—it will only work with radical solutions.
Personally, Vienna is not progressive enough in this respect. There is still the attempt to apply the watering can principle, where everyone has his or her spot and everyone should be supported. You don't want to step on anyone's toes.

Where would one have to start in Vienna in order to bring about changes in the mobility sector?

"The ideas for the measures are not lacking. The only thing missing is the will and courage to do something."

There are very conventional measures that people don't dare to tackle. The first would be to reduce the number of parking spaces in a much more radical way. What has become a matter of course in Amsterdam, for example, is met with opposition here. In Vienna, the districts have a lot of power in the transport sector, which should actually be raised to a legislative level. A transport department like the *MA18* should be allowed to conduct Vienna-wide planning that is then also implemented. The ideas for the measures are not lacking. The only thing missing is the will and courage to do something. I am deeply convinced that more beautiful environments and more space to stay and linger in public space are concepts that are accepted by the vast majority.

Is it up to the political decision-makers or the population to realise such spaces or to demand their realisation?

The change in value can only take place once things are worth something, also in the sense of monetary prices. We know that urban space, whether it is open space or residential space, is a precious and hard-fought commodity. But compared to the square metre of living space, we ascribe less value to the label "space in public space" via the lower price. And the population also perceives it that way, because the price tag is simply not right here. If we were to give public space the same monetary value as private living space, we would immediately talk about a different distribution of spatial resources, which is currently oriented towards motorised individual transport. ▪

Opportunities of design are also linked to opportunities of responsibility

Interview with **Mathias Mitteregger**—future.lab Research Center at TU Wien

MetroLab: In your 2020 publication *AVENUE21*, you argue that established territorial, institutional and organizational boundaries need to be challenged quickly to ensure a positive contribution from automated and connected transport. What does this mean for your approach to the Vienna metropolitan region? How is it defined in the context of your research project?

Mathias Mitteregger: We understand the Vienna metropolitan region as the "functional urban area" according to the *OECD* definition. For us as a project team, this is currently an exemplary area, on the basis of which we are investigating very concrete planning approaches and taking much greater account of the spatial conditions than has been done in the discourse so far. We ask: How could automated driving be used and implemented spatially in the context of the change in transportation, given the limited time frame we have left in the face of the climate crisis? What are the framework conditions that need to be set in order to avoid negative effects as far as possible? We were able to show that this is a planning task that can no longer be avoided in the future. Not planning at all is also a conscious decision.

What was your methodological approach in answering the above mentioned research questions and what was the overall goal?

For us, it was crucial that we as sociologists, architects, urban planners, traffic planners and architectural theorists tried to work together and that we had countless conversations where we did not have the expertise ourselves. You can see that the professional discourse on automated driving in the past was very much conducted from the technological and traffic planning perspective, and that a lot was lost in the process. This may be surprising, but we were the first study (in the field of automated traffic) to understand roads not only as transport routes, but also as living spaces.
The methods used correspond very much to the spirit of our times. Our intention was to use the general scenario technique in a different way and to focus on local design. We want to show that it is people who shape the future. ▸

In the end, the question is which voices are heard and which are not. Who gets to shape the future and who doesn't.

The city of Vienna, with its all-encompassing will to shape the future, is still rather paternalistic. Other cities entrust their citizens with more freedom, opportunities to have a say and to actively shape the future. Opportunities to shape things often create a personal bond instead of the expectation that someone will fix it. I don't think it is possible to move towards a climate-neutral future without this being a truly shared concern.

There is a lot of scope of action not only in technology, but also in politics, urban planning and administration. In your opinion, how should future settlement and mobility development in Vienna be structured in order to be able to design a well-integrated urban region? And what role will automated driving play in this?

The longer I work on the project, the more absurd I find the distinction between settlement and mobility development. These two areas are so fundamentally linked and simply have to be thought of together. In the same way, the difference between urban and rural areas is often emphasized today when it comes to the transformation of transportation. This difference is homemade, because it is largely the result of transport and urban development policy mistakes of the past. While (rail-bound) public transport was withdrawn from the area, uncontrolled housing development was allowed. It has always been known that this can only lead to a dependence on cars. We need to start thinking in an integrated way in order to develop the city and the countryside in a targeted way. What automated driving means for the development of Vienna's urban region cannot be clearly stated because, as I said, it is a design task. If nothing is done—as we were able to show in our publication—urban sprawl would be further intensified and centers and their lively street spaces come under massive pressure. But there are also numerous opportunities, especially in the public provision of suburban areas, where public transport is still unattractive today.

"We need to start thinking in an integrated way in order to develop the city and the countryside in a targeted way."

I think there will also be a need for pragmatic decisions in terms of transport policy in the future, especially with regard to climate change. We will have to set priorities and see where we can create attractive offers and alternatives to the car.

Current challenges are strongly linked to past failures. How do you think the long overdue change in transportation can be initiated? What role do digitalisation and automation play in this process?

There are two problematic approaches from the past that we must not repeat. The first is the fixation on a single means of transport. Secondly, we have to make sure that we plan a transport system in which cycling and walking are absolutely prioritised. We conclude that regardless of the technological possibilities, automated driving should

"Secondly, we have to make sure that we plan a transport system in which cycling and walking are absolutely prioritised."

only be used in parts of the road network to avoid the mistake we made with the car, namely, letting the car into every corner of the city and village.

Accordingly, the implementation of automated vehicles in the existing transport system is a planning task that involves understanding needs, developing criteria and assessing compatibility. It is important to create offers on a small scale, because the change in mobility will require cuts. However, if renunciations are demanded, alternatives must also be offered.

Is a paradigm shift in metropolitan planning emerging, or does it need to be initiated in order to achieve the goals you mentioned?

From my point of view, existing planning principles should not generally be called into question: first and foremost, it is about avoiding traffic. This can be achieved mainly by cutting down on land use and by promoting mixed cities and centers. Secondly, it is about shifting traffic and making as many trips as possible within the environmental network. Thirdly, roads must be seen as valuable living spaces and not as mere transport routes. Radical approaches are needed here—a few trees make little difference. We need completely re-designed roads. Much else is up for debate in a time of change we are in. It also makes no sense to strive for a city as it existed before the car. Because the truth is that we have a suburbia that people also like to go to. We have to recognize that it is in the suburban areas that the leverage should be applied. The city centers are mostly already well served. If we want even difficult transport policy decisions to be accepted by the majority of the population at some point, attractive alternatives must be available—everywhere.

"[...] roads must be seen as valuable living spaces and not as mere transport routes."

What is your vision of the Vienna metropolitan area?

We need a strong reality check in the development of visions. The city is a perennial and always unsolved problem. The exciting question is not only "where do we want to go" which is what all the strategy papers are for, but the question: "how do we get there?" And that's where the planning starts. It has to be said that the measures in the Vienna metropolitan region have so far been far from sufficient. Political borders, which are sometimes responsible for why Vienna and Lower Austria do not cooperate sufficiently, must also be moved aside, otherwise we have no chance. The reality is that mobility is changing—with and without automation. International companies offer mobility services that can be accessed with an app all over the world, while we in Austria still have a problem planning a trip with several means of transport across city borders. But this problem will hopefully soon be a thing of the past. ▪

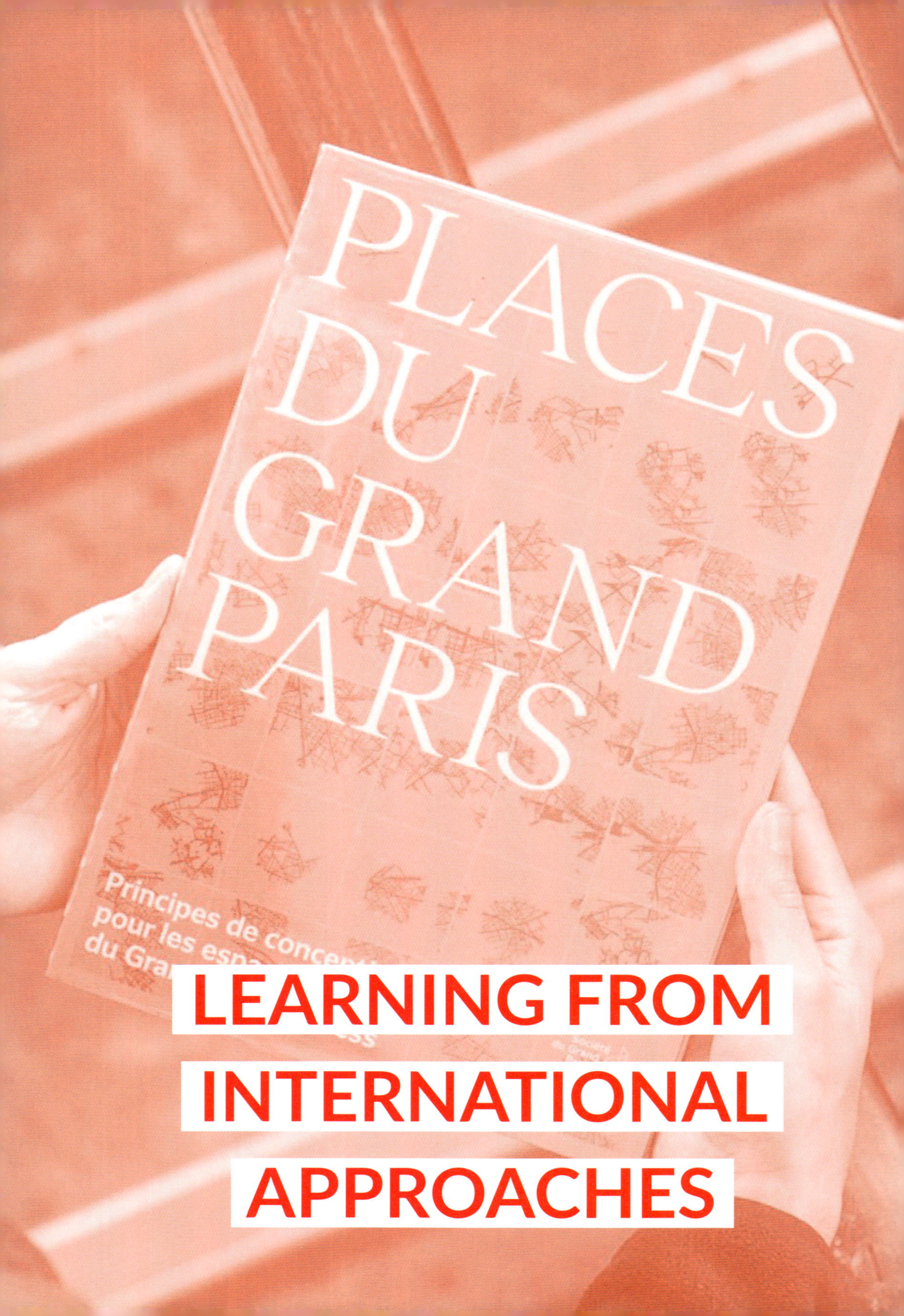

LEARNING FROM INTERNATIONAL APPROACHES

Les Places du Grand Paris—a universal vision of the public space around future stations

Alexandre Di Cocco—Société du Grand Paris

The *Grand Paris Express* is the largest infrastructure project in Europe. 200 kilometers of automatic lines and 68 new stations will be built in the Paris Region between 2021 and 2030. New public spaces will also be built around these stations to facilitate access and intermodality. They will be financed in particular by the *Société du Grand Paris* and *Île-de-France Mobilités* (transport authority), which must guarantee the quality of the solutions provided, adapted to each region.

By connecting to the existing network, the *Grand Paris Express* will strengthen the Paris Region public transportation network and profoundly change travel patterns. Alongside buses and bicycles, walking will become the main mode of transportation at future stations, for which more space must be created. Multifaceted mobility practices will continue to evolve after the opening of the lines, so it is essential to develop the integration of the new mobilities that find a place in these neighborhoods. Future public spaces must be capable of adapting to changing uses over time.

At the same time, public spaces will also become new urban centralities. The objective is not only to create new access points for future users of the network, but also to develop new spaces that meet the needs of all people, whoever they are: residents, travelers, passers-by, customers of a business, etc.. To make stations and their neighborhoods living spaces for users and residents, we are convinced that public space must be designed in its multiple dimensions. Their design should be consistent with the construction of the station and with the transformation of the surrounding neighborhood.

The *Grand Paris Express Station Design Reference*, published in 2011 and regularly updated, already stated that "*the Grand Paris station is designed as a route between the city and the trains*". In 2015, the publication *Les Places du Grand Paris* specified the urban ambition of the *Grand Paris Express* by outlining the first guidelines. Also in 2015, the *Société du Grand Paris* and *Île-de-France Mobilités* initiated a study program (68 hub studies) with the aim of defining, in collaboration with all partners, the program of intermodal facilities and equipment to be built within a 300-meter perimeter around each station.

These studies were discussed in a wide variety of geographical, sociological and political fields. In order to guarantee the overall coherence of the *Grand Paris Express* hubs in terms of the quality of the development of intermodal public spaces around the stations, the *Société du Grand Paris* decided to publish a reference framework for the Grand Paris squares. The aim of this guide is to pursue the creation of a shared vision of the urban and landscape integration model for the *Grand Paris Express* stations, in collaboration with the stakeholders of each area. The book proposes 40 operational design principles, 26 of which are essential, and a roadmap that will guide the design of the 68 *Grand Paris Express* squares. In order to maintain a common direction, three major ambitions, continuity, scalability and availability of public spaces underpin this shared vision and can be found throughout the entire project. ▸

A clear roadmap proposed in the hub's framework guides the delicate passage through the different structuring phases of a project (choice of designer, works, commissioning, management).

The reference plans of the hubs are the first step in affirming a common ambition. This starts with the hub studies, at the end of which the program of intermodal facilities and equipment to be built within 300 meters of the stations, as well as the estimated costs, financing and contracting authorities, will be formalized in a reference plan. This document forms the basis of a partnership commitment to the project and contributes to the development a shared culture of the public spaces of the *Grand Paris Express*. This will make it possible to align the urban design and landscape proposals and to envisage the principles that will form the basis for the operational phase.

As the quality of the project depends on strong project management, the *Société du Grand Paris* and *Ile-de-France Mobilités* invite the various stakeholders, once this reference plan has been drawn up, to develop a joint program and preliminary project for all the public spaces of the hub, either by appointing a single project or through a consortium.

UPSTREAM OF THE PROJECT MANAGEMENT PROGRAM: THE CHOICE AND PRIORITIZATION OF THE PRINCIPLES OF THE REPOSITORY

The principle selection phase is an essential prerequisite. Based on these principles, the *Société du Grand Paris* and *Ile-de-France Mobilités* validate the obtaining of subsidies for the design and realization of the hubs. In order to assess the relevance and priority level of each principle for a particular hub, a series of preliminary studies are carried out, ranging from an ecological diagnosis to a permeability study. These development orientations are then formalised into a list of principles which become contractual objectives in the project management programs, that are to be achieved.

SUPPORTING THE ACTORS IN THE SEARCH FOR INNOVATIVE SOLUTIONS

Les Places du Grand Paris, Design Principles for the Public Spaces of the *Grand Paris Express*, will help project owners in piloting, programming, designing and managing their public spaces. The design principles remain at a more abstract level in order not to trap future designers into a generic response, but to leave room for creativity.

Nevertheless, in order to foster shared reflection, the *Société du Grand Paris* and *Île-de-France Mobilités* will deploy a variety of tools to promote and initiate innovative approaches. Thus, in partnership with the *Association of Mayors of Île-de-France*, a call for innovation projects is launched each year, focusing either on mobility or on public space. The sum of these experiments will provide an overall vision for the success of future Greater Paris squares. The aim of the framework for the Greater Paris squares is not to impose on project owners who already know how to design and manage the public spaces in their area, but rather, given the specificity of a hub, to offer all the keys to success right up to commissioning and to ensure that each area has the same access to these tools. ▪

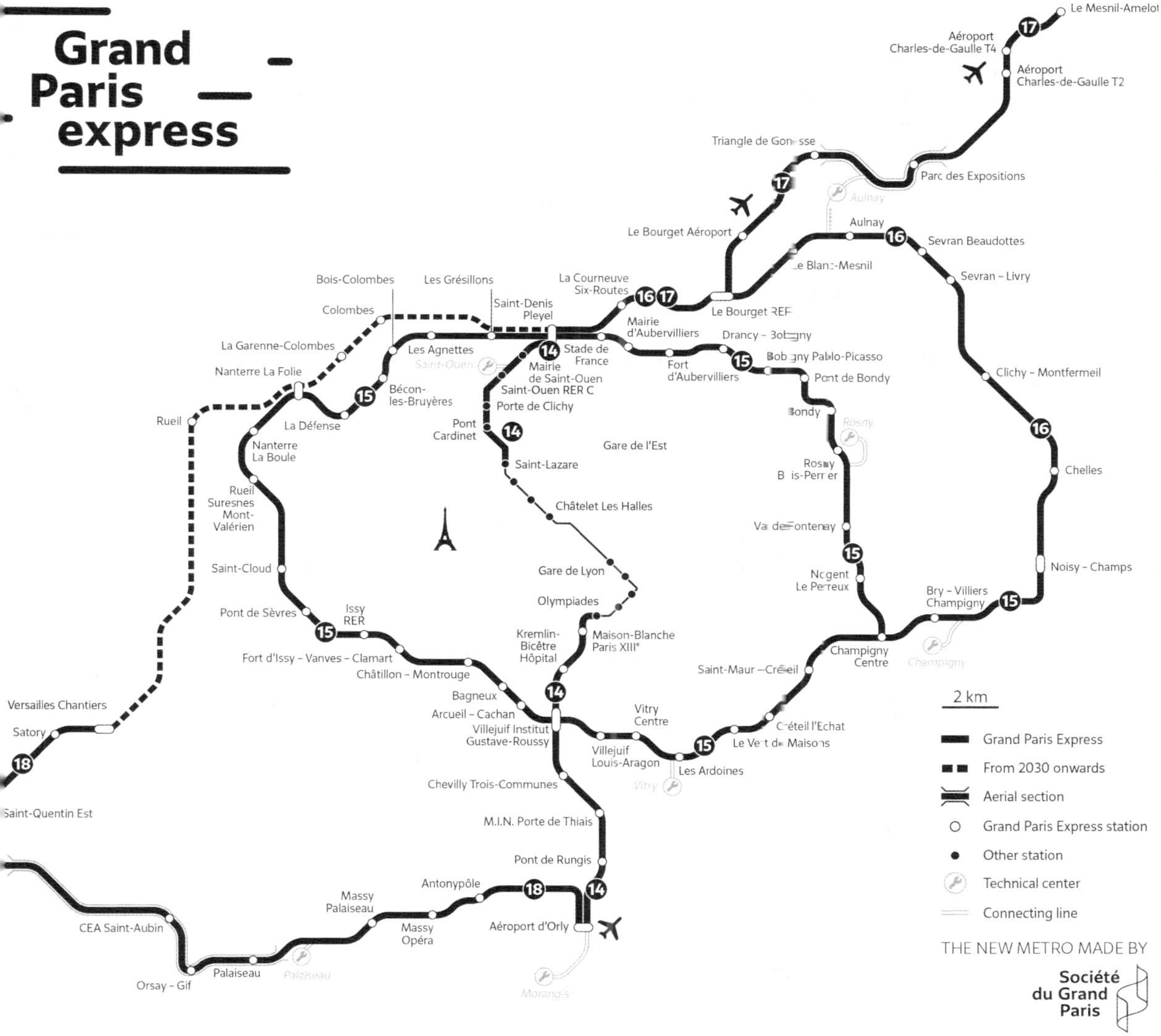

Figure 1: The Regional Network 2030
© Société du Grand Paris

Designing sustainable airports in the post-carbon era

Michaël Leymarie—ADP Ingénierie Paris

When one is immersed in one's own time, it is difficult to abstract oneself from it in order to project oneself into another, whether past or future. However, this is the exercise one must contemplate if the exit from our present era is not to be too violent.

ENTERING THE POST-CARBON ERA

While the Covid-19 pandemic may be seen as a harbinger of this change of era, its significance in terms of mortality is far less than that of air pollution, which itself is due to greenhouse gas (GHG) emissions, which, as the Covid-19 crisis has demonstrated, are the source of global warming. So, these are our two eras: the one that is coming to an end and the one that can be seen as an answer to the previous. And we are on a journey from one to the other (in search of the most effective response). The answer to this major problem lies in an ecological approach to the economy, best-known as the Post-Carbon era. Entering this new era not only means energy transition, sustainable development, but also green capitalism. The directions that the organisation of the world will take will question each of our territories, the dense concentration of people in large cities, the models of agricultural and industrial production, the distribution of wealth, cultures and the art of living, etc., but also all forms of transport.

THE CLEAN TRANSPORT REVOLUTION

All modes of transport will be redefined to be clean, without GHG emissions; each taking into account their capacity to carry passengers and their functional specificity in relation to their territorial scales. While this revolution will lead to the emergence of new modes of transport (such as UAM, "hyper-fast trains", airships, autonomous and connected electric vehicles, delivery drones, etc.), it will above all allow each of these modes to fit into or complement the transport matrix. Their starting point will be: interconnection and synergy. This interplay between each of the parts of this matrix will be all the more essential until each part functions effectively, using clean energy. And this is the case in the aviation sector, among others, where it will probably take more than 30 years to end greenhouse gas emissions. After 2050, this could be a new golden age for air transport, having overcome carbon.

THE GENERALISATION OF THE MULTIMODAL SYSTEM AT TRANSPORT NODES

The transport matrix cannot wait until each mode of transport is fully operational. Moreover, it is also easier to provide access to a transport node for a specific clean mode than to apply a specific clean technology to all modes.

A multi-modal transport system to enable inter-modality within the equipment of transport nodes is not new. There are such approaches in railway and bus stations and sporadically in airports.

THE THREE ISSUES OF THE REPORT TO DESIGN SUSTAINABLE AIRPORTS

Firstly, this report seeks to show the generalisation of the system of multi-modality through the following arguments:

1. The multi-modality of transport nodes: Each "station" facility must be able to be a node that allows for the greatest possible multi-modality. In this way, it creates a centrality effect within the territory.
2. The catalytic effect of a multi-modal node: the "station", becoming a central point, allows, on the one hand, easy access to its users and, on the other hand, a catalytic effect that attracts a whole variety of functions (shops, services, facilities, production, etc.) of which location is of strategic importance. Thus, the more the flows of activities that are concentrated there, the more complex and rich the "place-station" becomes.
3. Balance in the management of territories: The system allows for the possibility of embodying short circuits for territories that are both as autonomous as possible around each station (catchment area) and interconnected (inter-catchment area links).

Secondly, it demonstrates that multi-modality as a global flow management system is the best ally for developing an environmentally friendly approach to transport facilities (the airport platform as a whole). And in the specific case of airports and air transport, this multi-modal strategy is a structural means to mitigate GHG emissions by replacing domestic air links with rail land routes.

Thirdly, it shows that in the particular case of airports, approaching these facilities from the landside (or city side) is a reservoir for the development of their economy and the compensation of aeronautical resources when they are in crisis.

CONCLUSION: INTEGRATING THE HYPOTHESIS TO PRODUCE A NEW GENERATION OF AIRPORTS

This report assumes that the five concluding points must be integrated if airports are to be sustainable and fit into this post-carbon era:

1. Air-to-land transfer of domestic passengers: If achieving the "Zero Carbon Airport" objective (which is part of many airport programs) is limited to developing environmental approaches on the ground on the airport site without meeting the requirement to shift domestic (short-haul) ▸

Airport before and after development according to post-carbon targets
© ADP Ingénierie - Michaël Leymarie

flights to efficient ground transport, then airport managers are missing a major opportunity to reduce GHG emissions on the ground and even more in the air. The strategy proposed in this report aims precisely at shifting domestic air journeys to and integrating them with ground transport.

2. Air-Land Multi-modal Airports Platforms: In this way, airports would become *Air-Land Multi-modal Platforms (PMATs)* for connecting local land passenger flows with other points in the same regional area (medium-haul) or more distant points (long-haul) around the world. It would therefore be in the interest of each airport to develop both direct international medium- and long-haul services and to provide connections to local rail networks for domestic routes.
3. Reserves for economic growth levers: The large vacant ground surfaces of airports hold an extraordinary amount of development potential, as they can be resources for major economic growth. Also, multi-modal transport management is the best way to activate these growth levers.
4. The urban cluster at the heart of transport hubs: Nevertheless, if we do not change the culture in relation to the management of airports, leaving them trapped in an image of nuisance facilities without being determined to remedy this by studying the spatial artefacts and developing their territory, airports will not be able to integrate these levers of economic growth and they will progressively lose their activities.
5. The tripartite governance of the airport on the large scale of its territory: Finally, in anticipation of better times for the aviation industry, which must face the challenge of massive air transport without greenhouse gas emissions, the 2050 horizon is a period in which the synergy of actors and managers, air and ground transport, must be exploited through shared governance (*Tripartite Governance of the Contextualised Airport in its Environment TGCAE*) and a communitarisation of revenues and investments. This is a prerequisite for airports to be anchored in their territory as a major source of development while respecting its environment. ▪

Intersectional approach to understanding mobility

Floridea Di Ciommo & Andrés Kilstein—cambiaMO| changing Mobility Madrid

The mobility of care includes journeys to carry out errands, daily shopping (food, medicines, etc.) and visits to health centers, as well as accompanying dependent people (minors, elderly and/or disabled) on these same journeys, and also to educational establishments. These represent the highest percentage of journeys, which are, moreover, mainly carried out by women. Care mobility accounts, on average, for almost 40% of journeys in large cities, while journeys for work account for less than 20% of total trips—the rest of the journeys are distributed between study, leisure and personal management. Nevertheless, this type of mobility is neither correctly captured in the assessment of transport policies, nor in planning and design. Many of the tools used to collect data about mobility and design transport policies show a clear gender bias, by which mobility is understood through ascribing certain roles to men and women and troughout gender stereotypes. A good example to illustrate this gender bias is the design of services that focus on a type of trip commonly known as commuting. This implies an individual trip from home to work, without having to look after dependents, to central areas of the city, and with a commuting timetable that specifies peak hours of higher intensity in the early morning and late afternoon. This design based on commuting does not account for the different requirements of mobility of care. These trips tend to be less pendular, chained, entangled with activities or errands in between, and with high intensity in valley hours. The mobility of care exposes the presence of population groups with the greatest mobility needs: older people, children, and working and caregivers (women). The use of an intersectional approach, especially gender, ethnicity, age, and employment status in transport research, provide possible insights for policy makers. Working women and housewives, who assume the largest portion of these caring responsibilities, bear the costs of the failure in design, facing time poverty as a result of not catering services to all needs.

Additionally, with the breakout of Covid-19, frontline workers were particularly affected by the consequences of the pandemic, given that they could not work from home. Frontline workers are also a gendered group, especially when referring to health care and retail staff. his group had mobility needs that were not looked after during the health crisis, which clearly states that transport poverty goes beyond social poverty, and policy makers should set the population's needs as the starting point of planning. Making needs visible is essential for transport equity. Equity is a concept that has become relevant in transport investment assessment in recent years. Previous literature has shown that equity assessment in transport planning and infrastructure investment is crucial for identifying their impacts on society and the environment.

Reorienting transport planning towards the needs of mobility of care implies thinking of a network with diverse potential users, with different layers of use. It also implies considering the local scale and abandoning the hope that all possible improvements are related to the optimization of high-capacity road infrastructure. Some of the lessons and recommendations that can be taken from this are the following:

1. Women should be incorporated into the planning process as planners. There is an example of the city of Ha Noi, which has specific provisions to increase the employment status of women in the sector of metro rail. This implies new perspectives and insights for design and operation. Diversity is positive for any organization.
2. Design complete streets for walking, facilitating cycling, intermediate modes, and green, weather-resistant public transport. Complete streets entail mixed land uses, street life and the presence of different modes in the same space.
3. Develop whole communities by ensuring that land use and transport are well integrated. Transport-oriented land use ensures optimal urban integration. Encouraging innovation in planning developments with concepts such as the "15-minute city" led by the Mayor of Paris, is in line with our proposal.
4. Provide inclusive transport services that meet the diverse needs of travel beyond business travel. It should always be considered that caring is an essential activity in human societies, and trips with dependent people should be catered for.
5. Enabling progress in funding, education and outreach for inclusive sustainable mobility.

In summary, many activities needed for sustaining daily community life differ from business and leisure. Even when care-giving requires effort, time and dedication, these activities do not receive economic compensation and are often not considered as economic activities. Similarly, the care-givers' needs are not well accounted for in transport planning and need to be tackled in order to achieve transport equity, a fundamental concept in a wide theoretical framework. ▪

Barcelona's metropolitan avenues—a human metropolitan scale

Javier Ortigosa—Àrea Metropolitana de Barcelona (AMB)

Barcelona's Metropolitan Area is composed of 36 municipalities, has a population of 3.2 million inhabitants, and occupies 636 km2, 52% of which are natural and agricultural spaces. The metropolis is very dense—more than two thirds of the population live in compact urban fabrics with net densities of over 30,000 inhabitants/km2—and there are many historical centers with strong identities (PDU, 2019).

Given the compact nature of the different urban fabrics, many trips are done on foot, especially in the central conurbation where active mobility accounts for approximately 50-60% of internal trips (PMMU, 2016). However, most economic activities are concentrated in the metropolitan center and it attracts many commuters from a hinterland of 5 million inhabitants. Additionally, accessibility by public transportation outside the center decreases significantly (Recio et al., 2018), and most efforts in the past have been put into building a system of highways that has led to even more car demand, segregation of uses, and urban sprawl. As a result, in such a dense environment, the negative effects of traffic and infrastructure (e.g. pollution, space occupancy, segregation) have a very significant impact on the citizens' quality of living.

The structure and scale of cities has historically depended on the existing means of transportation. The expansion of many cities in the 18th and 19th century needed to accommodate flows of people and goods that travelled in streetcars and railways. That resulted in regional structures surrounding train stations and urban patterns composed of wide streets and avenues. Unfortunately, throughout the twentieth century, the spread of automobile use triggered urban sprawl, as well as a system of highways that segregated urban fabrics and promoted car dependency (Mumford, 1963). Consequences and impacts of this model are well known to us today.

The case of Barcelona and its metropolitan area is similar to many metropolises around the world (e.g. Herce, 2009; Corominas, 2017). The *Cerdà Plan* of 1858 proposed an expansion of the city based on a grid pattern and a system of wide avenues to support public space and public transport. A century later, however, the 1953 Regional Plan envisioned a metropolitan area structured by segregated road networks. That perspective was maintained in the *General Metropolitan Plan (PGM)* of 1976 (the current regulation), which led to the almost 300 km of highways and many other arterial streets that exist today in the metropolitan area of Barcelona. Although, in the last decades, measures have been taken to reclaim public space by pedestrianizing streets and squares (e.g. the Super-Block initiative), these efforts focus on city centers and do not address the metropolitan backbone, which is still based on street arterials.

It is crucial to get back to the "human-scale" to create inclusive and livable urban spaces and connections at the metropolitan level. ►

This article is based on the following:
Ortigosa, J., L. Pretel, N. Ginés, Sisó, R., 2020. Las avenidas y calles para la movilidad del futuro. ISUF-H Conference.
Ortigosa, J., 2018. Urban and metropolitan structure for sustainable mobility and livability in Barcelona.

Figure 1: Schematic view of a possible avenue
© PDU, 2019

Figure 2: Street potential map adding the standardized 12 indicators, thicker lines have higher score, colors represent different areas analyzed. ©PDU, 2019

This scope is the one that can bring substantial benefits by changing metropolitan mobility to a more distributed and sustainable phenomenon .

Currently, the metropolitan administration, *Area Metropolitana of Barcelona (AMB)*, is in the process of drafting a new master plan *(PDU)* which will define urban development in the next decades, and obviously transport issues are particularly relevant. One of the main proposals of the *PDU* is a network of metropolitan avenues that aims to structure the metropolis by transforming the road infrastructure and shifting towards a more sustainable mobility (see Figure 1). Many studies have highlighted the inverse relationship between road traffic levels and livability and activity in streets (e.g. Appleyard, 1981). The idea behind the network of metropolitan avenues is to transform both: the section and the perimeter. To do so, we want to create metropolitan avenues with urban intensity and mixture (demand for shorter trips) that ensure continuity and priority for sustainable mobility and support for a high- quality urban space. This "boulevarization" is not an isolated trend, rather the opposite.

Different European cities follow similar strategies such as Paris (APUR, 2015), Helsinki (Helsinki, 2013) and Lyon (see the European initiatives such as *Metrex* or *Urbact Riconnect*). Road networks are typically organized hierarchically according to traffic levels. This single-criteria structure influences the urban planning of entire regions.

Since the logic behind metropolitan avenues takes into account other perspectives, there are many factors that affect the choice of streets and roads which should be part of that network.

Figure 3: Metropolitan Avenues Network, 2019 proposal
©PDU, 2019

Our work consisted of creating a map to help decision making and validate the current proposal. A combination of 12 indicators was applied to all street and road segments (links between two intersections) of the entire Barcelona metropolitan area. These indicators are grouped in 3 categories according to: I) quality of public space; II) transport flows; and III) urban intensity and centrality. Results show that there is indeed potential to create an alternative metropolitan network based on active mobility, public transport and urban intensity (see Figure 2).

Moreover, it validates the strategic proposal presented in 2019 (see Figure 3) after a technical participatory process with urban planners from the 36 municipalities. We are also studying the intersections between the proposed network and the segregated system. Some of these points might become key nodes for intermodality and metropolitan centralities associated with new urban developments and transformations.

In short, metropolitan areas need to transform their road infrastructure networks towards more integrated streets that enhance urban life at their perimeters and promote more sustainable mobility. However, these networks of metropolitan avenues cannot be determined according to the classical traffic engineering fundamentals. For this transformation, new and more integrated urban science concepts need to be applied.

DISCUSSING THE FUTURE OF METROPOLITAN MOBILITY

We are not going to solve traffic issues with traffic solutions

Forum Discussion

What does the mobility hub of the future look like? How should public space be regulated around it? Will self-driving cars and busses replace individual car traffic? And can administrative borders be overcome when it comes to the extension of costly transportation infrastructure?
In the Forum Discussion of the first *MetroLab Forum*, we pursue these questions and shed light on how Vienna deals with the issue of current and future mobility from different perspectives.

"It's very important that we understand the urgency of change that needs to happen in the transportation sector."
Mathias Mitteregger

"It's very important that we understand the urgency of change that needs to happen in the transportation sector", says Matthias Mitteregger, project manager of *AVENUE21* at the *future.lab* Research Center of *TU Wien*, referring to the dramatically increasing greenhouse gas emissions. For Gregory Telepak, Speaker Mobility *MA 18 – City of Vienna*, fast action and the inclusion of everyday human life worlds in a sustainable mobility development is a top priority too. However, he also advocates that multi-modality should be understood in its various functions and at different levels, from the personal neighbourhood-related level to the cross-border national level. Accordingly, different context-sensitive requirements are placed on mobility and the development of mobility hubs and their environment.
Vincent Neumayer, Multi-modal Mobility Manager at *Wiener Linien*, Vienna's leading public transport company, is particularly focused on mobility points at the local level *"where we try to interlink public transport with sharing mobility as well as active mobility."* For him it is one of several pieces of a puzzle to ensure the quality of public space when developing multi-modal solutions. This includes the consideration of local businesses as well as the concrete design and intense urban development of surrounding areas.
Matthias Mitteregger and Stefan Mayr, co-founder of *MetroLab* Vienna, also agree that the key to a mobility and transportation change lies in rethinking the streetscape, as international pioneering metropolises have already demonstrated. This would provide the citizens of the Vienna city region with some extra space transforming their living and working environments into livable and healthy urban quarters.
While the moderator and co-founder of *superwien urbanism*, Roland Krebs, states that Vienna, in contrast to the *Métropole du Grand Paris* or *Àrea Metropolitana de Barcelona*, lacks a comprehensive metropolitan strategy in the sense of a *Greater Vienna plan* Stefan Mayr proposes a strong new element for the redevelopment of the Vienna-Bratislava-Lower Austria region: a *SuperRing*[1] in the form of a mobility loop connecting all the ▸

[1] The connecting SuperRing is presented as a metropolitan vision for *SuperWien* in the book *SuperWien Metropole. A new Capital for Europe* (2018) by Cédric Ramière and Stefan Mayr

core areas to one big metropolitan area. To transfer such a conceptual idea into a big infrastructure project would, on the one hand, not only emphasize the importance of developing urban design solutions for newly emerging centers around mobility hubs in surrounding municipalities, but also influence the behavior of people and the way they consume mobility. Relying on a needs-based approach would mean taking into account different user groups "*that usually don't show up in renderings of transportation hubs*", Mitteregger adds. Even though, from his perspective, new technologies such as automation and self-driving cars are not going to be the magic solution that can solve all our transportation issues, they bring with them a certain potential to transform suburbia. This future transformation, of course, needs to be guided and is strongly interrelated with social change.

Despite the partly different points of view that the invited podium guests took, they all agreed on one thing: We need to reflect on our values and principles, ask ourselves how and why people move and consequently focus on how mobility needs can be met, including how much we want to invest in it. Or, as Gregory Telepak puts it, "*we need a more honest discussion about the resources we commit as a society to transportation and to mobility.*"

"We need a more honest discussion about the resources we commit as a society to transportation and to mobility."
Gregory Telepak

Such a discussion would mean, on the one hand, admitting that traffic problems cannot exclusively be met with traffic solutions, and on the other hand, acknowledging the enormous potential of blending in the whole metropolitan picture when it comes to the integrated urban development of mobility nodes as well as political agreements between necessary stakeholders to coordinate costly transport infrastructure. Because, as Vincent Neumayer admits: "*from the governance point of view there is always room for improvement.*"

"From the governance point of view there is always room for improvement."
Vincent Neumayer

With this Forum Discussion the discourse on metropolitan planning was enriched by valuable arguments and ideas of how to understand, manage and design metropolitan mobility and thus is an important step towards a holistic metropolitan vision embracing the future chances and challenges of a successfully interconnected urban region.

To transfer such a conceptual idea into a big infrastructure project would, on the one hand, not only emphasize the importance of developing urban design solutions for newly emerging centers around mobility hubs in surrounding municipalities, but also influence the behavior of people and the way they consume mobility. Relying on a needs-based approach would mean taking into account different user groups "*that usually don't show up in renderings of transportation hubs*", Mitteregger adds. Even though, from his perspective, new technologies such as automation and self-driving cars are not going to be the magic solution that can solve all our transportation issues, they bring with them a certain potential to transform suburbia. This future transformation, of course, needs to be guided and is strongly interrelated with social change. ▪

Gregory Telepak
Speaker Mobility,
MA18 -City of Vienna

Mathias Mitteregger
Project Manager *AVENUE21*
future.lab Research Center, TU Vienna

Vincent Neumayer
Project Manager, Multi-Modal
Mobility Management,
Wiener Linien GmbH

Stefan Mayr & Roland Krebs
MetroLab, superwien urbanism

Scan to watch the documentation of the International Lectures and the Forum Discussion!

KEY FINDINGS ON THE FUTURE OF METROPOLITAN MOBILITY

1. CROSS-BORDER COOPERATION IS KEY TO BOOST MOBILITY DEVELOPMENT

Cross-border thinking and planning is key to developing a well-integrated transportation network and therefore an interconnected and well-functioning metropolitan area. Furthermore, defining functional areas according to the intensity of mobility movements (e.g. commuter flows) is a big chance to reduce inequality within a city region and thus to achieve a territorial rebalance. Since it can be assumed that the importance of urban regions in terms of transport and settlement policy will continue to increase, this aspect of transport equity is particularly important.

Strong urban-rural relationships and interdependencies make close cooperation between very disparate partners inevitable. Breaking with existing administrative delineations and artificially created divisions of competences means taking on responsibility in many ways and on many levels. Civil society as well as the private sector are equally challenged as decision-makers to look beyond their administrative borders and cooperate with their surrounding areas to finally boost mobility development and thus the engine for intra-regional growth.

2. RADICAL MOBILITY VISIONS MUST BE FOLLOWED BY BOLD ACTIONS

In the field of sustainable mobility development, more radical visions and utopias are needed to stimulate new, creative solutions and attract the attention of the population and decision-makers.

However, they should be followed by real strategies and approaches, that may well be disruptive (imagine, for example, what a metropolis without cars could look like), and show the way of getting there. This could be achieved by initiating pioneer projects, such as temporary pop-up bike lanes that can become permanent over time. In that sense, to develop visionary comprehensive development strategies requires the will to implement straightforward place-based solutions. Speaking out loud or sketching seemingly unrealistic but highly innovative ideas and visions is, in any case, essential to take a first step in this matter. All too often, the ideas and good intentions are already there, they just need to be highlighted and worked on. This is a plea for more courage in articulating, symbolizing and finally implementing visions, even if it means leaving the comfort zone of the strategic level.

3. MOBILITY AND SETTLEMENT DEVELOPMENT NEED TO BE CLOSELY INTERLINKED

Regardless of the mobility system in question, mobility development always serves as a driver of settlement development (and vice versa), which means that these two dynamics must always be thought of together. International approaches using mobility as a tool (e.g. the *Grand Paris Express*) show that this enables a healthy and climate sensitive living environment, but also avoids further urban sprawl. Building new urban centers around mobility hubs provides the ultimate opportunity to develop multifunctional polycentric zones with a high standard of living.
Moreover, transforming mobility systems means transforming spaces not only on the regional but also on the local level. The implementation of new mobility services should therefore go hand in hand with rethinking the streetscape on a neighborhood scale. Especially the transformative intervention in public space holds potential to make (already existing or new) qualities visible. The street must be reclaimed as an extension of living and working space.

4. THE RIGHT INCENTIVES MUST BE SET TO CHANGE MOBILITY BEHAVIOUR

Rethinking mobility infrastructure also means rethinking mobility behavior. It has been shown that people are particularly open to change in situations of transition, e.g. embracing alternative modes of mobility when moving to a newly developed housing area. Therefore, especially in those areas, there is a great opportunity to make changes in mobility behavior appealing. One way or another, using shared and active forms of mobility is a matter of values, not just the infrastructure provided as a hardware. Thus, in addition to setting the right incentives (e.g. new multi-modal offers or policies), awareness building is an important component of mobility change. If we want to change the mobility system we need to change how people move in space. Understanding and further developing use-based approaches will be the first step in expanding the range of (environmentally friendly and sustainable) services according to demand and steering them in the right direction—towards an ecologically just city.

5. MULTI-MODAL MOBILITY IS A MAJOR DRIVER OF SUSTAINABLE METROPOLITAN MOBILITY

The range of mobility options is becoming as differentiated as our society. It is therefore becoming increasingly clear that multi-modal, shared and connected mobility will be the future. Not only new technologies (e.g. automated or electric vehicles), but above all the stronger integration of different forms of mobility make it possible to develop adapted solutions for different spatial situations and needs.
Because mobility-on-demand transportation systems, such as multi-modal stations (hubs) consisting of a group of (mostly shared) vehicles, strongly relate to their surrounding public space, multi-modality is linked to the opportunity to achieve individual, place-based designs. This design has the potential to promote active forms of mobility and to ensure easy accessibility to the multi-modal offers. To make sure that users can easily plan, book and pay for their journeys with multiple types of mobility services, a specific service (Mobility-as-a-Service) that offers a joint digital channel is also needed in the long term. ▪

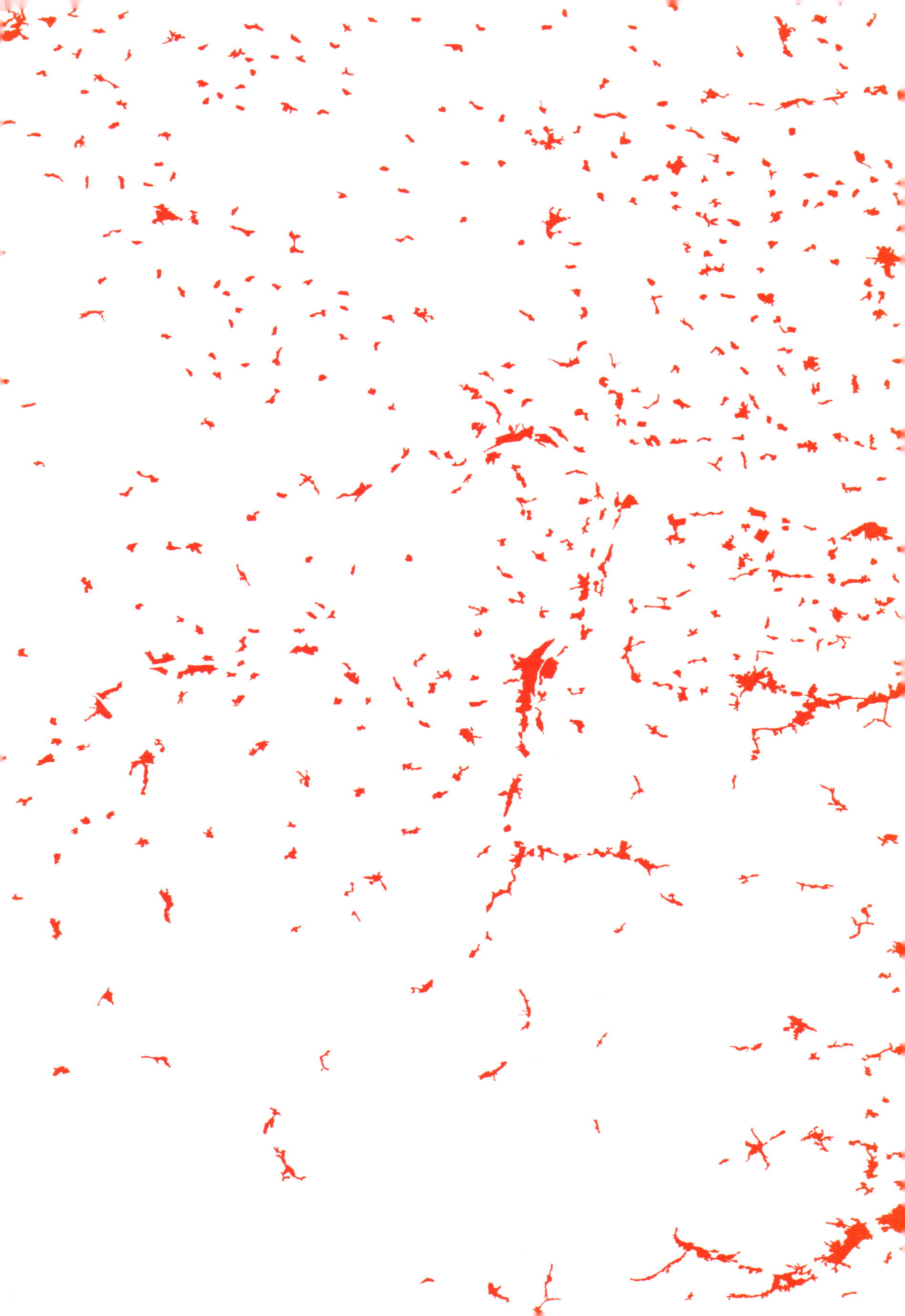

#2 GROWTH

MANAGING URBAN GROWTH

Flyer MetroLab Forum #2 GROWTH

How to manage urban growth?

In the last decades, the built-up area within the *SuperWien Metropole* has grown enormously. Despite all political intentions and regional planning regulations, increasing wealth is still accompanied by the consumption of land. Urban expansion has formed complex hybrid landscapes consisting of residential areas, commercial zones, agricultural plots, recreational and nature reserves. Many growing cities in the metropolitan area are already having problems handling the increasing demand for living and working space. *SuperWien Metropole* is a vision for the six million future inhabitants of the Vienna-Bratislava-Wiener Neustadt metropolitan region. It will incorporate the current growth of more than 50.000 inhabitants per year. One main goal is to reconfigure and strengthen the polycentric structure of the Metropole by following the principle of compact growth and concentrated densification. Together with international experts on housing, settlement development and metropolitan planning, we discussed the need of new forms of governance and co-creative planning tools.

UNDERSTANDING GROWTH

Co-creation means meeting at eye level

Interview with **Yvonne Franz**—Department of Geography and Regional Research at the University of Vienna

MetroLab: In the *MetroLab* publication *SuperWien Metropole. A new Capital for Europe* we first refer to the history of Vienna, which played a central role in the European network of cities, especially until the First World War. Since its integration into the European Union, Vienna has increasingly been seen as a mediator between East and West. What role do you ascribe to today's metropolis and what characterizes it?

Yvonne Franz: For me, on the one hand, there are hard criteria that define a metropolis, such as its size, area, number of inhabitants, functional connections and the transport network. On the other hand, there is a symbolic level, such as identity, that is, everything that one constructs for oneself, which is difficult to measure. Vienna often calls itself a metropolis, but I would say it is a big city. Vienna has elements of the metropolis, but they stem more from the past and are carried along. Much of this cosmopolitanism and melting pot, for example, comes from the migration history of this city. I could well imagine that Vienna was once more metropolitan in its influences and permeabilities, dynamics and inequalities. The city still lives very much from this identity today, however, it sometimes struggles with it. For me, migration in the sense of diversity, whether it is cultural or socio-demographic identity or symbolism, is what characterizes a metropolis and also its attractiveness as a place to work.

"Vienna often calls itself a metropolis, but I would say it is a big city. Vienna has elements of the metropolis, but they stem more from the past and are carried along."

In your opinion, what are the key challenges Vienna faces as an urban region?

In this context, I like to use the term "growing pains" for a growing city like Vienna. On the one hand, it is a matter of ensuring sufficient infrastructure and open spaces in the existing city; on the other hand, the enormous population growth, in quantitative terms, is primarily taking place in the urban development areas, i.e. often on former greenfield or industrial brownfield sites. "Growing pains" refers to this intertwining, the merging of what is already there and what is yet to come.
In central, well-connected development areas, for example in the *Nordbahnviertel* or *Sonnwendviertel*, these growing pains are not felt too much because the existing structure is very robust and can cope with the new development. ▸

Regarding urban development areas in Transdanubia, or in the south of Vienna, the crucial questions are: How do we connect these neighborhoods? How do we get high-quality public transport there? Is the educational campus that is planned there enough, or do we need to link it to the existing social infrastructure?
What does it mean for housing areas or allotments if an urban development area with 1,000 residential units is suddenly built in the direct neighborhood?
Even if population figures are currently tending to stagnate, they are still at a high level and pose a challenge. This involves everything from land policy to questions of financing and the social fragmentation and differentiation of the residential population with all its demands.

In order to make the growing urban region an integrated development area, we propose the idea of a *SuperRing*, along which a regional superfast train runs, and which defines focus areas of spatial densification with its stops (between Vienna Central Station, Bratislava, Eisenstadt and Wiener Neustadt). To what extent should the current and future residents of these areas be included in the growth policy of the agglomeration area, and what is the significance of participatory approaches in contemporary housing production?

Vienna has the distinctive feature of being dominated by social housing and plays a leading role here, both nationally and internationally. As a city that works closely with developers in urban development areas and stipulates that participation processes must be included in the development process, Vienna finds it much easier than other cities that have to deal with individual developers and cannot demand this through the gentle pressure of social housing. That makes Vienna very special. The blind spot here, however, is that you plan for people who already live in Vienna. Those who are not considered at all and often cannot participate in these participation and development processes are the newcomers, from apprentices and students to people with refugee experience. From this perspective, it would be really interesting to ask ourselves how we could create more inclusion. If one is aware that participation is not a one-time-only action, a lot has already been gained.

"I would strongly advocate that every participation process [...] should be open to anyone at any time and should pay particular attention to the social groups that are not seen or heard at first glance."

I would strongly advocate that every participation process, whether it is a neighborhood initiative or a formalized planning process, should be open to anyone at any time and should pay particular attention to the social groups that are not seen or heard at first glance. Vienna has a lot of opportunities for participation and encourages it, but this also makes the system very sluggish. In comparison, for example, to the Netherlands, where "active citizenship" and "co-responsibility" are emphasized, in Vienna one often finds "institutionalized" individual initiative, which often has to fulfill mechanisms that are too rigid to actually allow co-creation.

As *MetroLab*, we use not only participatory but also co-creative elements to develop urban strategies and place-based solutions. Thus, we leave behind the classical set of formal planning tools. How do you assess the openness for co-creation in Vienna and what do you generally understand by it?

"On the one hand, participation has legal formal legitimacy and is bound by sets of rules. On the other hand, the everyday reality is that we don't address all people when we apply this set of rules."

For me, co-creation means meeting at eye level, regardless of whether we are talking about the city administration, city politics or citizens. And that is the big difference to a participation process in which it is clearly delineated up to which street the residents and owners are involved. It's more about people who actually use the space and have an interest in it. Those are the different levels and I think it's important to separate that neatly. On the one hand, participation has legal formal legitimacy and is bound by sets of rules. On the other hand, the everyday reality is that we don't address all people when we apply this set of rules. That is why there are new formats that can be understood as co-creative.

You have also conducted research on urban living labs. What is their potential? And where do such approaches reach their limits? How can you convert these often temporary activities into long-term use?

Living Labs are an interesting tool that allow for a lot but also have their limitations. When the format was taken up by urban research about 10 years ago, it became fashionable to call something a "lab". Lab also means, and now we are at "enabling and experimenting", that failures, i.e. non-results, are also acceptable. In a formalized citizen participation process, that would be hard to argue with. In addition, Urban Living Labs also offer the possibility to cooperate beyond encrusted (institutional) structures, so that actors come together who otherwise tend to meet rather rarely.

Currently, it is often argued that Living Labs should be used as an incremental component in urban development processes, which means that they would have to be continuously financed for different issues and at different locations, and thus a constant exchange of knowledge could take place. ▪

Difficulties can be turned into opportunities if they are overcome with a good narrative

Interview with **Johannes Suitner**—Department of Urban and Regional Research at TU Wien

MetroLab: *MetroLab* approaches the metropolitan concept on a wide variety of thematic and spatial levels, thereby emphasizing the multi-layered nature of the term. Recently, the term "metropolis" has also enjoyed great popularity in political strategy papers such as the new coalition agreement for Vienna (Nov. 2020), where it is associated with topics such as health, culture, research and innovation. What is the very essence of the term for you?

"[...] it is important that all kinds of people can find themselves in such a narrative and aren't submerged in the idea of a metropolitan region that relegates them to the status of interchangeable cogs in a dystopian, mechanized production machine."

Johannes Suitner: In economic geography, the metropolis is, after all, a certain kind of location, a very well-connected and networked agglomeration with a disproportionately large number of high-level (decision-making) functions. But for me it is also a deeply political concept, a symbol of power, prosperity and certain hopes for the future. In the government agreement, of course, it's about the latter. It invokes a narrative that is linked to Vienna's prosperity and global reputation. I'm always interested in both—the metropolis as a measurable quantity and narrative. In practice, it is important that all kinds of people can find themselves in such a narrative and aren't submerged in the idea of a metropolitan region that relegates them to the status of interchangeable cogs in a dystopian, mechanized production machine.

How are these characteristics related to the Vienna metropolitan region? Is the metropolitan region spatially and also intuitively perceived as a coherent, integrated entity, as we outline it in the book *SuperWien Metropole. A New Capital for Europe?*

De facto, the Vienna city region is a European metropolitan region. The settlement area does not start and end at the city boundary but is highly integrated. The cultural and political significance of the region extends far beyond the borders of Austria. But it is true that there is a lack of perception, particularly at the local level. There is a lack of a common vision, a narrative of the future, which can also guide action for integrated city-regional development. It is a bit surprising that this is not the case in the Vienna city

"There is a lack of a common vision, a narrative of the future, which can also guide action for integrated city-regional development"

region, where the institutional basis for the development of such visions has actually existed for more than 30 years. In the past, however, the public discourse has unfortunately more often been about the demarcation between Vienna and Lower Austria, between the city and the country, than about the unifying factor. After the pandemic and with regard to the climate crisis, however, there is, in my opinion, a special need and also a special opportunity to develop a common vision, a narrative, and to draw a picture of a metropolitan region that is fit for the future. This is also necessary. A well-integrated urban region alone is of no use if it is not anchored in people's minds as a self-image.

The primary goal of the *SuperWien Metropole* is to create a functionally mixed and sustainable urban network that connects the various centers—high-density urban areas, suburban areas and also the natural areas—and thus enables coordinated development. What do you see as the biggest challenges in the integrated development of the metropolitan region?

In my view, the distribution of costs and benefits of integrated development is essential. It has always been a political killer argument when one side feels that it is paying the price. That's why we have to create scenarios that show who will potentially benefit from certain future developments and who might suffer as a result, and think about compensatory mechanisms in advance. In the end, everyone benefits more. This applies to the development of a climate-friendly, regional bioeconomy as well as to the exploitation of the tourism potential of the natural area surrounding the core cities of Vienna and Bratislava or the expansion of logistics clusters in the Vienna region. This must not be a competition between mayors or provincial governors.

In your work, you have looked closely at the potential of innovative city-regional competitions. Can you refer to best practice examples that promote such a balance in city-regional added value?

What is clear is that an instrument such as a planning value equalization or a budget equalization procedure, in which financial compensation is made, does not exist for the metropolis. But what I found interesting about the example of *Grand Paris* [see MetroLab Magazine Metro] is that the municipalities are very consciously throwing money into a pot for a joint competition in the region and thus getting away from the idea that each municipality only operates within its own sphere of influence. Instead, something is being developed collectively as a metropolitan region. A competition for the metropolitan region generates much more attention and is more likely to get the ball rolling than if, for example, the small municipality were to call a competition on its own. ▸

"A competition for the metropolitan region generates much more attention and is more likely to get the ball rolling than if, for example, the small municipality were to call a competition on its own."

What do you think would need to happen for greater attention to be paid to innovative approaches to metropolitan development? And how do you rate the chance of such approaches being included in Vienna's political agenda?

This always requires political commitment and a window of opportunity. In *Grand Paris*, for example, the initiative did not only come from the mayors of the region, but from the French president, who has made a lot of money available for the development of France's metropolises. I believe that nothing plays more into the hands of the development of the Vienna metropolitan region than the climate crisis, because projects for the integration of the urban region, which my colleagues in spatial planning have been demanding since the 1990s, can now finally be implemented under the pressure of the crisis without anyone losing face politically.

Behavioral economists argue that people show a strong preference for regional products in their behavioral change (especially in times of crisis). Not only regional products, but also the feeling for the region and the perception of its soft locational factors are becoming increasingly important. How do you see this trend towards regionalization or de-globalization and its impact on the development of metropolitan regions?

I am very ambivalent about this. Criticism of globalization is often very backward-looking and promotes a new nationalism that threatens to wipe away many of the social achievements of past decades. At the same time, we have to admit that something like a circular economy and a regional bioeconomy are needed for ecological and social reasons. These could become a new narrative for the metropolitan region.

“[...] we have to admit that something like a circular economy and a regional bioeconomy are needed for ecological and social reasons.”

In your past research on artistic-creative interventions that explicitly address metropolitan development, you described the *MetroLab* projects *TirolCITY* and *SuperWien Metropole. A new Capital for Europe* as unconventional sources of inspiration for city-regional development perspectives. What does it take to integrate such provocative approaches and atypical visions into conventional metropolitan planning?

"In every idea, no matter how abstruse, there is a spark of truth, a piece of metropolitan reality, so to speak, that can be implemented. The task of the planners is then to shape the path from the artistic idea to the formalized vision of the future."

The artistic formats provide an enchanting vision of what a metropolis could look like in the future. I consider such approaches to be essential. In every idea, no matter how abstruse, there is a spark of truth, a piece of metropolitan reality, so to speak, that can be implemented. The task of the planners is then to shape the path from the artistic idea to the formalized vision of the future. But to do that, the decision-making power would have to be taken out of their hands a bit. I have the feeling that in the past, more experimentation was done by forming planning communities across federal state borders. However, these then became more of a bureaucratic apparatus and political body. I would like to see another attempt to replace one of the old bodies in order to establish a platform for the metropolitan region that is given some room for maneuvre and money—and not just for art projects. ▪

LEARNING FROM INTERNATIONAL APPROACHES

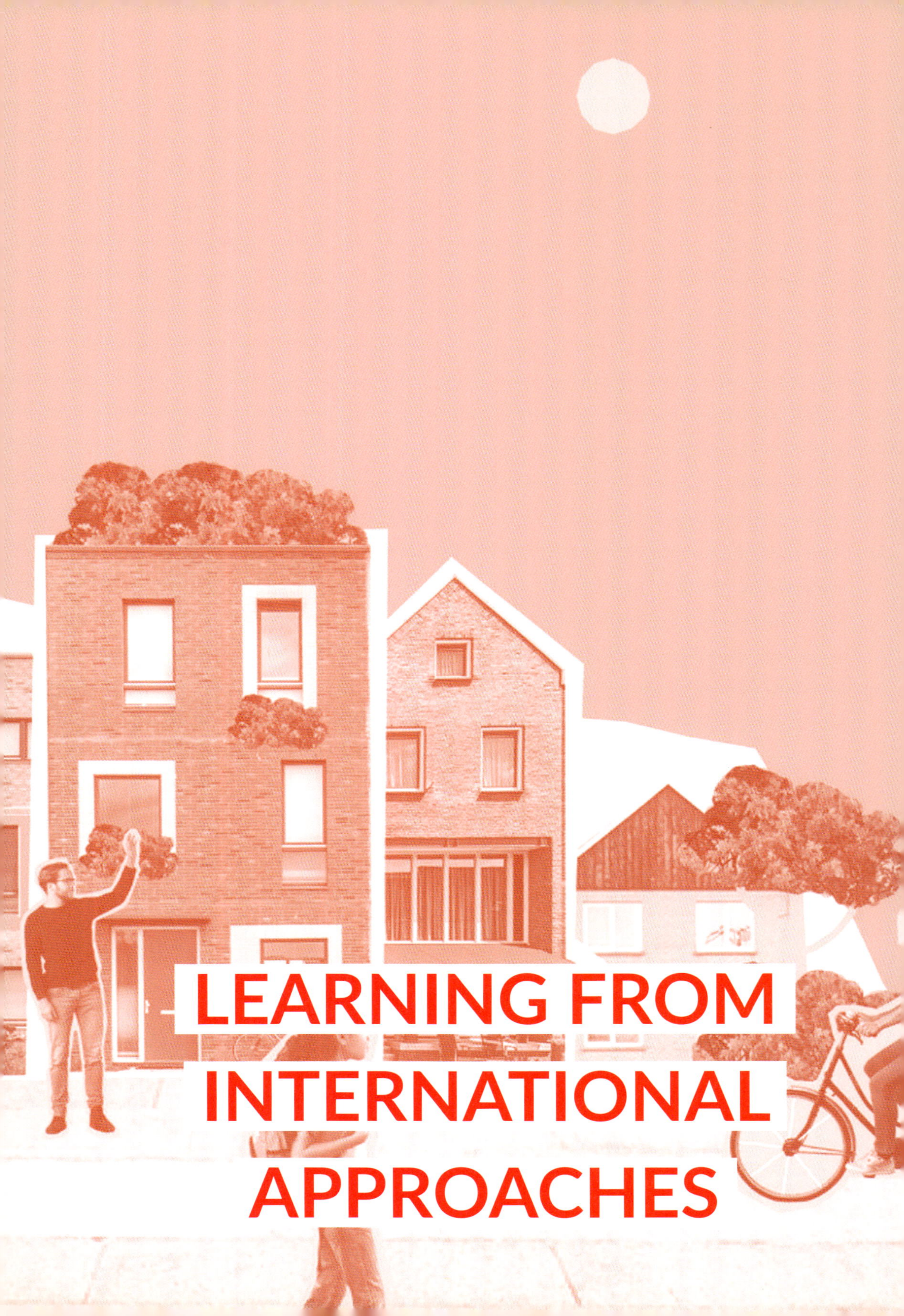

Rehearsing the future—exploratory scenarios as a tool to develop strategies for sustainable urban regions

Kersten Nabielek—PBL Netherlands Environmental Assessment Agency

In the policy domains of urban development, infrastructure and mobility, we are standing on the eve of a number of far-reaching developments that are difficult to overlook. While transitions, or system changes are needed in the fields of climate, energy and circular economy (IEA 2018, IPCC 2018, UNEP 2018, Watts et al. 2018) rapid technological developments are also taking place, for instance, in information and communications technology and transport technology. These technological developments influence daily lives as well as institutions (Van Dijck et al 2016, Crang & Graham 2007). In addition, social, cultural, political and economic changes are taking place, all of which increase the level of uncertainty that policymakers and planners are facing. And more recently, the Covid-19 pandemic has shown us that unexpected events can happen on top of more structural changes and developments.

In urbanized regions many complex developments come together. This often makes it impossible to "tame" uncertainty by providing more data, more advanced statistics or improved models. There is simply no reliable empirical data on transport modes that are only just being introduced or that are being tested. In addition, knowledge of interactions between various transport modes, changes in spatial circumstances and evolving needs of both citizens and businesses is often lacking.

In 2019 *PBL Netherlands Environmental Assessment Agency* published four exploratory scenarios for urban regions in the Netherlands in 2049. The research provides input for a debate on what we want our future urban regions to look like, what this means for various groups within society, what policy choices would be required to get there, and which dilemmas policymakers and planners may face in dealing with new challenges. The scenarios have a qualitative character and were developed in an interactive process together with experts and stakeholders, applying the morphological method for scenario building.

SCENARIOS AS A TOOL TO DEAL WITH UNCERTAINTY

Uncertainty is a fact of life when considering future developments. Acknowledging this can make policymakers feel uncomfortable. Their day-to-day tasks are complicated enough. Having to take into account the uncertainty of new developments, possible discontinuity of trends, and changes in the outlook on urban regions and mobility will make it even more complex. This makes it tempting to ignore uncertainty or to try to hide it.However, that does not make uncertainty go away. So, policymakers will need to relate to it, acknowledging that not exploring possible new challenges, views and policy options will only yield "present-proof" policies rather than "future-proof" ones. In order to help policymakers and planners gain insight into and anticipate a diversity of plausible developments, ▸

including possible paths for autonomous driving technology, exploratory scenarios on urbanization, infrastructure and mobility, titled *Bubble City*, *State of Green*, *Market Place* and *Our Neighbourhood*, have been developed.
These scenarios all have a qualitative and narrative character and were inspired by the work of researchers such as Townsend (2014) and Lyons (2015). Each of the scenarios is based on a certain set of societal values that was developed during the research. Moreover, none of the scenarios offers a perfect solution. Each scenario shows advantages and disadvantages and we were specifically interested in imagining and describing possible dilemmas that might arise per scenario.

WORKSHOPS WITH PLANNERS AND POLICY MAKERS

The publication of the project in spring 2019 included a printed handbook (PBL 2019a), a pdf publication of the full research (PBL 2019b) and a website (PBL 2019c) including five short animation movies. In July 2020 an English translation of the handbook (PBL 2020) was published. However, the project did not end with the publication of the project. As the scenarios were explicitly presented as a tool for planning, dialogue and involvement, we accompanied the publication with an open invitation to participate in scenario workshops. Many interested organisations, mostly municipalities, provinces and departments of ministries, responded to the open invitation and during 2019 and 2020 we organised more than 30 workshops, which we called "rehearsing the future". The workshops helped to widen the imagination of the participants and feed the discussion about possible futures of urban regions, underlying societal values and dilemmas that might arise in the process.

IMAGES AND NARRATIVES ARE CRUCIAL FOR THE FORMULATION OF URBAN VISIONS AND STRATEGIC POLICIES

In the face of deep uncertainty, well-informed images and narratives of future developments are crucial for the formulation of strategic government policies in the field of urban and transport planning. It is important to consider today's perspectives on problems and solutions in light of the longer term and to explore possible new challenges, views and policy options. In an era of deep uncertainty, data and quantitative models have limited value.
Qualitative and exploratory scenario research is a useful method that can contribute to dealing with the complexity and uncertainty inherent in transitions and to developing well-informed visions and resilient strategies for sustainable urban developments in regions, cities and neighbourhoods. ▪

Spatial design—from regional visions to design-based cross-border processes

Markus Nollert—urbanista.ch, Spatial Transformation Laboratories at ETH Zurich

In recent years regional visions and processes have increased throughout Germany, Austria and Switzerland. They illustrate the need for a conceptual understanding of larger metropolitan areas and cross-border regions and fill the gaps of other instruments of spatial development, which are limited to their sphere of influence. These concepts and processes demand a new understanding of the method of design, which is on the one hand capable of grasping, organizing and simplifying the sheer mass and layers of information of a metropolitan region and on the other challenged as a method itself out of the same reasons.

It seems, design on this level can and has to play different roles and fulfils multiple tasks, which should be taken into consideration for both, the design itself and the process underneath it in order use the its full potential. In the following paragraphs, I will try to distinguish and reflect these different roles of design and introduce the term of spatial design, which emphasis on supporting joint learning processes in multi-actor networks.

DESIGN AS A TOOL TO PUT REGIONAL DEVELOPMENT IN NEW (AND DIFFERENT) PERSPECTIVES

The first and central function of regional design is to introduce different and new perspectives to the development of functional regions, which are normally seen as a multitude of single spatial units, that are divided by borders and competences. By approaches like ignoring the borders, concentrating on crucial information, using metaphors or simply imagine a possible development, they set a spotlight on development potentials, functional links and options of collaboration, which mostly weren't there before. The *Städtebauliche Vision—Neue Stadt im Glatttal* of the *Group Krokodil* (see Figure 1) and the *Metro Map* of *Superwien* (SuperWien Metropole – a New Capital for Europe 2018) can be seen as examples of this type. Here design plays a bigger role as an outcome—without saying that the process of elaboration can be very complex, time-consuming and elaborated.

The design objects speak for themselves, offering new ways of looking at the development of a certain region: Seeing Vienna, Bratislava and its surrounding regions as one metro-system shows, how differently the metropolitan region could be organized, if seen without borders and as on organism or city. In the case of the Glattal, the urban design vision shows, how it would be possible, if one would treat the different municipalities as one "urban body"—referring to the often-used term of the *Glattal-City*, which doesn't find its way to everyday planning practice.

While the power of this kinds of design lies in opening a discussion and confronting planning and politic practice, they face difficulties to serve as a basis of further planning actions. The reason for this difficulty might been found in their simplicity—which is undoubtfully also their strength—and in their elaboration ►

This article is based on the following: Markus Nollert, "Raumplanerisches Entwerfen: Entwerfen als Schlüsselelement von Klärungsprozessen der aktionsorientierten Planung – am Beispiel des regionalen Massstabs" (Dissertation, ETH Zurich, 2013)

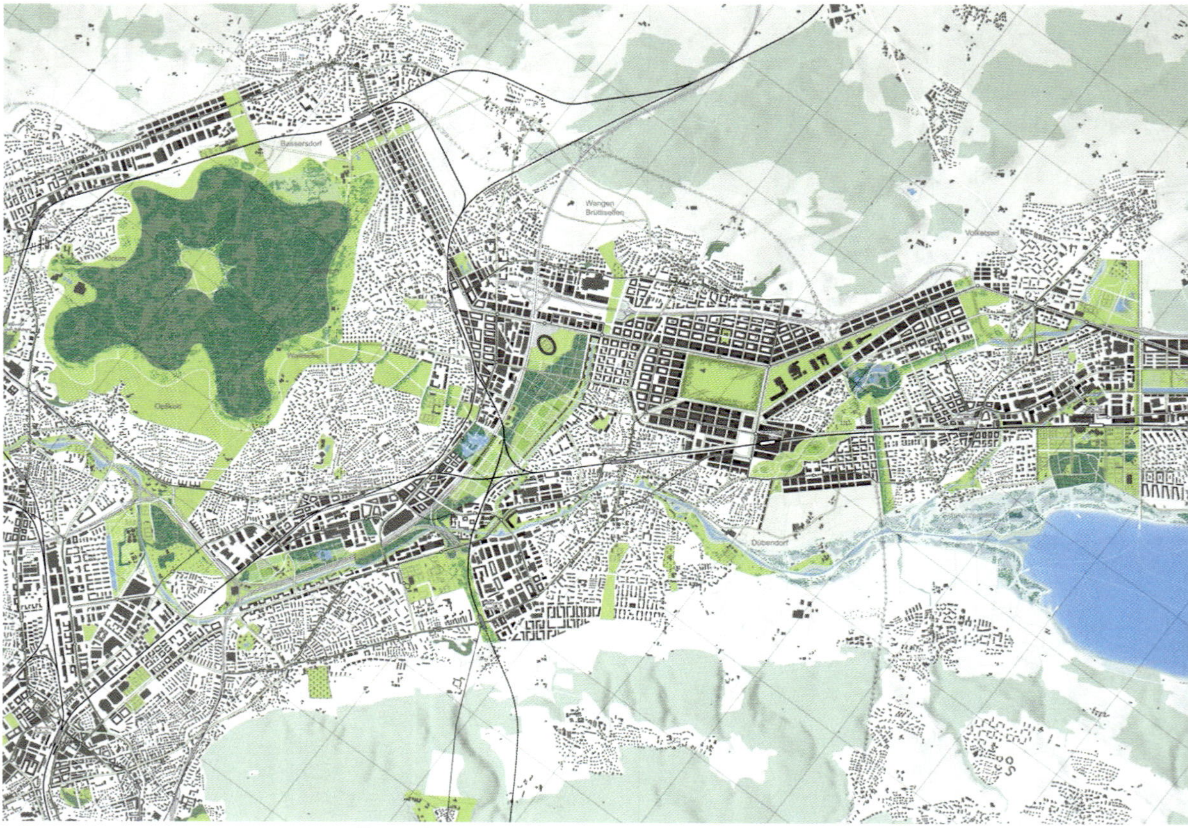

Figure 1: *Städtebauliche Vision - Neue Stadt im Glatttal* of the *Group Krokodil*
© Adam, Hubertus 2011

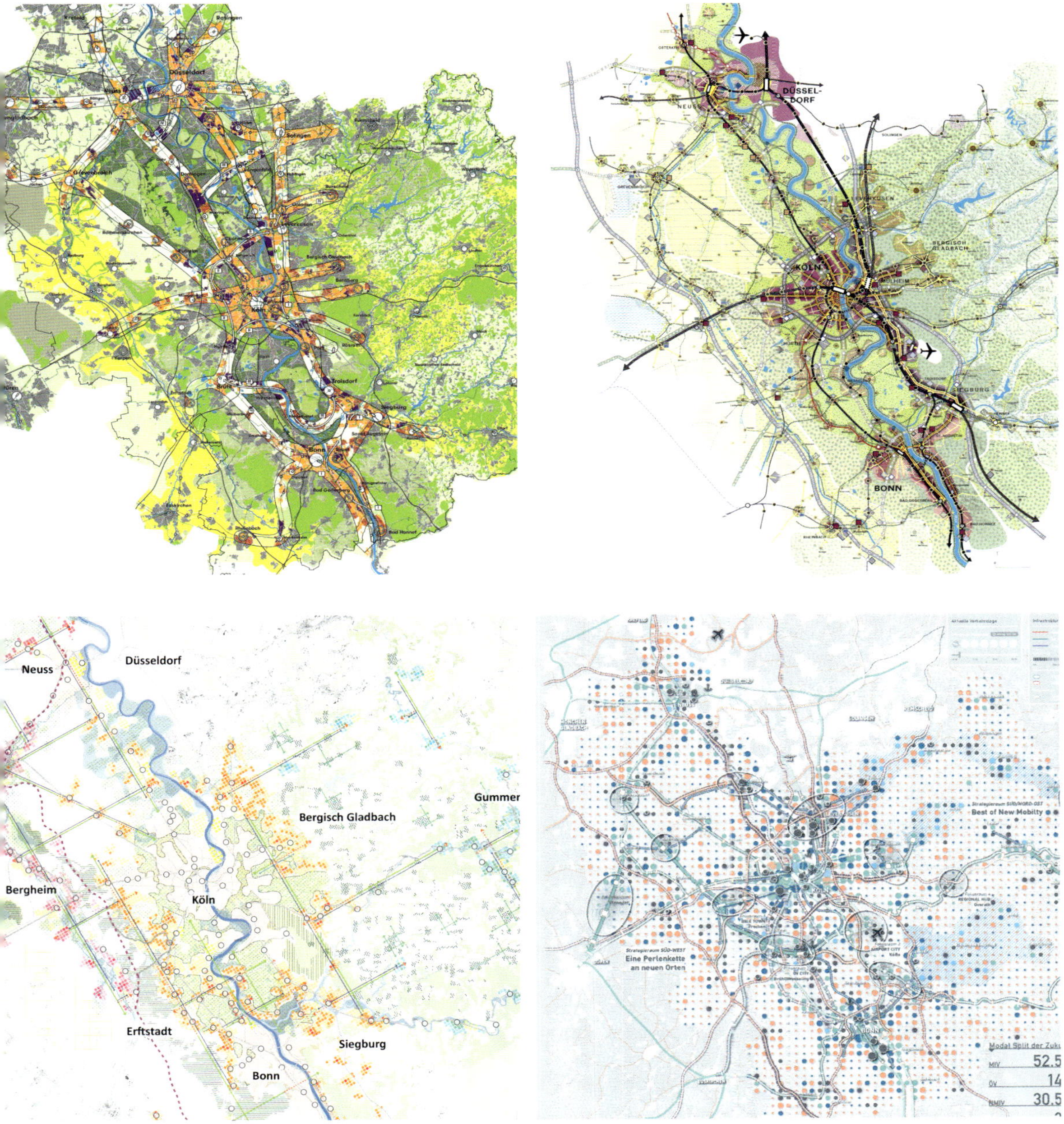

Figure 2-5: The *Rhenish Ladder*: The four contributions for the process "Agglomerationskonzept Köln-Bonn",
© Region Köln/Bonn e.V..

as a work of a group of architects and planners in their "atelier" which didn't take interests and objections local actor-networks into account—which is a strength, too. Hence, one could say that these kinds of regional design can start a discussion, but might not work as a foundation for a further collaborative process.

DESIGN AS BASIS FOR MULTI-ACTOR CROSS BORDER PROCESSES

The *Renish Ladder* (see Figure 2-5)—a perspective for the future development of the region between Cologne, Bonn and Dusseldorf, doesn't look much different from the upper examples. In fact, it was designed with the same intention, to break with common perspectives, especially the monocentric one of cologne. Therefore, it also used a strong visual language and the kind of exaggeration and simplification (Region Köln/Bonn 2019). The main difference is, that this concept was designed in a process of one and a half years, which integrated regional planning authorities and local politicians into a joint discussion over possible development paths of this region, organized by the Region Köln-Bonn e.V. In this process the design-team could discuss several states of their work with the actors, explaining central thoughts of their work and receiving quite an amount of critical comments and questions, which they could integrate into their further steps. Even as important as the integrated design processes was the fact, that it was not a single concept to be elaborated and discussed, but four of them, without the intention to choose a winner. This concurrence not only allowed the actors to compare different approaches to one another simultaneously and recommend further actions, it also gave the designers the freedom to emphasis on issues they think are important for the future development of this region and discuss them with the actors, which not only in this case proved to be a vital element of successful multi-actor processes.

West of the Cologne-Bonn area, in the Rhenish mining district another regional development process took place in which different actors could participate. The scale was the same if not larger and the task was also similar. Three teams were asked to develop a regional development strategy, showing possible ways to overcome the structural change which is expected with the end of brown coal mining and energy-production (Zukunftsagentur Rheinisches Revier 2022). To mitigate the expected negative effects the federal government provided a special fund of 14 billion Euro. Hence the expected "spatial image" [Raumbild] was not only a new perspective but also was elaborated in the light of a parallel discussion about what this money should be spent on. The result looks different as the "Renish ladder"—almost like a map of the future. This might be a result of the enormous scale or also of the diversity of topics it had to address: How can mobility be managed in a car-oriented region? Which kind of growth strategies are suitable for residential and commercial areas? How to become the desired first climate neutral region in Europe? Besides the questions of "what", "where", "how" and "why" the question of "when" played a crucial role in the design-process. Especially the future development of the opencast mines of Hambach, Inden and Garzweiler proved to be a challenge. Until the last mine will become a full lake—offering tempting development potentials—it will be 2090! A time too far in the future to think about now. Yet the design teams were confronted with numerous projects and visualizations of how these regions could look like and part of our job as planners was to put these images into perspective (see Figure 6).

Despite many parallels, design seems to serve different goals in this cases, which sometimes aren't that visible in its visual appearance but in the underlying process of their elaboration and the approach designers might have. ▸

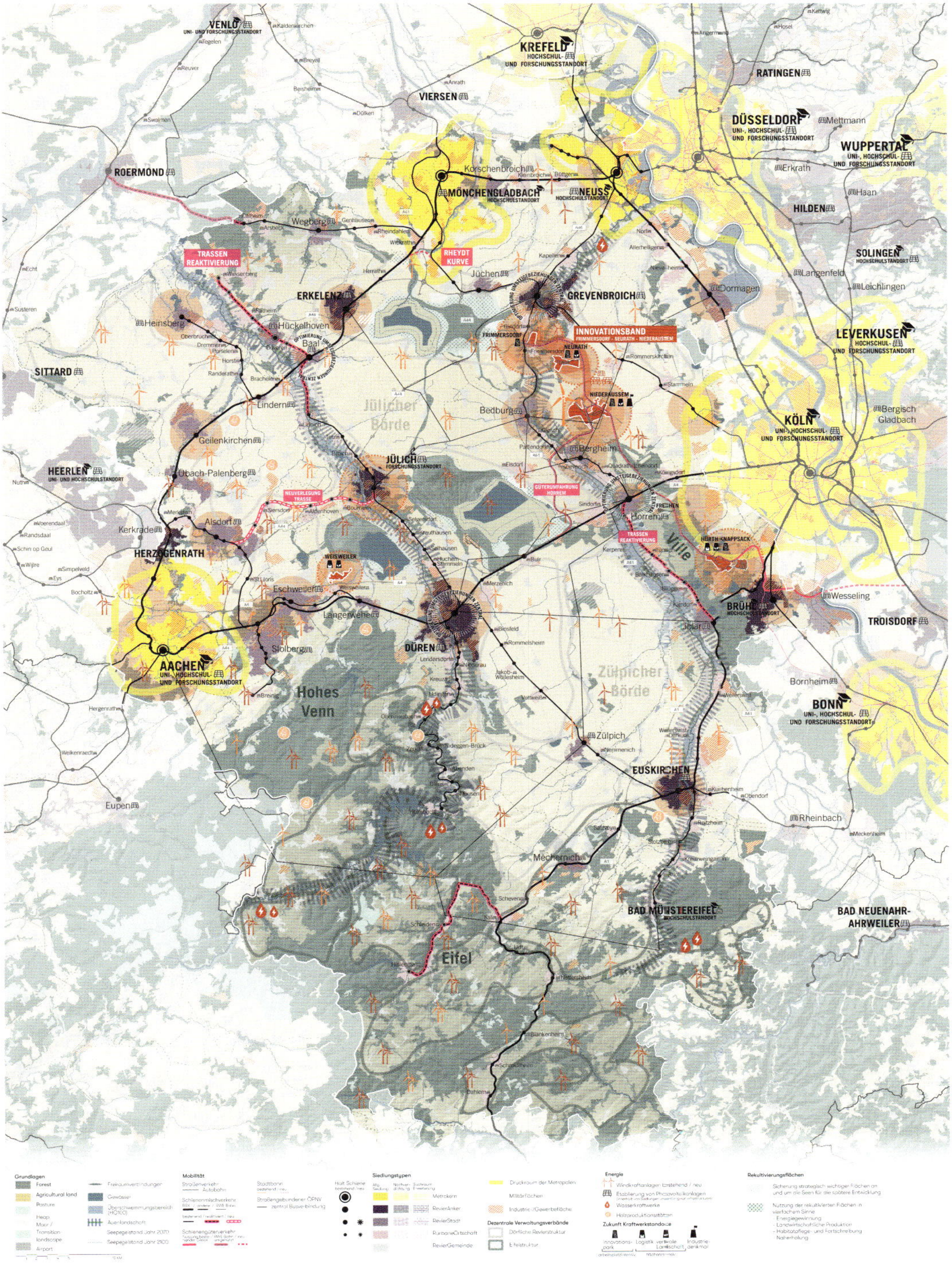

Figure 6: The "Strukturbild" as one of three contributions for the process "Raumstrategie Rheinisches Revier 2038+"

SPATIAL DESIGN—A COLLABORATIVE LEARNING PROCESS

Using the method of design inside cross border multi-actor processes does not necessarily aim at the production of an image ore a plan but at the revelation of "knowledge of action" [Handlungswissen]. The design itself is only the one mean to represent central development principles, findings, proofs and arguments, the main work and outcome lies in the process of design, its findings and the exchange with the affected actors. This means to work not only in the designer's "atelier" or "workshop", but integrating the actors' interests actively into the design process. This is of course done in other design-tasks, too, but maybe in a different way. One difference lies in the active discussion of the design team with the actors and the fact, that they aren't direct commissioners as e.g. in the design-process of a house. Even if the figures of the two presented cases show "designs" (as plans) the main and decisive media of both processes were the presentations. Here the design teams could explain, why they chose certain development paths and why they rejected others. Likewise, the actors could apply their concerns and criticism leading to fruitful (but not always conflict-free) discussions.
Another difference is the importance of the explicitness of the design-process itself and one of its major advantages: The productive handling with failing. In regions like Cologne-Bonn, the Rhenish mining district or Vienna-Bratislava, the matter is so complex, that its simply not possible not to fail while designing. But these fails often are the basis of new findings or the discovery of tasks, which weren't visible before. In the best manner of solving "wicked problems", as Rittel (Rittel 1973) called them, the best way to define a problem—or in other words: a task—is trying to solve the visible part of it and maybe fail. By discussing a preliminary state of a design alongside with findings of tasks, possible options of action, failed attempts and different opinions, the process of design becomes an outcome in itself. Together with the discussions mentioned above it can then lead into a collaborative learning process for both, actors and designers (see Figure 7).
To enable this learning process, designers have to make their process of design explicit and show assumptions, unfinished and preliminary elements—which is why, I also like to refer to the term "draft" or "drafting", which is included in the German term "Entwerfen". Being "unfinished", the draft fosters a discussion, especially in these complex tasks and scales, while "final" plans might hinder it. In doing so it allows designers to change their ideas early in the process and thus save their limited resources. Also, spatial design is much more than elaborating plans and principles: Designers have to use their skills to identify crucial problems, to develop arguments for or against certain actions and to find a suitable narrative in order to transport the main ideas of their concept.
On the other side, spatial design has to be embedded in a process, enabling discussions between designers and actors in an organized way and laying ground for an open exchange between all parties involved. These discussions are not only about the design itself. Especially in the case of the *Raumstrategie Rheinisches Revier 2038+* one important task for the designers was to identify arguments against existing ideas of other actors, because they would lead to unsustainable developments. It needs a series of exchanges in order to establish a dialogue which is capable of handling these kinds of discussions. Also, certain ideas need an "incubation time"—they won't be accepted at first glance but with time (and better arguments by the designers) they can thrive. To create the needed open dialogue and the freedom to test and fail these processes can't define a winner in the end. A competition that could be won by one team would eradicate all that is important for these collaborative learning processes: no design team would mention "new problems" they discovered, no one would criticize or reject existing ideas or projects and no one would be open to test bold hypotheses not knowing if they lead anywhere.

Figure 7: The interplay between different roles of design.
©Markus Nollert

Nevertheless, the concurrence of several design teams is a crucial element for these kind of collaborative learning processes. Only in the comparison between different ideas, strategies and perspectives experts and affected actors can identify viable strategies and proposals. Furthermore, more perspectives on the same task help to prevent overlooking important aspects of development.

One family of processes suitable of providing these features was "born" in the City of Vienna, called the *"Wiener Modell"* (Freisitzer, Maurer 1987) and is now known as "test-planning" [Testplanung] or "concurrence of ideas. These processes aim for discussing options of action with stakeholders, identifying common ground and conflicts among actors, testing possibilities and the preliminary approval and rejection of solutions—without selecting a winning concept. Being a known element in Switzerland in the last decades, this kind of processes start to also be conducted in Germany and Austria again.

DESIGN | DRAFT | TEST—PROCESS

The aim of this short reflection was not to judge certain forms of regional designs and choose a favorite. Its more about being conscious which role and outcome several forms of design can have, especially in metropolitan, regional and cross border situations. It wouldn't be too surprising, if it needs an impulse of a design like the metro-map of *Superwien*, to start or support a discussion about the integrated development of a region across borders—which then could be transformed into a process described in the paragraphs above. It is important to know what outcome is desired and what form of design and which process is suitable for it. If it is to be part of a collaborative learning process, it must be integrated into the stakeholder networks from the beginning

Above that, design can play so many more roles which couldn't be discussed here and we are only at the beginning to understand the potentials and restraints of the method of design in complex (regional) tasks. So, every time we start a new design task, we're part of a much bigger design-based process about design itself. We try, we succeed, we fail, we learn. ▪

Bordeaux Métropole—fifty thousand homes along public transport routes

Jérôme Goze—La Fabrique de Bordeaux Métropole (La Fab)

With 65 kilometres of tram lines, 2 651 kilometres of roads, 152 million passengers on the public transport network, nearly 4 000 social rental housing units built each year, 420 000 jobs, 140 kilometres of walking paths in the green belt and 150 parks and natural spaces, the metropolitan area of Bordeaux is a dynamic territory. It is also a territory that boasts an outstanding architectural heritage, with its *UNESCO*-listed eighteenth-century historic centre—the *City of Stone*—as well as low-density neighbourhoods, where three storeys are considered a high-rise building.

But there is another side to the metropolitan region. Firstly, the waiting time for social housing is more than three years, which affects about 80% of the French population entitled to social housing. Secondly, there are growing difficulties in housing the middle classes of the conurbation. Housing is becoming too expensive to stay in the metropolis, so they often have no choice but to move to the outskirts, where there are fewer public facilities and poorer infrastructure.

This is reflected in frenetic consumption of farmland, heavy rush-hour traffic, long commuting times and, ultimately, a lower quality of life. Looking at the local economy and people's purchasing power, the majority—around 70%—of households in the metropolis can spend up to € 250 000, which is equivalent to 58 m² of new housing today. Accordingly, the majority of households can no longer afford to live in the metropolitan area. The discrepancy between the metropolitan and the suburban area is made clear in the following example: for about € 185 000, one will find a flat of 60 m² in the metropolitan area, but if one moves around 15 kilometres away from the metropolitan area, one can afford a flat of 90 to 100 m². So, if we want to keep families in the metropolitan area, avoid morning and evening traffic jams, fight urban sprawl and protect nature, landscape and the environment, we need to be more competitive in what we offer. That means we have to build more, cheaper and better, which is what happened in the metropolitan area in 2010.

The programme *Living and Thriving—50 000 Naturally Accessible Homes* was initiated by *Bordeaux Métropole* and aims to counteract urban sprawl by producing housing differently. The goal is to nurture the emergence of innovative housing developments, meeting the needs of future residents, entrepreneurs and users and providing homes which are economically accessible, located in immediate proximity to existing and future public transport lines. The five main objectives were:

1. To support the ambition of the *Bordeaux Métropole*, because without political will, there is no change.
2. To provide new answers to the need for housing, which is one of the most important economic and social issues, along with the necessity to contain global warming.
3. To question our way of shaping the city through housing.
4. To strategically reflect on the metro-politan area by comparing local operational situations.
5. To answer basic questions such as, "Do we know how to build the housing we would like, so that we can all live in *Bordeaux Métropole*?" ▸

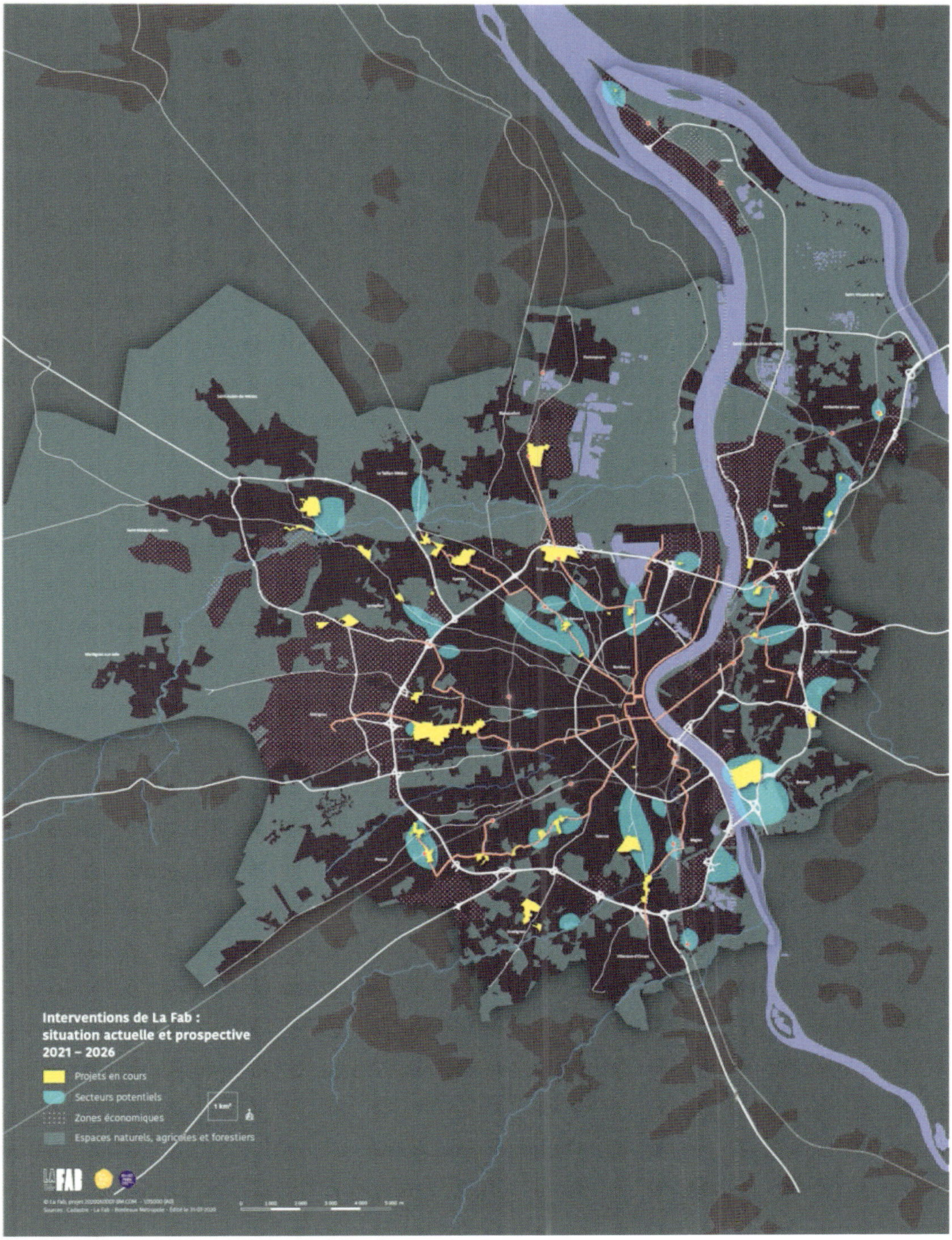

Figure 1: Interventions by La Fab: Current and Future Situation, 2021-2026
© La Fab

Despite the naivety of the question, the needs of the population, such as the desire for a safe and beautiful home and the desire for the city, come to light. The public authority has surrounded itself with experts to develop a working method and tools to ultimately achieve these objectives.

Five international teams were selected for their vision and their responses to the challenges, by taking urban reality as a basis, making use of the mobility infrastructure, highlighting new types of places to live, and applying a useful approach by studying a wide range of building typologies.

Their method was to take urban situations and create conditions to produce tailored responses, such as to build in the suburbs, to build to define the boundary between city and nature, to build on a car park, to build to accommodate changing family forms and so on. The five teams set the themes defining the quality of housing. Working on specific project sites as unique urban situations required answers in relation to mobility and parking, privacy and sociability, environmental performance at the service of housing, etc.

The teams determined how to improve the urban, architectural and landscape quality through housing design taking into consideration specific requirements in regard to density, diversity, and accessibility, and the environmental and climatic conditions of Bordeaux.

The following mission and specific targets to contribute to an attractive and balanced metropolis and its neighbourhoods on a local scale were defined by *Bordeaux Métropole* and the 28 municipalities:

1. A breakdown of the programme into three parts, namely social rental housing, affordable homes and private housing
2. A significant proportion of housing for families
3. A selling price for affordable housing of around € 2 500 € per m^2 compared to € 4 300 per m^2, which is the average price per m^2 in the conurbation
4. A maximum of one parking space per flat

At the same time, a consultation on fifteen trial blocks has been launched to mobilise project owners and project managers in different locations and municipalities, starting with those on land parcels over which we as the city of Bordeaux have control. In parallel, we are working and looking at different approaches that require more complex arrangements.

The bottom line is that 42% of private housing means that we have 58% price-controlled housing, which is made up of social housing, first-time buyer housing and affordable housing.

In conclusion, it is crucial to stimulate discussions and exchange ideas and, at the same time, to never stop demanding high-quality housing for everyone, to respect urban situations and human narratives, to respect the people who are already there and those who are just moving into the area. With this in mind, never insult the future with ready-made answers when we have not even asked all the questions yet, and remember that contradiction is often the most obvious path to truth. ▪

Model of the Route de Toulouse Project
© LaFab

Le Bouscat - Libération
© LaFab

Mérignac Langevin
© LaFab

Cité de la gare
© LaFab

Bordeaux Résisdence du lac
© LaFab

The disciplinary approach to a metropolitan qualified way of life—projects & tools

Antonella Contin—Department of Architecture and Urban Studies at Politecnico di Milano

I want to introduce the Metropolitan Approach to Complexity. Regarding the *Großstadt* of the last century, I have to point out a discontinuity. That is why we say that we are dealing with a Post-Metropolis Era, and not with a polycentric city. Instead, nowadays, Metropolis is a net-city. It is not only referring to nodes and poles but the space in between the infrastructure—the body of space, as D.G. Shane (Shane 2005) called it in 2005—which we have to reconceptualise. Nevertheless, we are not referring to a conurbation, but we have to understand a new entity with a new DNA, and we need new tools to comprehend and design it.

METROPOLITAN ARCHITECTURE PROJECTS

In the current metropolitan dimension, we can follow two different active paths of research. One is dealing with policies at the government/sub-national level and the other with actions, namely the implementation through Metropolitan Architecture Projects, which is our research field of action. Our research questions are related to how it is possible to give order to the explosive growth, which means arguing how we can structure the knowledge related to the metropolitan region. Then, we investigate the metropolitan principles and issues, in order to be sure that our metropolitan project will be sustainable. Also, we investigate our values and what the notion of public and common good mean at the metropolitan scale. We also define a possible metropolitan scope as the Metropolitan Architecture Projects' field of action. Thus, we figure out new tools to understand the impact of metropolitan processes and dynamics on the territory for the realisation of meta-projects. That is "how" the Academy can intervene in the metropolitan arena, providing meta-projects as negotiation support for the dialogue among the different metropolitan agents.

GREEN-GREY INFRASTRUCTURE AS THE GENERATOR OF A NEW URBANITY

Today we are dealing with a new metropolitan nature, which is defined by the structure or architecture of our city framed by the green-grey infrastructure continuity: the wet and drylands, the scarcity of the resources, the wellness and the welfare that means water capital and management, renewable energies and pollution prevention.

We have models. Looking at the image of Madrid's chessboard and the Filarete' section, the city is always related to geography and water. The *Madrid Metro-Matrix* (Ortiz 2014) is the geographic structure for the mental map of a metropolis, but, at the scale of metropolitan architecture, it can also prefigure something more "modern" than the traditional concept of the metropolis. Looking at the Madrid diagram, the mental grid disappears but the linear city rooted in its territory through metropolitan centres rises. A city without administrative boundaries, the continuity of the green and blue infrastructure, a city of exchanges of flows and defined places. We classify the metropolitan paradigms of city structure related to the revolutionary cultural eras in order to address the understanding of growth issues. Analysing the scales-progression towards the threshold of discontinuity, we observe how the compact shape of the city walls had been transcended during the eighteenth century. Nowadays, the challenge we face is to move away from the broad and de-regulated shapes of the diffuse urbanisation of the second post-war period. Regarding our categories we can say that the identifying name of the historical Evo is the Regional Net-City linked to the network of the cities of the word; the Shape and Structure Paradigm is the Archipelago for the practice of the *Tele-città* supported by the green-grey infrastructure; the Scale, so the character of the urban space is the electro-telematic Scale of the just in time; the Idea of Citizenship is the Utopia of cosmopolitan citizenship, and time is the Metropolitan Unit of Measurement. Four Metropolitan Contexts shape our set of landscapes and our field of action:

1. The semi-sprawl along the main roads (Venturi's Las Vegas Strip)
2. The hyper-oriented and planned space of the grey infrastructure (Moses's New York grey infrastructure)
3. The new centralities (the Lille TGV station and its neighbourhood by Koolhaas)
4. The eco-armatures.

The section strategy is the connection between them. It is a critical section that links the lithology of the ground, the water, the grey infrastructure, nature and agriculture, and finally the layer of the landscape. That allows us to think about transative territories (Zammataro 2020) where the project operations determine a relationship between inhabitants and the environment not only through efficiency and economy but also considering cognitive and perceptual aspects.

Our research question is also related to the conditions of providing a metropolitan urbanity or intersomaticity (Choay 1992) through the Metropolitan Architecture Project; it usually acts in the hybrid territory in between urban and rurban; rurban and rural; rural and natural identifying their linkage. So, we are trying not only to identify which functions are needed but also a new typo-morphological invention. Nevertheless, we consider the green-grey infrastructure as the generator of a new urbanity. In our project, we interconnect the regional (commuter), metropolitan (metro), urban (BRT-LRT-Bus-Taxi) to the micro-urban (Bicycle-Pedestrian) scales. So, the grey infrastructure guarantees performance and feasibility of the railway; the environment deals with the physical structure of a fragile context, and finally the urban settlements re-organise a scattered territory. Thus, we achieve urban-rural organisation with the creation of new linkage patterns. Our results are land properties, tenure formalisation and governance, the creation of hierarchies and performative connections. Our Metropolitan Architecture Project, subsequently, must reinforce the urban-rural linkage pattern's water networks. In India, for example, we studied the Desakota region as a best practice and a systemic approach to implementing territorial resources.▸

NEW URBAN MORPHOTYPES

The Metropolitan is a phased project, and we have defined new morphotype patterns. Starting with the categories of the Japanese author Fumiko Maki (1964) and then Frampton's definition (1999) of the new built form types as megaforms, we argue that something that was related to the morphology of the city right now is miniaturised and included inside the metropolitan new typologies: the New Urban Morphotypes (D'Alfonso 2000). These must re-connect the anonymous urban city-fabric within the city centre in a new syntax and unit. According to Fenton (1985), we can catalogue them in three categories: the fabric, a fence and traditional typologies integrated inside (the Rockefeller Center); the graft, building as layer-machine (The United Nation Headquarter); and finally the newest the monolith that combines different functions and times of use in the same "big" form through multiple pockets of space (the Lilla of Moneo in Barcelona).

These new patterns of land use and morphotypes represent an evolution of the TOD centrality that must include in its pattern green and blue infrastructure, not such as an embellishment, but as fundamental elements grounding the project to the territory. Our metropolitan digit covers more or less 1 km x 1 km. A rail or commuter transportation system station is at the centre and the green-grey continuity is provided by the connection between the urban park and the regional park through the new built form type of the Metropolitan Architecture Project. Ours is a cognitive approach. Starting from strategic and structural plans, we must deal, then, with the local, territorial intelligence which constitutes variant elements at the local scale that we have to maintain, develop or radically transform to be the invariant elements at the Metropolitan Scale. That avoids generating a generic city again (Koolhaas 1995).

METROPOLITAN CARTOGRAPHY

The maps potential produced through our methodology tool, the Metropolitan Cartography, is expressed in the research and analysis of open-source data. We express the intrinsic meaning of the data, not only the alphanumeric descriptive ones but also those that contain the relational and spatialising value of the implicit properties of the territory. This study makes it possible to generate synthetic, non-thematic maps that attempt to express the information of the analytical maps through the representation of the implicit connections between the levels of information, keywords and related concepts, organised in the software of Glossary. It is difficult to assess the vulnerability of the Metropolis through the limited availability of data. However, a study focusing on the environmental, social, political and

economic management issues in the exposed metropolitan context could be the key to promoting more specific and inclusive policies for the benefit of the host communities and migrants. Our epistemological approach drives us to always demonstrate the reasons why we select specific data and indicators. The Protocol Maps are maps that show the fundamental relationship between the elements that make up the metropolitan system and reveal its structure through the stratification of the physical aspects of geographical and historical data. We conceived eight protocol maps at XXL, L, M scale. The maps of dynamics, instead, are maps which represent the factors of mutation of the landscape over time. These are the result of the synthesis done by the metropolitan expert towards the different perspectives done by the other team members, who see the metropolitan issues from their specific disciplin's point of view.
By using alphanumeric data, the metropolitan cartography selects, orders and relates the unexpressed quality values of the territory. Therefore, it tries to evaluate and represent the qualitative-relational data through a logical sequence of choices. Due to the software of Glossary, from the semantic package obtained through the metropolitan discipline evaluation, as a container of keywords (categories) to which the specific concepts of the descriptive variables of metropolitan complexity correspond, it is possible to take a further step: to initiate the selective process. However, we must clarify specific details in order to understand the general structure of the process since the Semantic Package is a set of possible concepts applicable at a global level to identify current scenarios or changes in the metropolitan territory. The semantic package can contain related concepts for each metropolitan dimension: physical, social, economic and governance, according to the classification by each category. The correspondence of the concept and the information level layer on the map is not always immediately perceptible, as intangible economic and governance factors cannot always be spatialised. However, metropolitan cartography provides an opportunity for the immediate representation of quantitative economic values, which help to adequately describe the properties of the metropolitan reality, since the conversion of the mental map, the semantic package, into the metropolitan cartography, is a synthetic result of the representation (Contin et al 2020).
In conclusion, starting from the need for interconnection among the different *SDGs*, which describe the sustainability regarding the four metropolitan dimensions: physical, social, economic, and governance, our metro-dology provides the decision making for *SDGs Assessment*. Through interconnection, merging the elements of our cartography within the *SDGs*, their targets and indicators, we can define which areas of activity must be reinforced with new policies actions. In short, from the projects to the policies, not vice-versa. ▪

Kersten Nabielek
PBL Netherlands Environmental Assessment Agency

Jérôme Goze
La Fabrique de Bordeaux Métropole

Antonella Contin
Department of Architecture and Urban Studies (DAStU), Politecnico di Milan

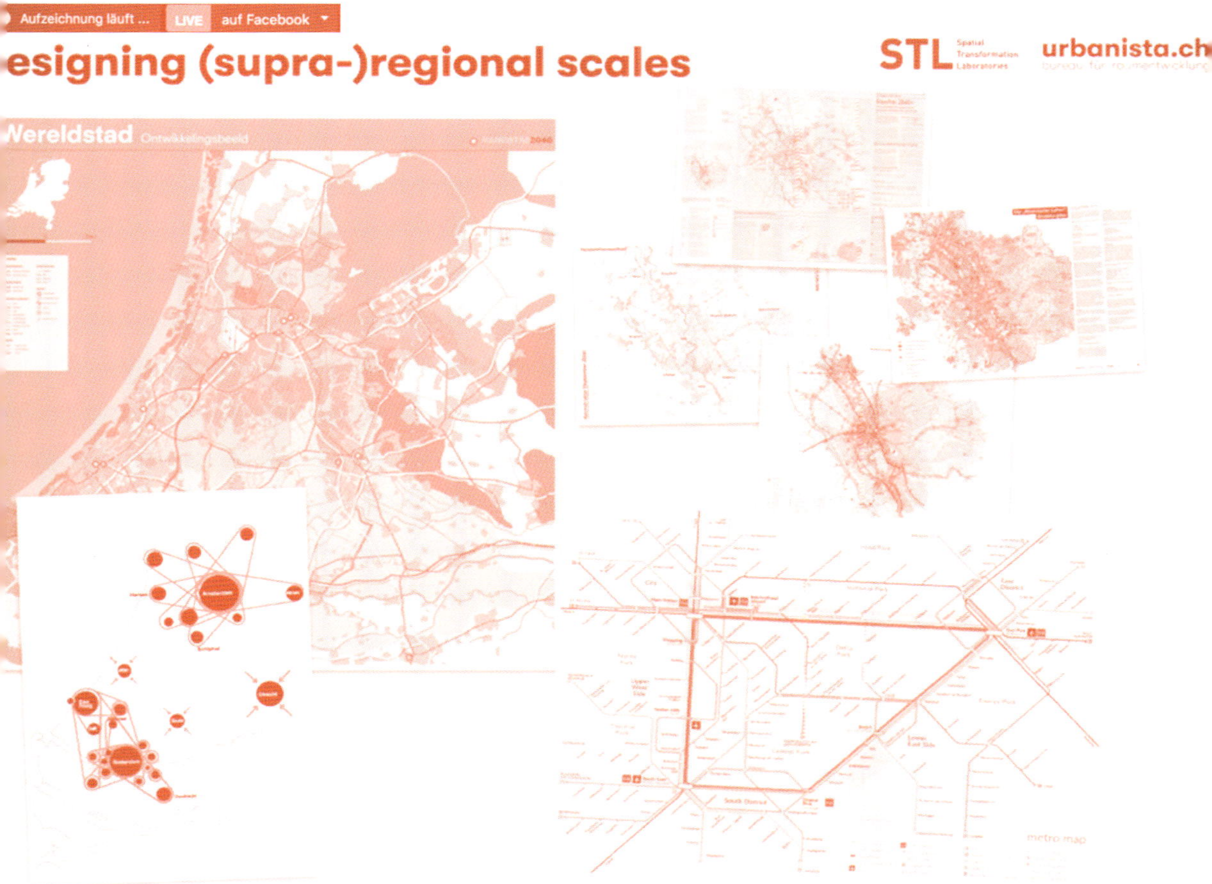

Markus Nollert
urabista.ch, Spatial Transformation
Laboratories, ETH Zurich

DISCUSSING URBAN GROWTH

The City of Vienna is a strong believer in the regional dialogue

Forum Discussion

What new demands must be placed on urban governance to ensure a high-quality and affordable living environment? How can existing standards in housing be maintained while fostering compact growth? And how can decision-makers be sensitized when it comes to coordinated settlement development within urban regions?

These are some of the key questions raised during the Forum Discussion of the second *MetroLab Forum* which was devoted to the management and design of rapid urban growth. Five experts from the fields of city planning, housing development, urban geography and urban design contributed, from their professional perspectives to the challenges and limits of growth.

At the very beginning of the discussion, Michael Rosenberger, representing the *Urban and Regional Development Unit* of the *City of Vienna*, took the opportunity to look beyond the administrative borders of Vienna. Relating to the challenge of managing growth within the city limits and not only to grow in size but also to increase density, he stated that we are currently confronted with a "running-out-of-space-phenomenon". However, the biggest obstacle in providing people with qualitative and well-connected places for living and working is not a lack of space itself, but more a lack of willingness to cooperate within and between cities, towns and their surrounding areas. By stating that "*the possibility to look at the metropolitan dimension to accommodate growth*" has not yet been considered, he supported the idea of finding "*other modes of growth*" which are more oriented towards functional interdependencies.

According to Rosenberger, the prerequisite for a strong metropolitan plan would be to establish a common ground aligning the individual motives of the different entities of one metropolitan region:

> *"We don't all have the same interests and desires. So, I think the task is to create this common narrative and understanding of what a metropolitan region could look like."*
>
> *Michael Rosenberger*

Then he added: "*if we want to become a metropolitan region of six million with Bratislava and all the partners in the region then we have to arrive at a shared kind of spatial vision.*"

Important steps in this direction have already been taken with the help of the *BAUM* project, said Marek Dinka, the initiator of the *Bratislava Region Management* and city planner of the *Division of Spatial Planning* at the *Bratislava City Administration*. Although his wish for a joint master plan for the cross-border city region of Bratislava and the surrounding municipalities in Lower Austria and Burgenland was not fulfilled, the platform now offers the framework for a trustworthy and cooperative partnership. According to Dinka, the joint project office and the international team function as a "hub" ▸

[1] The connecting SuperRing is presented as a metropolitan Vision for "SuperWien" in the book *SuperWien Metropole. A new Capital for Europe* (2018) by Cédric Ramière and Stefan Mayr

and are less concerned with suburbanization issues than with cross-border pilot projects on mobility or culture.

It is the soft factors, according to Yvonne Franz, working for the *Department of Geography and Regional Research* at the *University of Vienna*, which, from the perspective of Urban Geography, help establish a shared identity and visibility. This is especially true for the terms we use to describe the metropolis: relations, networks, connectivity etc.

Even though municipalities are spatially interconnected, they often have very different legal, administrative and institutional systems, making the successful transferability of best practice implementations difficult, Kurt Hofstetter argued. The Senior Coordinator of the *International Building Exhibition Vienna 2022* further stated that the key to a coordinated urban development avoiding urban sprawl lies in a well-connected public transport system and the commitment to meet at eye level:

"We do not only need the infrastructure and the public transport system, but also the willingness and the understanding of developing things together."

Kurt Hofstetter

From the perspective of an urban designer, Nela Kadic, Senior Lecturer at the Institute for Urban Design of the *Vienna University of Technology* argued that large-scale visions, which are mostly elaborated on the level of metropolitan regions, need to consider concrete design solutions for the local environments.

This not only includes the proposal for built structures, but also considerations about transportation, connecting and linking different spatial units, establishing (social) infrastructure, logistics of production etc., which has been demonstrated during the Urban Design Studio organized in collaboration with *MetroLab*. Very satisfied with the students' designs, which deal intensively with the facilitation of slow mobility and lively public spaces, she spoke out against the outdated top-down Masterplan, but admited:

"Somehow we started to rely only on the strategy itself and today have forgotten to make a design proposal."

Nela Kadic

Designing the hardware as well as the software of our living environments in an innovative way means being courageous enough to leave constraints behind, to think outside the box and, above all, to establish a solid and inclusive communication structure in favor of building trust and mutual knowledge exchange. This is the only way we can succeed—and all experts agree on this—in developing shared future visions representing not only the perspective of urban planning professionals, but of local experts who live on the ground. Leaving the comfort zone of one's own discipline and introducing bottom-up and co-creative tools such as urban living labs or urban design competitions that include workshops with citizens enable the opening up of new and unconventional forms of living and dwelling. Here a certain degree of irritation can be quite helpful, as Yvonne Franz pointed out: *"I love provocation, because it starts new debates and new perspectives."* ▪

Scan to watch the documentation of the International Lectures and the Forum Discussion!

Kurt Hofstetter
Senior Coordinator, International Building Exhibition Vienna 2022

Nela Kadic
Senior Lecturer, Institute for Urban Design, Vienna University of Technology

Yvonne Franz
Senior Lecturer, Department of Geography and Regional Research, University of Vienna

Michael Rosenberger
Urban and Regional Development Unit - City of Vienna

Marek Dinka
Division of Spatial Planning, Bratislava City Administration

KEY FINDINGS ON MANAGING URBAN GROWTH

1. A METROPOLITAN NARRATIVE SUPPORTS COMMON DEVELOPMENT PERSPECTIVES

As functional regions often break with existing administrative delineations, there is not only a high demand for coherent spatial development, but also for the creation of common development perspectives for all places within the extended urban area. A shared metropolitan narrative is essential to drive coordinated spatial development on a larger scale and to face metropolitan challenges such as jointly designing and managing urban growth or coordinating land use and transportation projects across municipal boundaries.

In order for the metropolitan region to be increasingly perceived as integrated, it is important to emphasize commonalities. This includes unifying hard factors such as infrastructural or economic connections, but also soft factors such as culture or leisure. The definition of an inclusive metropolitan narrative should be framed as an open process so that all stakeholders, political decision-makers as well as citizens can co-create it and find themselves in it.

2. DEFINING SPATIAL AND THEMATIC FOCUS AREAS MAKES THE NARRATIVE APPLICABLE

Based on the joint metropolitan narrative, a comprehensive strategy with tangible objectives and fields of action needs to be defined in an intensive negotiation process between different stakeholder groups as well as the civil society. To better coordinate growth and initiate joint projects, both spatial and thematic focus areas should be identified at the metropolitan level. They must be well aligned with each other. In particular, the mutual influence of settlement development and mobility as well as green space development, agriculture and production must be considered and synergies between these different sectors created. The public transport network should serve as a basis to manage settlement development and define centers in which growth is to be forced and a spatial as well as functional density (living, working, production) is to be promoted. As a counterbalance to dense urban centers, generous natural spaces and agricultural areas must be preserved and developed.

3. TRANSLATE METROPOLITAN STRATEGIES INTO PLACE-BASED ACTION

The definition of focus areas provides an important strategic framework, but needs to be translated into place-based projects. One way to turn metropolitan strategies into local action is to organize cross-border, metropolitan planning competitions based on the spatial focus areas. The innovative housing program *50 000 Naturally Accessible Homes* initiated by Bordeaux Métropole, demonstrates that a coordinated approach can be more effective in combating urban sprawl by quality densification than if spatial units act individually. Taking into account specific local requirements in terms of density, diversity, accessibility, environmental and climatic conditions, tailored responses could successfully be developed in different urban situations. Finally, transforming focus areas into place-based projects enables compact, socially, and economically mixed centers within the polycentric network of the metropolis.

4. INTEGRATIVE PLANNING INSTRUMENTS ARE NEEDED TO BALANCE GROWTH

To proactively balance metropolitan growth, the inter-municipal mobilization of financial resources is needed to jointly respond to challenges related to uncoordinated urban growth, such as the increasing consumption of land, as well as spatial and social fragmentation frequently leading to unequal living conditions. A shared budget allows for the integrated and targeted development of the metropolitan area to be driven by different political stakeholders meeting at eye level. Moreover, compensation mechanisms that balance profits and costs between urban centers and surrounding and structurally weak municipalities such as an inter-municipal financial equalization have proven to be an effective instrument to support more sustainable spatial development. In addition to formal financing instruments, regional associations that promote the joint coordination of land policies as well as informal instruments such as strategy papers enable coordinated and balanced territorial development.

5. INCLUSIVE METROPOLITAN AREAS DEMAND CO-CREATION

One of the main challenges of urban growth is integrating expansion areas into the built city and overcoming or preventing dissatisfaction or even protests by residents in the surrounding area. To create more inclusive and just neighborhoods, it is necessary to also involve those groups who are not seen or heard at first glance as well as those who do not live there yet. As institutionalized participation is limited in its reach, new, more engaging formats should be integrated into day to day and formal planning processes to overcome these hurdles. The advantages of co-creative approaches, such as Urban Living Labs, lie in their experimental character, the opening of new perspectives and the productive handling of failure, whereby the process itself becomes the actual result. The openness of such dialogue-oriented formats enables the exchange and cooperation of stakeholders across encrusted structures and, thus, also stimulates collective learning processes and knowledge spillovers. Further, the possibility of co-creation also strengthens the identification of the participating actors with the common metropolitan area. ▪

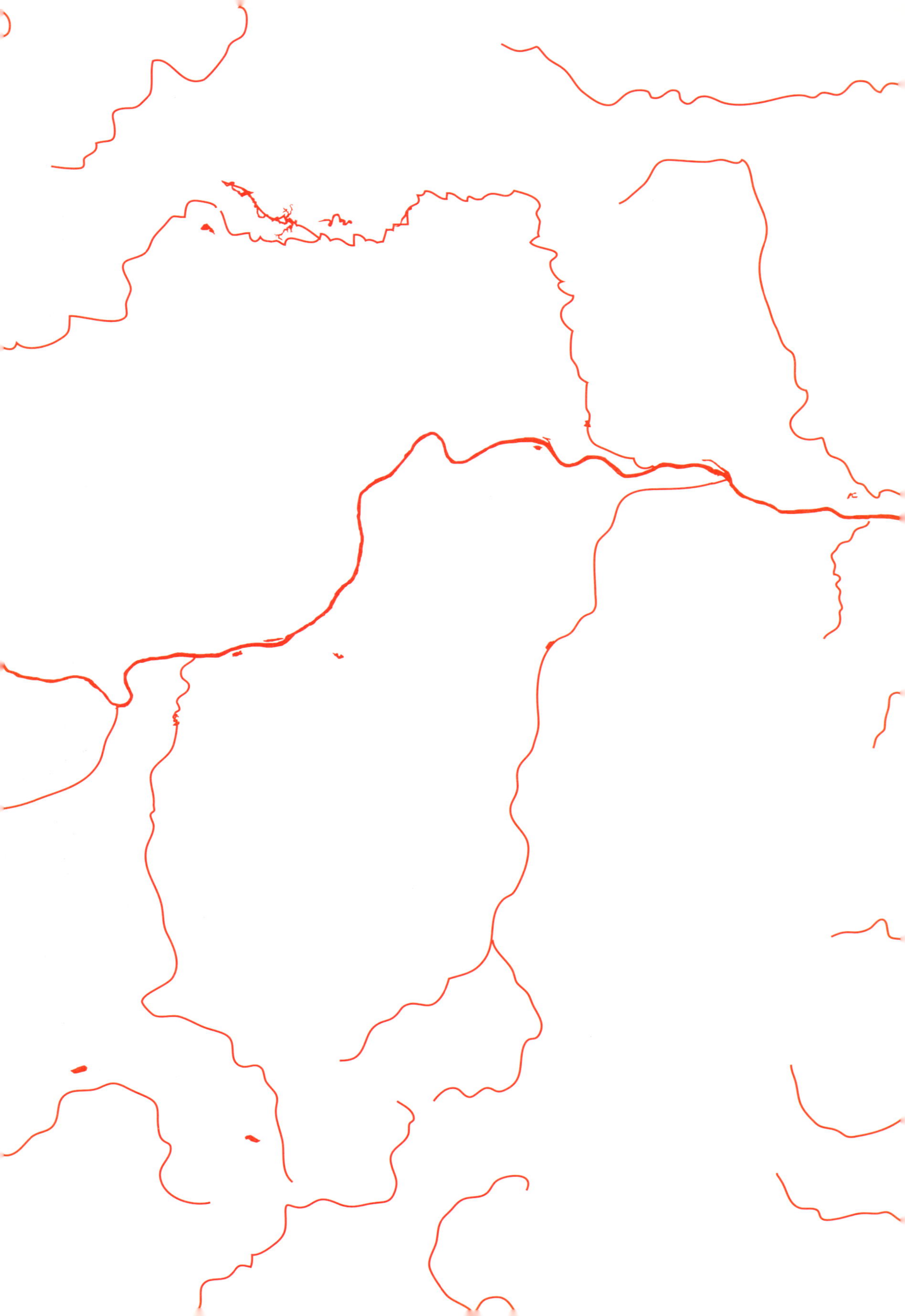

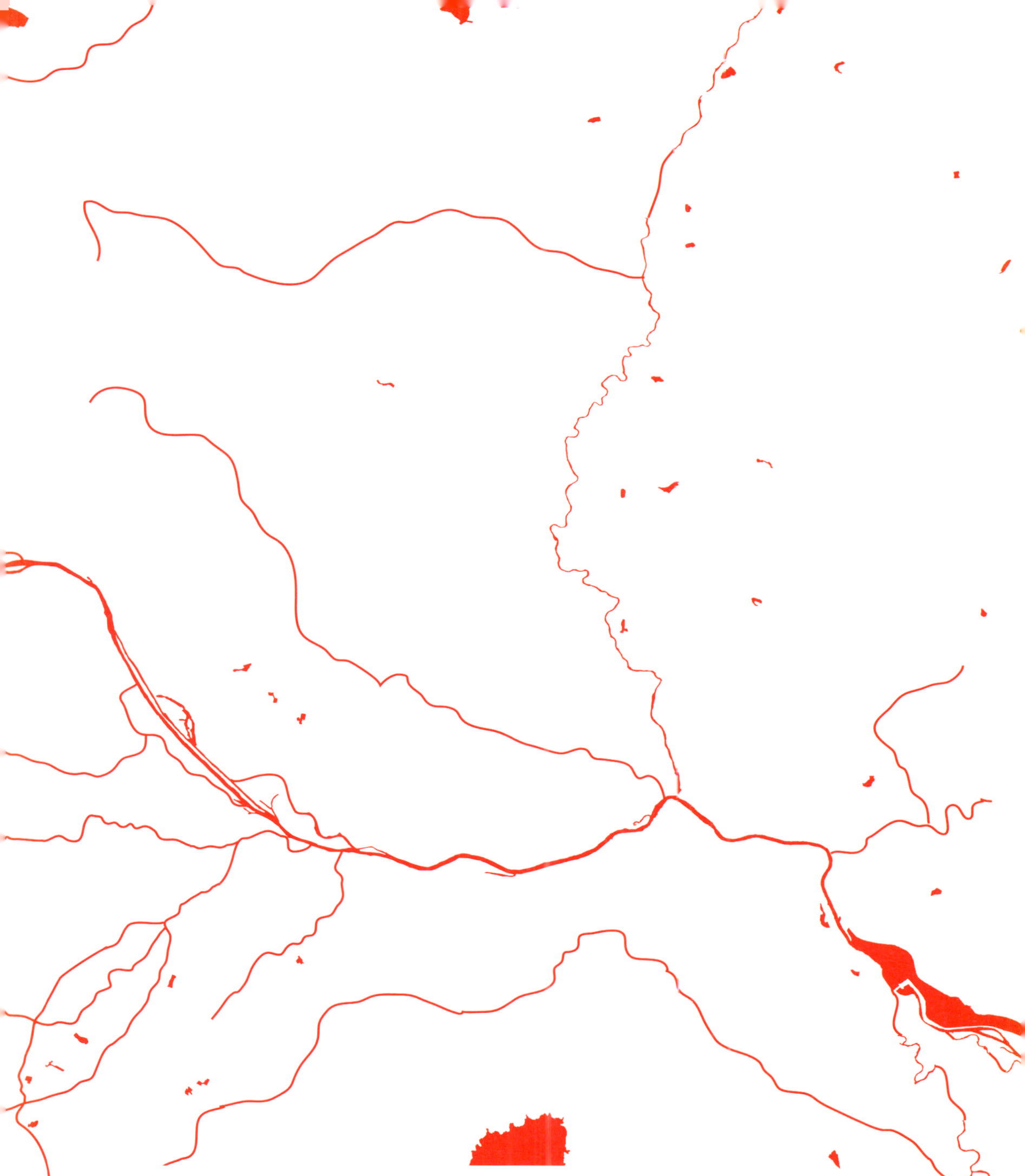

#3 DELTA

THE RESILIENCE OF METROPOLITAN LANDSCAPES

METROLAB FORUM

International Dialogue on Metropolitan Planning

04.10.2021
17:00-18:30

METROTALK WORKSHOPS

***Philipp Loidolt-Shen**, Azolla Ecosystems, Vienna*
***Vanessa Giolai & Daniel Löschenbrand**, Urban Food Atlas, Vienna*
***Christoph Fink,** Metropolitan Cooking, Vienna*

19:00-21:00

MOVIE NIGHT

Everything's coming together while everything's falling apart: The ZAD, AT/DE 2017, 36 min, OmU (engl.)
So this is where we are now, AT 2020, 20:53 min, OmU (engl.)

05.10.2021
09:30-12:00

METROPOLITAN WALKSHOP

***Regional Park DreiAnger**, with **Christina Stockinger**, City of Vienna, and **Renate Zuckerstätter**, SUM North*

17:00-19:30

INTERNATIONAL LECTURES

FERTILE SOILS
***Hélène Coussedière**, BASE Landscape Agency, Paris*

"NEULAND GEWINNEN" - HOTSPOTS OF TRANSFORMATION
***Siri Frech**, Raum+Strategie - Office for Coproductive Urban & Rural Development; Neuland gewinnen e.V., Berlin*

MUCH ENERGY, LITTLE SPACE: METROPOLITAN STORIES ABOUT WIND POWER
***Pia Kronberger-Nabielek**, PBL Netherlands Environmental Assessment Agency*

NEW LIFE TO MARKETS BETWEEN LOCAL AND GLOBAL DISTRIBUTION SYSTEMS
***Daniela Patti**, Eutropian Research & Action, Rome*

REVITALISING FORMER MILITARY CAMPS AS AN ECOSYSTEM NETWORK
***Paraskevi Tarani**, RiConnect, Major Development Agency Thessaloniki*

FORUM DISCUSSION

Herbert Bartik, Urban Innovation Vienna, **Anna Detzlhofer**, DnD Landschaftsplanung, **Andreas Gugumuck**, Future Farm Vienna, **Helga Kromp-Kolb**, Climate Change Centre Austria, **Christina Stockinger,** City of Vienna

Flyer MetroLab Forum #3 DELTA

Can metropolitan landscapes become resilient?

The quality of life in the *SuperWien Metropole* is not only defined by its urban centers, business districts and working areas, but also, to a large part, by its different types of landscapes—delta areas and large-scale parks are complemented by urban agriculture and vineyards. Considering the increasing consumption of land and the challenges related to the climate crisis, it is a shared responsibility to preserve green and blue infrastructure to create a resilient metropolitan area. These landscapes are not only of high recreational and leisure value for the local population, but also attractive for visitors and tourists. There is also a significant need to rethink urban food systems and ensure a sustainable and affordable energy supply. Together with international experts on environmental, energy and landscape planning, we discussed spatial strategies towards an integrated and climate-friendly metropolis.

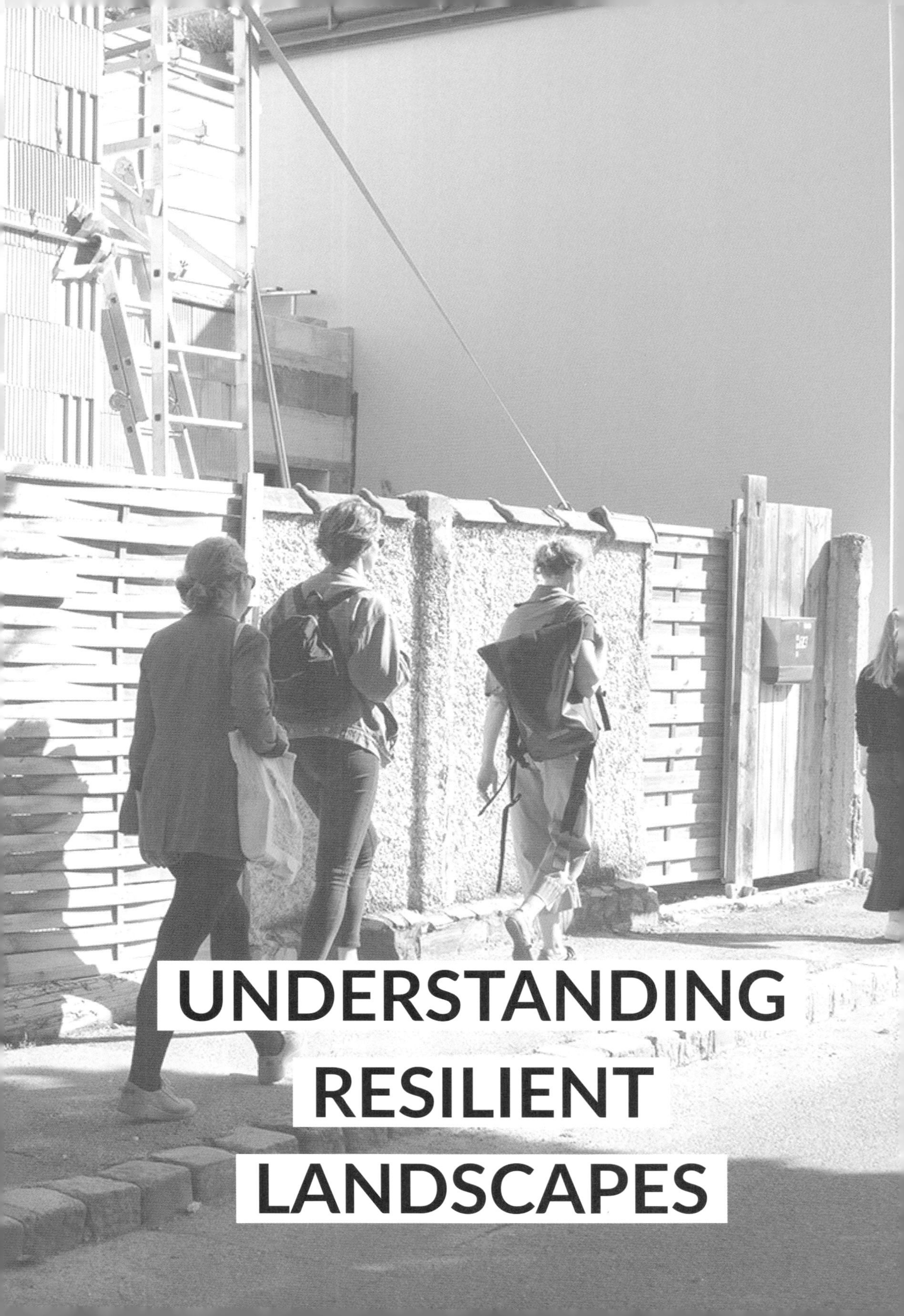

UNDERSTANDING RESILIENT LANDSCAPES

Vienna has some catching up to do in cooperating with the city region

Interview with **Christina Stockinger**—City of Vienna

MetroLab: The quality of life in the *SuperWien Metropole* is defined, to a large part, by its different types of landscapes. Considering the increasing consumption of land and the challenges related to the climate crisis, green and blue insfrastructure must be preserved to create a resilient metropolitan area. What do you see as the main challenges and opportunites for the *SuperWien Metropole*?

Christine Stockinger: Vienna certainly has some catching up to do when it comes to cooperating with the city region. This works very well in terms of mobility and economy, but on many topics the exchange is not yet there. The *Biosphere Park Vienna Forest*, which extends across Vienna's city limits, is a historical joint product that was secured ages ago. We also cooperate with the province of Lower Austria on the *National Park Donau-Auen*. However, the cooperation with the surrounding municipalities works on a good-will basis; there is no formal regional level in Austria, as there is in Switzerland or France, for example. This means that such cross-border projects greatly depend on the commitment of the individuals involved, and there is a risk that projects will falter if the person, for example the mayor, or the political party changes. The informal character has advantages and disadvantages; if the cooperation works well, decisions are quickly and easily made.

"Such cross-border projects greatly depend on the commitment of the individuals involved."

What is special about the *Regionalpark DreiAnger* as an instrument of regional development? Were there any (international) role models for it?

The *Regionalpark DreiAnger* is about jointly developing and preserving the landscape reaching from the Bisamberg in Vienna Floridsdorf to Gerasdorf bei Wien to the Norbert-Scheed-Wald in Vienna Donaustadt. In contrast to protection projects such as the Donau-Auen, this is a very vibrant area, whose dynamics are to be preserved. The term "Regionalpark" comes from Germany and served as a model to try out the concept in a smaller framework for the first time. ▸

Within the framework of the *Regionalpark DreiAnger*, administrative boundaries are to be overcome through cooperation between the *City of Vienna*, the Province of Lower Austria and the municipality of Gerasdorf bei Wien. What does it take to successfully implement cross-municipality/cross-state projects? What do you consider the central levers and also challenges?

"The concept of the regionalpark also underlines the importance of cooperation between municipalities, disciplines and also stakeholders for its realization."

Green and open spaces are a generally positively perceived topic. Cooperation is much more complicated when it comes to more unpopular topics such as settlement development. Initially, of course, there was a certain skepticism, but this quickly dissipated once the advantages of integrated development were communicated. The commitment and re-election of the mayor in Gerasdorf and the district leaders in Floridsdorf and Donaustadt were also decisive. If there had been a major exchange of political actors, there would have been a risk that the objectives would also have changed. Depending on the territory, the financing of the implementation measures is borne by the districts of Donaustadt or Floridsdorf or Gerasdorf bei Wien. Here, the administrative boundaries become clearly apparent. I do not exclude that there will be a common budget for the development of the regionalpark, but this certainly takes time.

Which tools did you use in the development of the regionalpark? What tools for city-regional cooperation have been tested?

"Initially, projects that could be implemented quickly, such as finding a common name and installing a wayfinding system, were launched to position the regionalpark and make it visible and tangible to the public."

In a first step, a landscape plan with visions and concrete ideas for the cross-border recreation area was developed with the involvement of various stakeholders from agriculture, civil society, administration, economy and also committed residents. For this purpose, a steering group consisting of key stakeholders from the province of Lower Austria, the municipality of Gerasdorf bei Wien and the two Viennese districts, the Marchfeld Canal operating company and the *Stadt-Umland Management Vienna/Lower Austria* was set up to develop and coordinate ideas. In a two-day ideas workshop, citizens were able to bring in local knowledge. Their ideas were presented and discussed at a green-space-conference to which a wide variety of stakeholders and NGOs from Vienna and Lower Austria were invited. In addition, stakeholder discussions were held, among others with farmers. It is important to note that the goal was always to preserve agriculture and merely to give it a face with the development of the regionalpark in the sense of making it tangible. In parallel, a landscape planner developed ideas for the landscape. The actions and instruments in order to achieve the goals are specified in the action plan. Initially, projects that could be implemented quickly, such as finding a common name and installing a wayfinding system, were launched to position the regionalpark and make it visible and tangible to the public.

What is your vision for the *SuperWien Metropole*?

"It is important to first secure and connect the green spaces and then think further in terms of settlement development. [...] the chances for such a development in Austria are good, if the pressure of suffering becomes greater."

My vision for the metropolitan region is that both thinking and acting will be much faster. I believe that green spaces are a particularly important topic for the city region, because otherwise there is a danger that the settlement cores of the cities and the surrounding communities will merge at some point and no green spaces have been secured. It is important to first secure and connect the green spaces and then think further in terms of settlement development. In my opinion, the chances for such a development in Austria are good, if the pressure of suffering becomes greater. The pressure of suffering is not yet great enough to recognize this and make it a priority. Of course, I hope that the *Regionalpark DreiAnger* will serve as a role model and show how city-regional projects can successfully be implemented. ▪

The regionalpark DreiAnger as a showcase for interregional cooperation

Metropolitan Walkshop through the Regionalpark DreiAnger

The *Regionalpark DreiAnger* in the north of Vienna is designed as an inter-municipal recreational area. It connects not only the three historic "Anger" villages Stammersdorf (Floridsdorf, Vienna), Gerasdorf (Lower Austria) and Süßenbrunn (Donaustadt, Vienna), but also the European nature reserve Bisamberg and the recreational area Norbert Scheed Forest. Thus, it forms the missing link to the historical idea of Vienna's green belt.

Guided by the aim to activate this landscape, taking into account the existing agricultural activities and to make this area more attractive for people seeking recreation, the Regionalpark was developed within the framework of the EU project *LOS DAMA*.

What opportunities but also challenges does the cooperation between Vienna, Lower Austria, the districts of Floridsdorf and Donaustadt and the municipality of Gerasdorf hold? How are conflicts of use dealt with and what is the importance of securing green space for a city? Together with the project coordinator Christina Stockinger from the *City of Vienna* and the *Metropolitan-Area Manager* Renate Zuckerstätter, a group of about 15 people explored the regionalpark. In conversation with *MetroLab*, they gave an insight into the special characteristics and potentials of this area on the fringe of Vienna, but also explained what needs to be considered when implementing cross-border projects and what the chances are for further cross-border projects in the Vienna Metropolitan Region. The 3,000 ha landscape area is characterized by a special dynamic: In addition to small villages with agricultural fields, which plays an important role in feeding the metropolitan region, there are wide settlement areas with single family housing and *"some kind of density"*, as Renate Zuckerstätter explains. The settlement pressure on the fringe as well as in the surrounding municipalities is steadily increasing, not least due to the pandemic. At the same time, the regionalpark is an important habitat for numerous animal and plant species and a local recreation area for Viennese and Lower Austrians.

> *"There is no such thing as a strategic agglomeration plan. The regionalpark is one of the few projects where the municipality of Vienna works together with a municipality in the sourrounding."*
>
> *Renate Zuckerstätter*

One of the main challenges in the development of the project was due to the fact that the municipality and districts involved are located in two different federal states and, thus, have different nature protection laws, as well as spatial planning and building laws.

Both, Christina Stockinger and Renate Zuckerstätter agreed that the regionalpark is a very special project that tested a novel way of co-operating in the cross-regional border area. A lot can be learned from this project for future cooperation within the Vienna Metropolitan Region. ▪

Scan to watch the video documentation of the *Metropolitan Walkshop!*

METROTALK

How to feed the future metropolis?

In times of increasing ecological threats and social challenges, it is important to develop ecologically and socially sustainable solutions for shaping our common future. In order to highlight the importance of a successful cohabitation of future communities and their surrounding ecosystems, we launched the *MetroTalk*[1], revolvig around the question of how we want to feed the future Vienna metropolitan area. The workshop series took place in the courtyard of the gallery *Die Schöne* and served as a kick-off for the two-days *MetroLab Forum*.

By inviting different practitioners from Vienna who deal with the topic of metropolitan food cycles and aim to build awareness in the field of urban food production, we expanded the transdisciplinary platform of knowledge exchange by opening up the discussion.

The *MetroTalk* was launched by the construction of a recirculating aquaponic system, followed by an interdisciplinary food mapping workshop. The event was accompanied by an experimental cooking session. Thus, we did not only learn about new concepts of sustainable food production and the food cycle system in Vienna, but also explored how delicious food from the metropolitan area can taste. ▪

Scan to watch the video documentation of the *MetroTalk!*

The MetroTalk was supported by the call *Creatives for Vienna* by the Vienna Business Agency with a special focus on Future Communities.

AZOLLA ECOSYSTEMS

Philipp Loidolt-Shen

"fof one" - MODULE ON
(prototype)
Production capacity per year:
300-900kg fish
6.336-19.200 salads
612-1920kg fruit or vegetables

Sooner rather than later, conventional, harmful farming practices will have to adopt more sustainable approaches in order to prevent our climate from collapsing. The future oriented farming module, "fof one" is a prototype to demonstrate the potential of decentralised, small-scale and environmentally friendly methods of food production.
Azolla Ecosystems enables gastronomers and supermarkets to grow their own produce, on demand, always fresh and right where it's consumed or sold. This system has the potential to save food waste and CO2, but also to curb the exploitation of our waters and degradation of soils. Additionally it contributes to local food sourcing and -security.
The aquaponic systems (a closed cycle in which fish produce the nutrients for plants and they in return clear the water) will be installed inside supermarkets and gastronomy and provide a steady supply of fish and veggies, herbs and fruits.

URBAN FOOD ATLAS

Vanessa Giolai & Daniel Löschenbrand

Feeding the city or even a metropolitan region in a sustainable way is one of the crucial challenges of the 21st century. How food and space can be interwoven, where connections, dependencies and resource flows exist, how food-related urban typologies can be classified and assessed on the basis of climate-friendly, resilient development is the main focus of the *Urban Food Atlas*. The project exerts a mixed quantitative-qualitative methodology (cross-media mapping, interactive workshops, interviews with experts, collective data acquisition) with the following main objectives:

» Create a visual image and analyse the food perceptions related to space of the Viennese population, with approaches of citizen science.
» Conceptualise the spatial implications of food-related urban typologies to address resource sharing from the urban planning perspective.
» Enable communication and knowledge-sharing between civil society, practitioners and the planning community by producing a prototype that creatively intertwines bottom-up and top down approaches.

METROPOLITAN COOKING

Christoph Fink

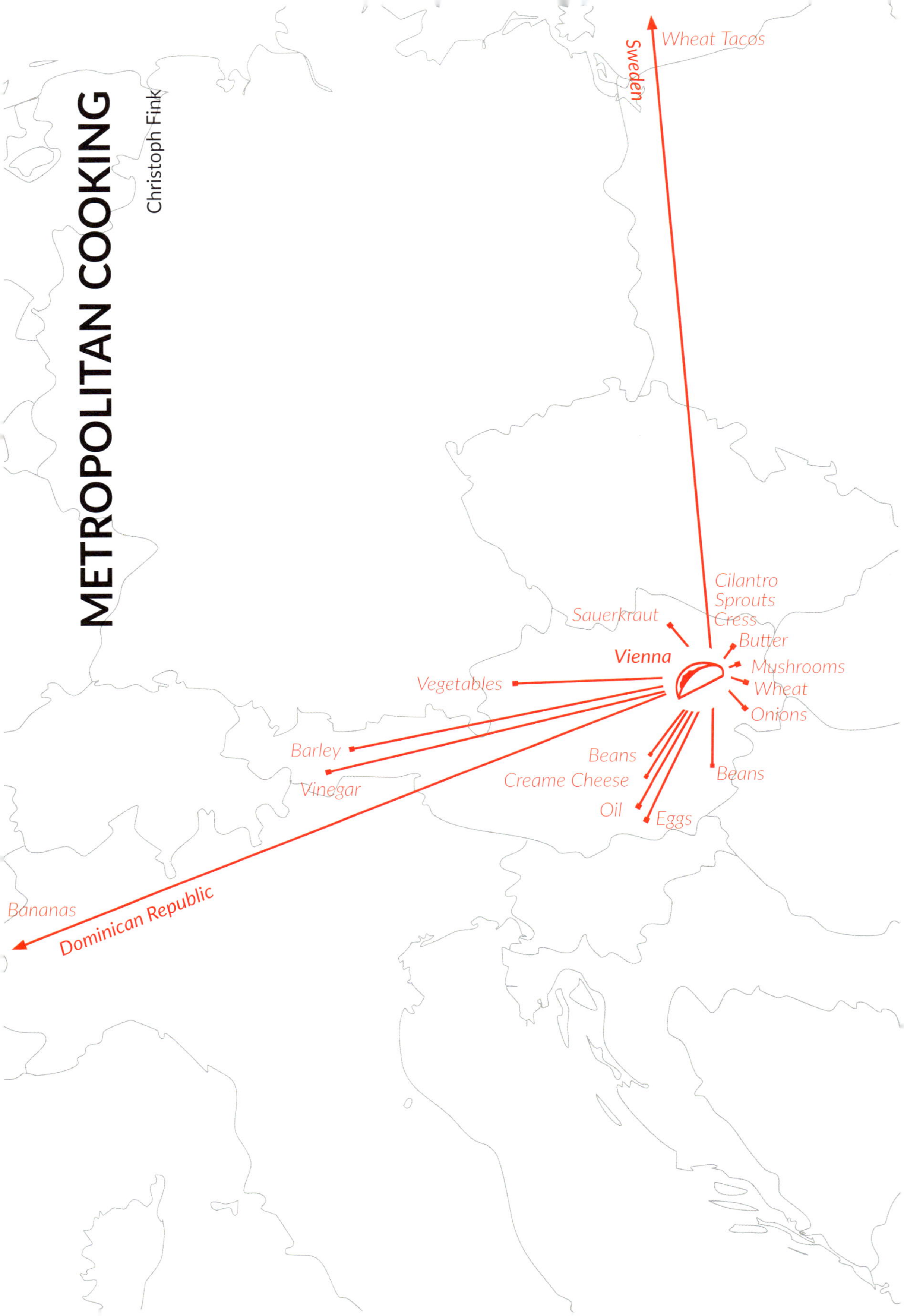

INGREDIENTS OF THE METROPOLITAN TACOS:

- **Nutbutter-Mushroom-Cream Cheese with crispy Sauerkraut**
  Butter (Upper Austria), Cream Cheese (Styria), Mushrooms (Lower Austria), Sauerkraut (Lower Austria)
- **Cumin-Sourdough-Miso-Bean Hummus with Miso-Mayo, Crispy Onion & Cress**
  Wheat (Lower Austria), Barley (Tyrol), Beans (Styria and Burgenland), Oil (Styria), Vinegar (Tyrol), Eggs (Styria), Onions (Lower Austria), Cress (Vienna)
- **Pulled Banana Peel-Chili with Sour Cream, Red Bell Pepper Jam & Cilantro**
  Bananas (Dominican Republic), Mushrooms (Lower Austria), Sour Cream (Styria), Vegetables (Austria), Beans (Burgenland), Cilantro (Vienna)
- **Green Pea Guacamole, Union Pickle & Pea Sprouts**
  Peas (Lower Austria), Oil (Styria), Onion (Lower Austria), Sprouts (Vienna)

LEARNING FROM INTERNATIONAL APPROACHES

Let's conquer the soil—the new fertile soils chain

Hélène Coussedière—Landscape Agency BASE

How can we design urban planting projects without sacrificing the fertile and living soil coming from the stripping of agricultural and natural areas?
We have been asking that question, at *BASE*[1], for over 5 years and responded by creating a local fertilization chain for sterile and inert deep land in Lyon, coming from the excavated lands of the metropolis.

"60.000 ha of agricultural and fertile land, the size of a French department, is artificialized every seven years." (Europe 2016)

This statement is commonly linked to the issue of disappearing agricultural land, but is less often associated with the consumption of fertile soil used for the construction of public spaces and parks. In order to guarantee adequate planting soil, we, as landscape architects, must dictate the use of topsoil for the development of urban projects. In the absence of any other supply, the soil for artificial design comes from the excavation of agricultural and natural land. By trying to increase the quality of life in the city, we paradoxically participate in the rarefaction of a unique resource that is taken away from the living milieu by consuming fertile land.
The pressure on this resources creates three major problems, which we already face: rarefaction of the resource, inflation of its price and high carbon and ecological costs. The key now is to identify and qualify potential local land resources, as well as to encourage institutional authorities to cooperate with private sector actors. This constant exchange, between field data and stakeholders, is the ideal recipe for a process that is tailored to the territory and particularly flexible for its development on a larger scale.
In Lyon, this approach has allowed the development of the *Productive Landscape©* concept—a pioneering landscape that creates economic and ecosystem values. Economic progress is created by providing a methodology for setting up local reuse networks that generate fertile soils, biomass-energy, phytoremediation, among others. This approach is being applied in Lyon with the *Terre Fertile 2.0* platform , which was installed on the urban sites Vallée de la Chimie and Champ de la Confluence

STRATEGIC DEVELOPMENT OF THE FERTILE EARTH SECTOR

In order to strategically develop the fertile earth sector, we at first need to look at the composition of the material "soil'. If we dig beyond the first 30 centimeters, we will find soil unsuitable for planting. The organic material is low in air and water concentration and consequently devoid of any microbiological life. With an appropriate technical process for soil amendment, it is possible to catalyse their fertilisation ►

[1] BASE is a landscape agency founded in 2000 with more than 70 landscape architects, designers, architects and engineers in three offices in Paris, Lyon and Bordeau

Figures 1&2: Soils of the Chemical Valley and Creation of Fertile Land at the Chemical Valley (before and after) © BASE

in a relatively short time to conform the expected qualities of the topsoil for planting. This excavated layer is abundant on the metropolitan territory. By collecting and re-using road and building materials, it would be possible to set up a local land industry in Lyon for the construction of public spaces.

During our work on the *Chemical Valley 2030* master plan, we have brought together a network of political, private, technical, economic and scientific stakeholders on this topic. Together, we enumerated the available excavated soil resources, and identified the topsoil required for metropolitan development projects. This work made it possible to create a link between the absence of silty excavated earth and its local reuse after fertilization. We used the technological risk prevention plan to create storage for the land factories in the valley, made out of excavated lands. A way of fertilizing the soil has been developed on two metropolitan sites: the Vallée de la Chimie and the Champ de Confluence

TECHNICAL SET-UP ON TEST SITES

With the support of a call for projects *L'Appel des 30* we selected companies developing or wishing to develop economically profitable technical processes for the fertilization of excavated soil in the Vallée de la Chimie. Under our leadership, two pilot projects for the recycling of excavated land were launched:

» The *"Lône de Pierre Bénite"*: refertilization of extracted soil to create extensive wood biomass plantation, to provide boiler rooms in the metropolis (Suez - Valterra - Société Forestière)

» The *"Terre Fertile 2.0"*: platform for the fertilization of excavated soil from organic amendments, reusable in the plantation of public space (*Economic Interest Grouping (EIG) Terres Fertiles 2.0*)

Champ de la Confluence in Lyon is another experimental urban site, where industrial wasteland is transformed into a new district. Buildings will be located in an urban forest.

As the duration of the urban project created vacant spaces, we used a platform in these areas to experiment with the reuse of the excavated loams. Soils were mixed with organic materials in different ways and laid out in windrows: a transitory landscape able to arouse people's curiosity. In this project, the Productive Landscape consisted of a pioneering experimentation of uses: one of these examples was the Station Mue. Designed by the collective *Bruit du Frigo*, it's a hybrid public wood structure that speaks about the Champ de la Confluence and the values it carries. It is designed to host workshops and animations with the actors and associations of the area, like a real Agora.

IMPORTANCE OF THE LOCAL CONTEXT

From this experience we can learn the importance of local anchoring: knowing and considering the available resources, identifying the necessities and the actors that animate the territory. This is the importance of operating within a chain logic: collegial composed of strategic and technical-economic points of view.

This alchemy must form the basis of an approach that aims to share an evolutionary process, rather than a fixed project image.

Beyond the question of soil fertility, we are trying to develop tools within the *Productive Landscape* that allow other ways of thinking landscape design. We could envision a landscape practice that prepares territories and people for the rapidity of the new urban transformations, including climate change. ▪

Neuland Gewinnen—hotspots of transformation

Siri Frech—Raum+Strategie—Office for Coproductive Urban & Rural Development, Neuland gewinnen e.V.

There are two sides to my work as a planner. On the one hand, I develop and design plans with a focus on strategic spatial development and process design with a special preference for spaces that have fallen out of the classic planning cycle. On the other hand, I support people in becoming creatively active themselves in their living environment, their region, and in changing and further developing their own spaces together with other people. These are small niches where new things are tried out and often realized.

A graphic in the *Flagship Report* of the *German Advisory Council of Global Change* shows the influence that these niche experiments can have on global developments and that this work in niches should not be underestimated. Perhaps my work with these niches could also be called supportive planning. Here I am not the designer, but I accompany people to realize their own development ideas. In view of the enormous challenges posed by climate change and the socio-economic changes it requires, it seems to me that there is hardly any other way than for many people in their regions to work together to shape these changes. Every creative force is needed here. And the connection between metropolises and surrounding areas will play an important role in this.

LOCAL ACTORS BRINGING ABOUT LOCAL CHANGE

A groundbreaking approach to supporting these local changes is the *Robert Bosch Stiftung's Neulandgewinner* program. It was developed in 2012 for rural areas in eastern Germany and I have been intensively accompanying it since 2014. The approach is not to support topics and projects, but to find the people in the regions who recognize potential for change for the community and develop and implement suitable projects together.

The rural areas in eastern Germany are a special area in terms of transformation. Here, it was not only the agrarian-industrial transformation that changed almost all historical structures. The peaceful revolution and the end of the GDR in 1989 brought about a complete collapse of social and economic structures. So, these are spaces with cracks, gaps, and fractures. Ideal breeding grounds for new niche developments. The *Neulandgewinner* program seeks and supports actors in these spaces who test new things for themselves and the community and establish them if they are successful. We spend a lot of time tracking down these people through an elaborate selection process and then actively support them over a period of two years. The support is divided into three areas:

» There is financial support for the implementation of projects. The money can also be used for living expenses so that there is enough time and energy for the realization of the project. In addition, no personal contribution has to be made and the money is transferred in advance so that no out-of-pocket expenses are incurred.

- The creation of a strong network between the actors is actively supported. There are several networking workshops and an annual festival. In addition, an association, Neuland gewinnen e.V., was founded to expand this networking beyond the circle of supported people. Thus, a network of over 120 actors has been created so far.
- Every *Neulandgewinner* receives two years of mentoring. In other words, personal support during the funding period that responds to their individual needs and current developments in the project.

This new, person-centred approach makes it possible to really find the people in the regions who can take other people with them and bring new things into the world.

And since the focus of the programme is not on the projects but on the individual approaches of the actors, the results are also very colourful and the fields of impact very broad:

- New infrastructures—such as the construction of the first e-filling stations on the island of Usedom or the opening of an open workshop for wood and metal work and the pressing of juices.
- Revitalisation of vacant buildings—here new development concepts for hard-to-develop properties are found and established through testing, sometimes over many years. New festival sites and cultural hubs for the city are being created.
- New educational venues—where new forms of knowledge transfer for young and old are rehearsed and established by opening new schools, testing new educational offers and developing teaching units where young people learn how to find a job in the region so they don't have to move to the city.
- New mobility—which not only connects place, but also people or new and old forms of sharing.
- New Culture—whose projects range from highly professional Mirco Operas in empty churches to free instruments and free lessons for all children in the region.

LOCAL CREATIVITY PROMOTES SELF-EFFICIENCY

Through these projects many new forms of local creativity are emerging. By establishing new offers, strengthening new engagement and highlighting new opportunities, new cultural creativity emerges. Social creativity is strengthened by activating village life and local culture or by establishing new cooperations. And through the new spaces and places that are created, a spatial creativity grows through which new resources are discovered. These important developments can also be concentrated on one point: It is the strengthening of local self-efficacy. ▸

Figures 1&2: Joint Development of New Ideas and Local Projects in Rural Regions of East Germany © Neulandgewinner e.V.

People and regions that have experienced that they can influence and shape their own future will deal with future challenges differently. They know how to react to changes or even use them for their own benefit. This is an important basis for resilient regions.

Strengthening self-efficacy is also the most important goal in the participation processes that I develop and accompany.

The aim here is not only to strengthen individuals, but also entire regions by jointly developing a concept for the future and the necessary projects. One example of this is the project *Zukunft Goldberg-Mildenitz*, in which 36 villages and a small town jointly developed a future concept. We worked on three levels at the same time:

» We established a long-term new culture of communication by setting up citizens' councils.
» In different steps we have tested and established a new culture of cooperation. Here, issues are discussed together and projects are developed.
» And a new structure has been established for the long-term implementation and monitoring of the projects developed, so that the many voluntary efforts are given a professional framework.

SUPPORTING BOTTOM-UP TRANSFORMATION

Finally, I would like to emphasize once again how valuable this actor-supportive planning and promotion is, because it is always the people who initiate and realize change. And for major transformations, we need a lot of people to tackle this in their own way. The experts alone will not do it. My credo in conclusion: Build niches and develop micro-utopias. They will work! ▪

Lots of energy, little space: metropolitan stories about wind power

Pia Kronberger-Nabielek—PBL Netherlands Environmental Assessment Agency

A lot of energy is still needed to transition our fossil-based energy systems. With the 2015 *Paris Agreement*, international energy politics have shifted to a more implementation-oriented course of action. Our most urgent task today is to reach countries' climate mitigation pledges. There are, however, no simple and ready-made solutions. Energy trajectories—defined from an international perspective— are not easily translated into local and place-based implementation pathways. Current attempts of goal achievement often have to cope with unforeseen problems and lock-in effects. We can calculate desired energy futures yet to keep implementation in pace with the complex realities of energy and social practice is another matter.

Concerning implementation practices, much can be learnt from wind power. Wind turbines were once considered the iconic image for successful energy transition together with the Danish "energy" island of Samsø. While wind turbines represented the most modern generation of green energy plants, Samsø communicated the idealistic image of rural communities that are 100 percent energy self-sufficient. Both represent early considerations when dealing with sustainable energy trajectories: the economic concern of optimal utilization of technologies for harvesting energy (choosing large-scale wind power), the territorial concern of governing the allocation of energy plants (focusing on thinly populated areas) and the social concern to allow for local participation (creating win-win situations). Yet these early answers to implementation problems appeared to be tricky. In the space of only two decades, wind power has become one of the most contested topics in today's societal debate about energy. It also has become quite obvious that the Samsø concept alone won't do. In the long run, energy-consuming metropolitan areas must sincerely contribute to climate mitigation. Post-2020 energy trajectories have to cope with little space and increasing complexity. Earlier experiences with wind power are an important source of knowledge to understand the spatial and social challenges of these newest implementation strategies. Through wind power, countries such as the Netherlands have learnt that the regional level is key for locally supported planning decisions. Wind power also provides for much experience with spatial and legal instrumentalization, for example the widely applied practice to restrict renewable energy to so-called suitability (or preference) areas. These earlier decisions have created clarity about location-choices yet introduced new path-dependencies. One of greatest challenge for next-generation metropolitan plans is therefore to cope with earlier implementation practices, and conditions that seriously restricted the amount of leeway when it comes to searching for alternative solutions. Current attempts are therefore much more concerned to give room for 'negotiation' between the a large spectrum of actors and their diverging stakes. Promising strategies foster regional cooperation, instrumental diversity and alternative technologies and thus, a wider and regionally varying spectrum of possible courses of action. Future energy trajectories are hopefullymore aware of imper-fectness and allow for flexibility while, at the same time, create commitment. ▪

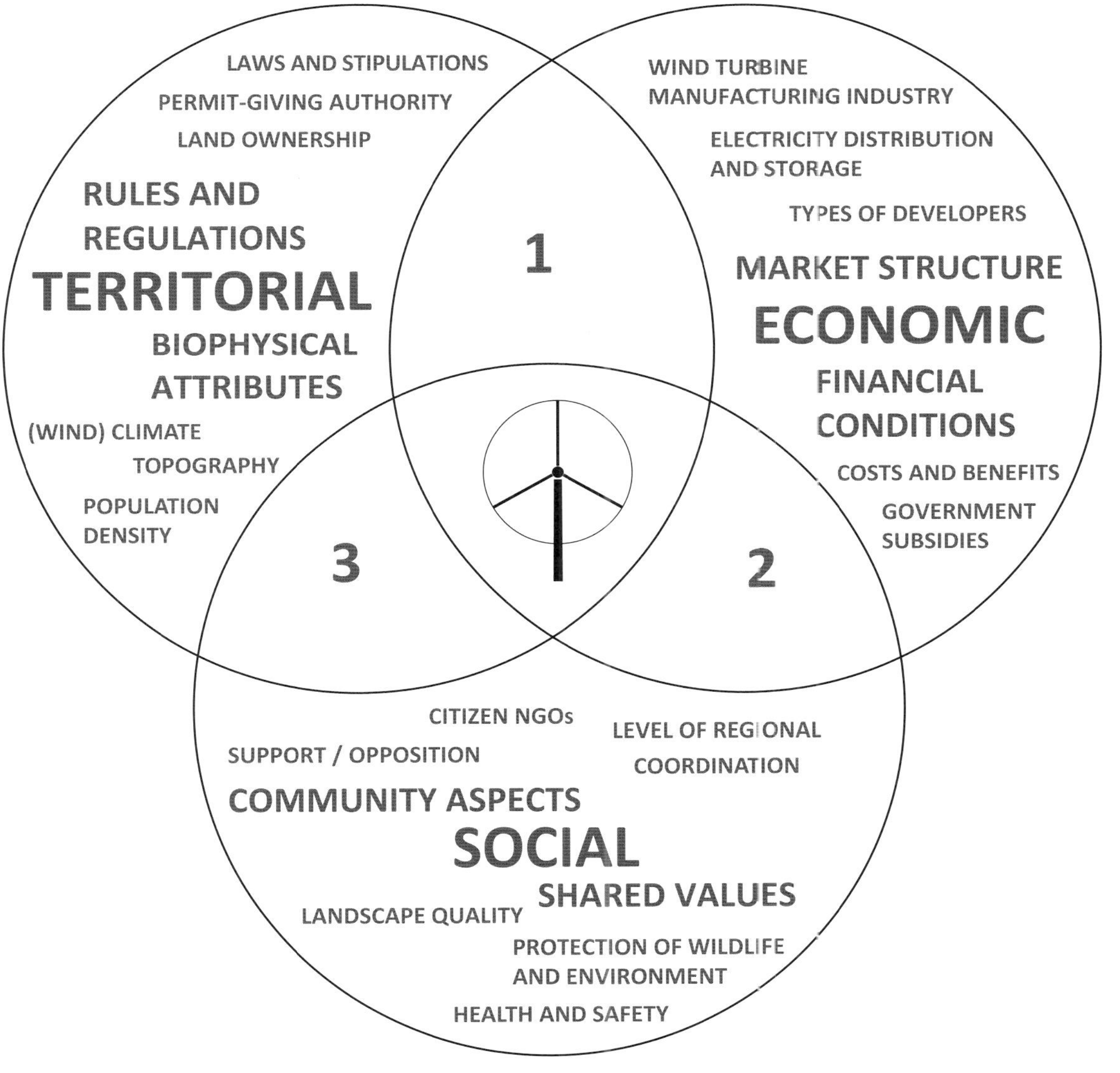

Figure 1: The three dimensions of the spatial aspects of wind power

Revitalising former military camps as an urban ecosystem network in Thessaloniki

Paraskevi Tarani—RiConnect, Major Development Agency Thessaloniki

Ecosystem functions provide a robust framework for addressing complex ecological challenges associated with modern metropolitan areas. A comprehensive approach to urban ecosystems considers specific urban areas, such as nature-occupied urban brownfields, as valuable natural resources linked to the overall urban environment and aims to provide strategic solutions for enhancing integrated ecosystem services. This paper argues that we should consider ecosystem functions in the metropolitan area as dynamic, hybrid, and living ecosystems that are well connected and located between the city and nature. This approach offers key new considerations for policy makers and planners, especially as urban sustainability, resilience, and environmental crises increasingly reshape metropolitan areas and increase consideration of these issues.

URBAN ECOSYSTEMS, ECOSYSTEM FUNCTIONS AND SERVICES, AND THE SIGNIFICANCE OF THE URBAN BROWNFIELDS

Planet Earth is increasingly becoming an urbanized landscape, occupying about 3% of the Earth's land area, with more than half of the human population living in cities. The Earth's population living in cities has more than doubled in the last 40 years, from 1.5 billion inhabitants in 1975 to 3.5 billion in 2015, and is projected to reach 5 billion by 2050, almost 55% of the world's population (OECD 2020: 10). The explosive urbanization and especially the state of continuity of urbanized areas have caused enormous and diverse environmental problems. The purely natural areas of the planet are constantly shrinking, and natural ecosystems continue to be under pressure from urbanization. The greatest threats are the climate crisis, unsustainable resource use, and inadequate urban planning. Cities are becoming increasingly unsustainable, unsafe, and vulnerable, which is why achieving sustainability and resilience in cities must be at the top of every government's agenda.

Life forms on planet Earth are now forced to live and adapt under these new conditions of dense and ongoing urbanization. Evolutionary biologist Menno Schilthuizen presents a new and appealing argument in his lively book on urban evolution, Darwin Comes to Town: "We need to embrace and harness the evolutionary forces that are shaping novel ecosystems here and now, and work towards allowing nature to grow in the hearts of our cities" (Schilthuizen 2019: 26). Schilthuizen, far from seeing big cities as enemies of nature, advocates the idea that many species adapt to urban conditions and create new biodiversity.

Based on the above, we can say that cities depend on natural ecosystems outside the city limits, but also benefit from internal ecosystems and natural resources of all kinds, such as riparian areas, rivers, lakes and streams, wetlands, urban forests and lawns or parks, fallow land used by nature, but also street trees and cultivated land.

Ecosystem assessment literature generally uses the terms "structure" and "function" to describe natural systems. These are characteristics of natural complex systems that result in the

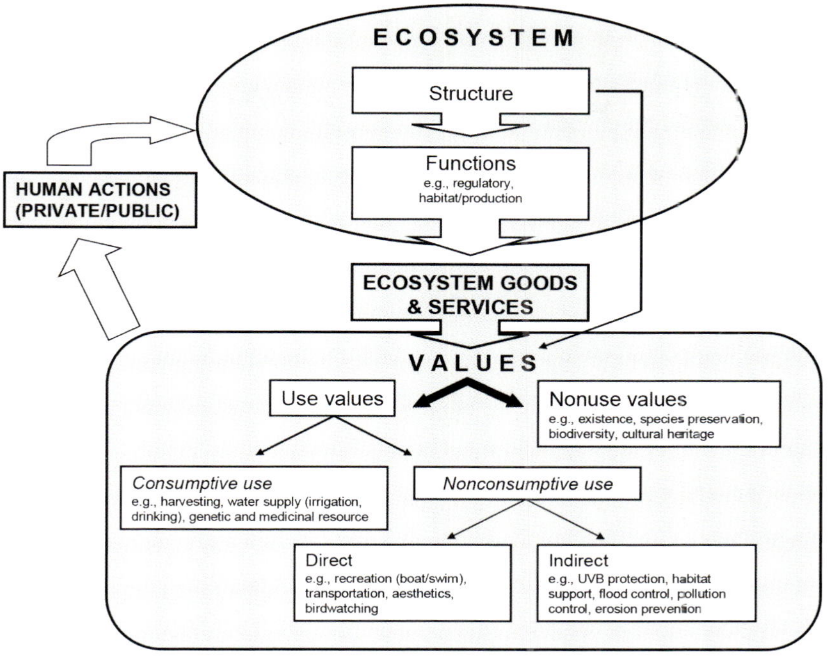

Figure 1: Explaining the connections between ecosystem structure and function, services, values, and policies. Source: (NRC, 2005 p.241)

provision of goods and services that, in turn, can be valued by humans. Identifying ecosystem structure and function is the useful starting point for subsequent mapping of ecosystem goods and services.

Ecosystem structures: it is difficult to define clear boundaries for urban ecosystems because many of the relevant flows and interactions necessary to understand their character extend well beyond the urban boundaries defined by administrative, spatial, or biophysical factors. The relevant scope of urban ecosystem analysis therefore extends beyond the urban area itself; it includes not only the ecological infrastructure within cities, but also the surrounding areas that are directly affected by them (Pickett et al. 2001: 129), and therefore the metropolitan dimension is very important for environmental planning and management.

Ecosystem functions capture the role that water and vegetation within or near the built environment play in providing ecosystem services at different spatial scales (building, street, neighborhood, and region). This includes all "green and blue spaces" found in urban and peri-urban areas.

Ecosystem services are defined by Daily et al. (1997) as "a broad range of conditions and processes by which natural ecosystems and their associated species help sustain and fulfill human life." These services support the production of ecosystem goods such as seafood, wildlife, forage, timber, biomass fuels, natural fibers, and many pharmaceuticals, industrial products, and their precursors. Taylor (1986) argued that the sustainability of ecosystem services can be viewed in two ways: (1) with an anthropocentric approach, which assumes that natural capital has value only because of its benefits to human well-being, or (2) with a biocentric approach which assumes that natural capital also has non-consumptive value, value that cannot be readily priced in specific market products but should be considered in policy decisions and strategic plans. ▸

Based on the above, the *U.S. National Research Council*, in a consensus study entitled "Valuing ecosystem services toward better environmental decision making" (NRC 2005: 241), illustrates the linkages between ecosystem structure and function, services, policies, and values that represent the current state of knowledge about urban ecosystems (Figure 1). Recent research has highlighted the role that urban brownfields can play in maintaining biodiversity and providing ecosystem functions in urban areas. Large and well-connected brownfields appear to be a significant source of urban biodiversity, acting at two scales. At the local level, where site size, soil characteristics, vegetation cover, and microclimate are dominant factors, and at the urban level, where geographic or planned connectivity with other natural resources can influence the overall urban ecosystem.

THESSALONIKI: GEOGRAPHY, NATURAL ADVANTAGES, AND URBAN SHAPE

Thessaloniki is a medium-sized city in northern Greece, on the Thermaic Gulf, part of the Aegean Sea. It is the second largest city in Greece, with a population of 1.12 million. The city extends around a coastal arc at the tip of the Thermaic Gulf. A major spatial feature of the urban area is its expanse and multifunctional coastline that connects the various urban activities, most of which are of regional and national importance, such as the Axios river delta, the port of Thessaloniki and the Macedonia airport.

The urban form of Thessaloniki differs from other European cities that extend circularly around their historical center. The city necessarily stretches between its natural boundaries, Mount Chortiatis and the Thermaic Gulf, and is conceived as a linear city whose activities are more or less arranged in a line along the sea front. A closer look at the urban hinterland inevitably leads us to a butterfly pattern, whose mechanical skeleton consists of the public transport networks. Indeed, the city seems to align symmetrically along the sides of a central axis (Vougias: 2010).

Another event that shaped the form of modern Thessaloniki is the fire that broke out on August 18, 1917, destroying 128 hectares of the historic center, including the commercial area, and leaving 70,000 people homeless. As a result, an international commission was set up to replan Thessaloniki, headed by the French architect Ernest Hébrard, who happened to be in the city as head of the archaeological service of the Armée de l'Orient. The implementation of the new plan resulted in a radical modernization of the urban form for the "intra muros" city. The old spatial patterns were eliminated, the urban fabric was homogenized and a new urban space was created (Hastaoglou-Martinidis 1997: 497).

DEFINING THE ECOSYSTEM SERVICES OF THE FORMER MILITARY WASTELANDS IN THE GREATER THESSALONIKI AREA

Due to the importance of the Thermaic Gulf and its advantages as a place to live, numerous settlements developed around it, dating back to the Neolithic and Bronze Ages, which formed the beginnings of the city of Thessaloniki. The Romans contributed to the rapid growth of the city. The construction of the Via Egnatia (146-120 BC), which connected the eastern with the western part of the Empire, contributed to make Thessaloniki an important commercial, cultural and military center.

From the 7th to the 10th century, Thessaloniki developed in every aspect and often played a leading role, which underlines its great importance and position. It was the gateway to the Balkans and again played a leading role as a center of military operations.

During World War I, Thessaloniki served as the military operations center of the Macedonian front and hosted the famous *Armee d'Orient*

Figure 2: Thessaloniki metropolitan area. geography, natural advantages, and urban shape

(Army of the Orient), allies of the Entente. In the outskirts of the city there were numerous English and French military camps. As a result, today there are 15 plots of land that used to be military camps and are now abandoned. Problems with ownership and the questioning of their urban character have resulted in these former military sites lying unused in the dense urban fabric of Thessaloniki.

The former military camp *Pavlos Melas* covers an area of 35 hectares in a central location in the northwest of the metropolis of Thessaloniki. The former camp has been declared as a historical site and some of its buildings have been designated as historical monuments. Today, a master plan has been developed that focuses on land use priorities and reuse of the historic buildings. With a design logic based on the idea of preserving and strengthening the natural ecosystem that "occupied" the vacant land, the *Metropolitan Park Master Plan* serves to develop a public place where nature and human activities of recreation, culture, and sports can harmoniously coexist.

The former military camp of Kodra, located in the east of the metropolis, was already the largest camp in the Balkans at the time of the Turkish occupation. Most of the remaining buildings date back to the beginning of the 19th century. The former military camp of Kodra is ►

today an open space of great importance within the dense urban fabric of Thessaloniki, due to its location, archaeological interest and natural beauty. During the pandemic period, the site was claimed by hundreds of users for various activities. The Municipality of Kalamaria is now in the process of developing a local urban plan for the redevelopment of the camp. Based on the *NRC* diagram (Figure 1), we attempt to define the ecosystem services of the abandoned former military site of Thessaloniki by grouping its values (Table 1). Consumptive use involves the extraction of a component of the ecosystem to support a specific anthropocentric purpose. This type of use involves a withdrawal and thus a reduction in the amount of available resource. Nonconsumptive use, on the other hand, directly uses the services provided by abandoned former military lands without removing the resources and reducing their availability. A responsible planning and reuse process must consider the non-consumptive uses that may degrade the quality of these ecosystems through pollution or other externalities.

This methodology can improve our understanding of how important the natural environment is to human communities and view urban ecosystems as natural capital and one of the city's most important assets. In addition, this comprehensive approach can support decision making and planning based on the specific character of each ecosystem function in each former military camp. The absence of any form of management and conservation away from any human activity has resulted in the transformation of the former military camps in the Thessaloniki metropolitan area into rich natural ecosystems, which are richer than most other heavily managed urban green spaces and therefore much more heterogeneous in their structure and composition. This characteristic is a significant advantage for service delivery, as it is well known that the most complex ecosystems are also ▸

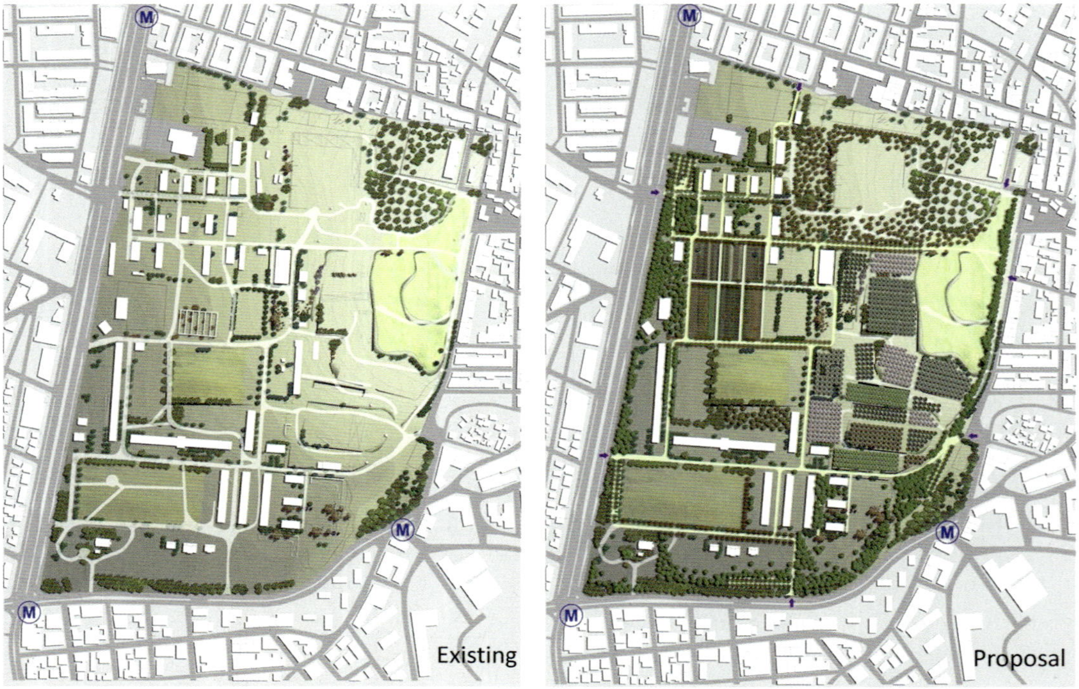

Figure 3: Master Plan of the Transformation of the Former Military Camp of Pavlos Melas to a Metropolitan Park

Figure 4: Regeneration Project of the Former Military Camps of Kodra,
Municipality of Pavlos Melas &. Nikiforidis – Cuomo, Architects

Figure 5: Regeneration Project of the Former Military Camps of Kodra,
Municipality of Pavlos Melas &. Nikiforidis – Cuomo, Architects

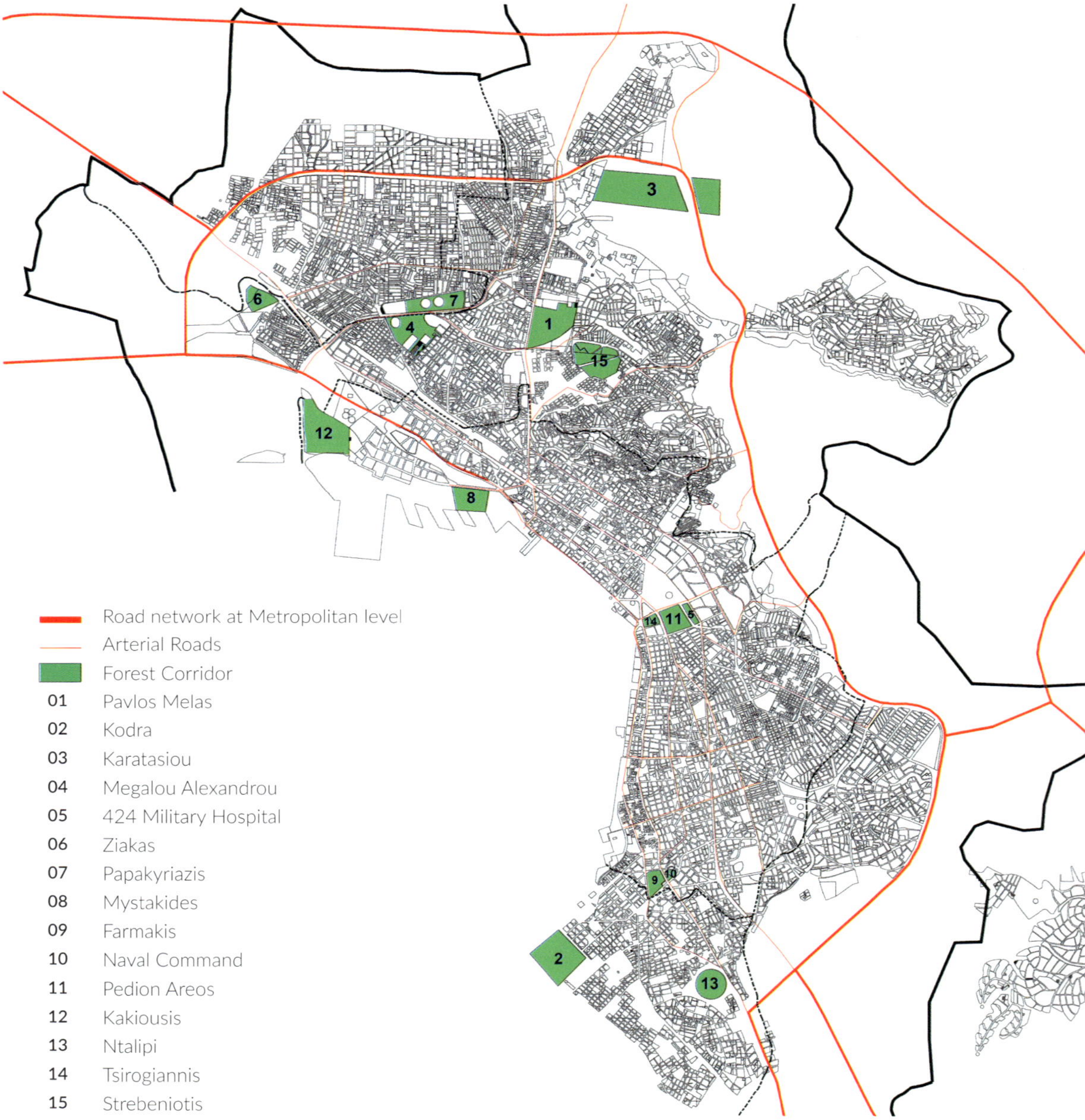

Figure 6: Thessaloniki former military camps

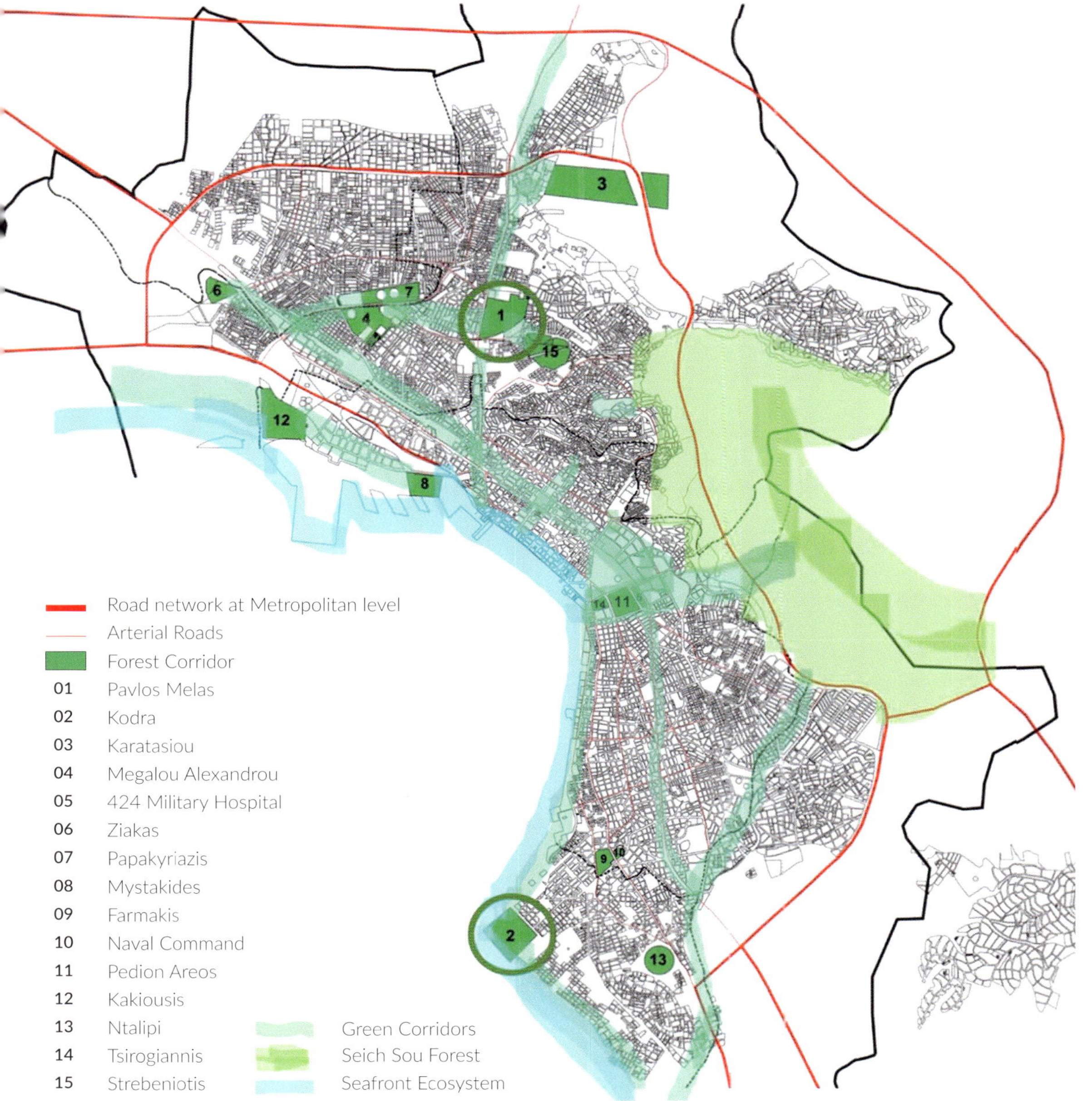

Figure 7: Mapping an indicative network of ecosystem functions for Metropolitan Thessaloniki.
Source: MDAT, RiConnect Thessaloniki Integrated Action Plan.

the most ecologically interesting (Harrison et al. 2014 and Machon 2021: 14). In addition, because of their size, former military camps can play an important role in providing ecosystem functions and services at the urban scale, such as climate change support and regulation, temperature regulation, urban heat island protection, air pollution regulation, carbon storage, and, of course, wildlife and biodiversity accommodation.

THE RICONNECT METROPOLITAN CITIES NETWORK AND THE RISE OF AN IDEA

The former military camps, located as "islands" in the dense urban fabric of Thessaloniki, allow the development of a series of collective public green spaces, interconnected as an ecosystem network. Natural elements, ecosystem functions, collective activities and green open spaces can find their place between the original landscape and the historical substance.

The initiator of this idea is the *RiConnect* project, in which the City of Thessaloniki participates through the *Major Development Agency Thessaloniki* (MDAT S.A .). *RiConnect* is a network of eight metropolitan cities whose goal is to rethink, redesign and integrate mobility infrastructures in order to reconnect people, neighborhoods, cities and natural spaces. It is an *URBACT* project co-financed by the European Regional Development Fund. *RiConnect* develops planning strategies, processes, tools and partnerships to promote public transport and active mobility, reduce externalities and social segregation, and unlock opportunities for urban regeneration. The long-term vision is a more sustainable, equitable, and attractive metropolis for all.

As part of the *RiConnect* project, Thessaloniki aims to develop an integrated action plan for the city's former military sites, with the following objectives.

- » To make people and authorities aware of the overall planning of the former military areas, which are not considered separately, but as an ecosystem network
- » Consider the former military camps as available land on which to develop a network of new collective green spaces in conjunction with the city's existing natural resources
- » Promote inter-municipal collaborations and projects for green infrastructure and collective green spaces at the city level.

Former military camps in the Thessaloniki metropolitan area provide valuable opportunities for biodiversity conservation and the provision of ecosystem functions and services. At the metropolitan scale, they represent habitats that urban planners must consider and incorporate into dynamic urban planning, along with other urban and peri-urban natural resources.

Ecosystem functions provide a robust framework for addressing complex ecological challenges associated with modern metropolitan areas. A comprehensive approach to urban ecosystems considers specific urban areas, such as abandoned former military camps, as valuable natural resources that are connected to the overall urban environment and aims to provide strategic solutions for enhancing integrated ecosystem services. This paper argues that we should view ecosystem functions in the city as dynamic, hybrid, and living ecosystems that lie between the city and nature. This approach offers key new considerations for policy makers and planners, especially as urban sustainability, resilience, and environmental crises increasingly reshape cities and bring consideration of these issues to the forefront.

Ecosystem functions and new governance:
The dynamics of urban ecosystems need to be addressed through a new systemic approach to both analysis and policy decisions. There are no one-size-fits-all solutions for adding ecosystem functions, as they are living organisms in a constant process of change, with their essential

Use Values			Nonuse Values
Consumptive	**Non – Consumptive**		Habitat / biodiversity
Availability of urban land	**Direct**	**Indirect**	Living space for wild plant and animal species
Nature products and trees	Land for public space and recreation	Urban heat control	Providing opportunities for cognitive development
Fresh water	Tourism activities	Urban heat island protection	Resources for future generations
Raw materials		Carbon storage	Scientific and educational opportunities
Building stock for reuse		Water preservation	Natural heritage
		Air pollution regulation	Architectural heritage
		Soil improvement	Inspiration for creative activities
		Biological pest control	Nature and city, health, and quality of living

Table 1: Ecosystem Services of Thessaloniki's former military land. adapted from National Research Council (NRC) 2005: 46 and Barbier (1994)

elements interacting and feeding back positively or negatively on a daily basis. For this reason, the policy approach to ecosystem functions and services must bridge the gap between bottom-up investments in infrastructure and an understanding of the emerging structures that result from the activities of all stakeholders in the area.

Ecology for the City—A Planning Concept: This concept can be seen as a new planning paradigm that emphasizes how the interaction between environmental, place-based science and the actions of decision makers are the key drivers of urban ecosystem design. Like natural ecosystems, urban ecosystems have inputs, throughputs, and outputs that are openly interrelated with their surroundings. Multiple layers and levels of the system must be integrated to form a complete complex system. Such a systemic approach is inherently capable of ensuring resilient solutions to urban problems. ▪

The condition of local food markets in Rome

Daniela Patti & Levente Polyak—Eutropian Research & Action
Manuel Torresan—Confcommercio-Imprese per l'Italia

With 39% of the metropolitan area of Rome being agricultural land (PTPG 2010), the city is one of the biggest agricultural municipalities in Europe. This brings along the importance of the agricultural sector, which has recently undergone strong challenges. Over the last 10 years there has been a relatively small diminishing of the agricultural land in comparison to the drastic reduction of the number of enterprises, where very small land owners sold their property to larger ones. This has fostered an increase of the average plot size, which remains nevertheless very small in Rome, with less than 5ha.

This is a farm typology covering nearly half of the agricultural land in the metropolitan area. Yet the other half of the territory is owned by farming enterprises with over 50ha of land, which make up for only 2% of the total number of farms in the territory (ARM 2013), the reason for this to be traced back to the history of its aristocracy and clergy. Within such a scenario, there has been a recent return towards agriculture especially from younger generations, as a result of the economic crisis. This has brought to the competition for cooperatives of young farmers to run farms on public abandoned land. In 2014 four plots of land were identified within the boundaries of the City of Rome for which hundreds of applications were submitted, showing the increasing interest of young people in the possibility of working in the agricultural sector. This initiative was the result of pressure coming from a civic network advocating for a better use of public abandoned land.

With food production and short distribution chains gaining increasing attention from the public in Rome, initiatives and projects related to markets also started taking place. In fact, the City of Rome has a remarkable infrastructure of 119 food markets distributed over the entire municipality, with 27 covered markets, 33 kiosk complexes and remaining street markets. As Figure 1 illustrates, covered markets are predominantly located in central neighborhoods, whilst kiosk complexes can be found in more peripheral social housing areas and street markets, which make up for nearly half of all markets in the city, are located predominantly in central areas (Torresan 2019).

Despite the great potential, walking through large part of the markets of Rome, there is a visible condition of decline and abandonment. Currently markets risk of disappearing due to shopping malls in the periphery and due to fancy window shops in the city centre, to which a micro-commercial activity as those in markets, often family run, cannot compete (Terra!Onlus 2018). On the one hand it is possible to see the low investment on the side of the public administration towards the maintenance of the structures, often valuable from an architectural point of view, and on the other the large number of empty stalls that show the difficulty that most vendors have to respond to the current demand within contemporary society. In fact, many markets operate with an extremely limited number of vendors, often below 15 units, hindering the economic attractiveness of the market. Under such difficult conditions, there has been some attempts from vendors and local inhabitants to relaunch the markets. Whilst this is undoubtedly necessary in Rome, the models and programs to be pursued require

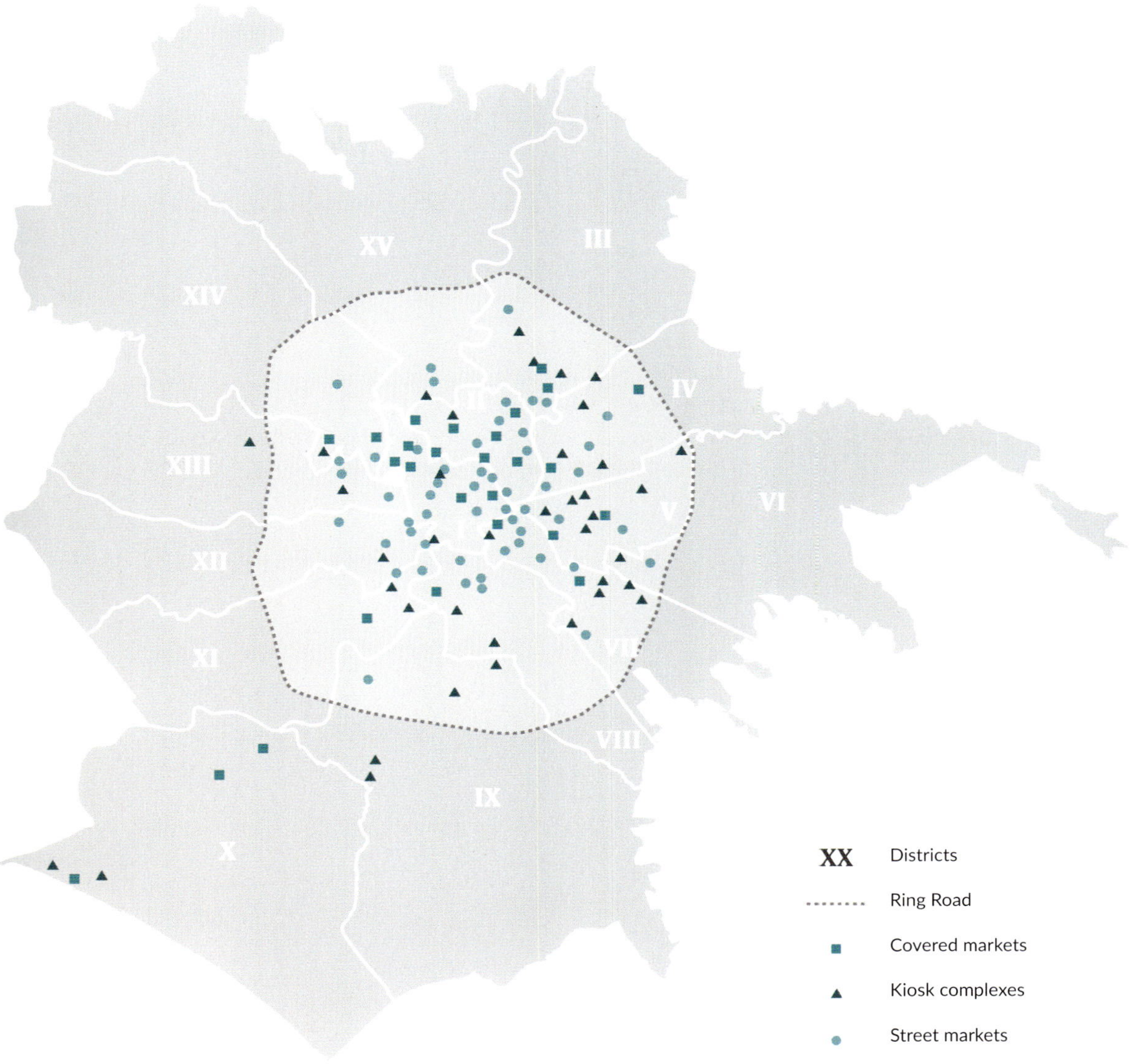

Figure 1: Map of markets in Rome according to typology.
Source: Torresan (2019)

a thorough thought in order to respond to the spatial, socio-cultural and economic conditions in which the different markets are positioned. With such a strong agricultural identity and such a diffused market infrastructure throughout the city, the relaunching of market structures in Rome could be an opportunity to improve food accessibility, in terms of costs and quality, but also to reactivate neighbourhoods in terms of employment and socio-cultural offer. ▪

Siri Frech
Raum+Strategie, Neuland gewinnen e.V., Berlin

Hélène Coussedière
BASE Landscape Agency Paris

Paraskevi Tarani
Ri-Connect, Major Development Agency Thessalonik

International Lectures on Resilient Metropolitan Landscapes at the *MetroLab Forum #3 DELTA*

DISCUSSING THE RESILIENCE OF METROPOLITAN AREAS

There is this gap between what we want to achieve and what we do to achieve it

Forum Discussion

What are the main challenges for metropolitan areas in dealing with the climate crisis and biodiversity loss? What measures can be taken in urban planning and development to meet these challenges and what role does a shift in thinking towards a circular economy and self-sufficiency play in this?
Inspired by the international contributions, the panel discussion on resilient urban landscapes explored some of these pressing questions of our time.
Even though Vienna has maintained its relatively high level of green space of about fifty percent of the city's size over the past few decades and is committed to provide a certain amount of green space per person, it faces major environmental challenges just like other cities around the world.

"We have two parallel crises: the climate crisis and the biodiversity crisis"
Herbert Bartik

says Herbert Bartik, representing the *Future Cities* department of the *Urban Innovation Vienna*. While Vienna is already strategically and practically addressing the climate crisis, he stresses that the city should also be seen as a place of biodiversity, accommodating an even greater variety of species than rural areas that are dominated by industrialized agriculture. Therefore, the integration of the issue of biodiversity and urban agriculture in urban development concepts and strategies, such as the new *Urban Development Plan (STEP 2035)*, should be one of the top priorities when it comes to protecting green spaces and rethinking land management within the metropolitan area. The reused organic farm *Zukunftshof/Future Farm*, located on the southern outskirts of Vienna in an urban development area with 120 hectares of fertile soil, serves as *'a kind of flagship project for urban agriculture'*, says Andreas Gugumuck, urban farmer and snail breeder who runs the farm. His cooperative relies on the principles of the circular and sharing economy to help make the metropolis more self-sufficient:

"Our goal is to make urban agriculture a big issue for the city."
Andreas Gugumuck

He also advocates vertical farming along buildings and raises awareness about local food production. Producing food, not only for the world market but also selling it locally, would be one way of making regional agricultural production more tangible while contributing to the identity of the metropolis. Christina Stockinger, who works for the *Department of Urban Development and Urban Planning of the City of Vienna*, agrees that agriculture has an identity-forming character for the city region and thus contributes to the common metropolitan vision. Nevertheless, she points out that it is particularly important in agriculturally dominated areas to coordinate different use demands and to cooperate with local farmers to mediate between them and the residents. According to her, campaigns that draw attention to agricultural activities near recreation areas are an important measure for conflict prevention ▸

"It should be a win win situation for everyone who uses the land."

As far as achieving climate targets and sustainability goals is concerned, on the one hand Helga Kromp-Kolb, chair of the *Climate Change Centre Austria*, argues that experimenting with different forms of circular economy at the neighborhood level is an important start, but needs to be expanded to the level of metropolitan areas to achieve real change. Anna Detzlhofer, on the other hand, argues that city-regional strategies need to be translated to the local level in the form of concrete projects, such as the *Coole Straßen/cooling miles* that she and her team at *DnD Landschaftsplanung* are implementing in various Viennese districts to help cool down heat islands in the city. She believes that the high level of appreciation of these innovative measures, which improve the microclimate is a sign that;

"Landscape planning changed from a 'nice to have' to a 'must have'."
Anna Detzlhofer

The pressure of suffering due to the oppressive heat in dense neighborhoods has become so great, that in inner-city locations it is no longer necessary to discuss if a tree or a parking space is more important. But since this is not the case for all places, Helga Kromp-Kolb is convinced that *"we urgently need to rethink how we want to live and what we want to achieve."* This requires a certain mindset that is no longer based on the idea of exploiting our natural environment, but rather acting in its favor.

From an urban planning perspective, Kromp-Kolb suggests, it would be helpful to *"[...] think about what the city of Vienna could look like in 2040, which is the date the Austrian government has set for net zero carbon dioxide emissions."* Since we would have to reduce emissions by 95% to ensure a healthy environment by then, this would mean that we don't have to discuss new roads, but how to preserve green spaces, reduce parking areas and shopping centers. Creating more resilient urban landscapes therefore implies that we need a more resilient economy, even if that means breaking with traditional growth paradigms, as Kromp-Kolb insists:

"The way we currently run our economy, the way we run our finances essentially is based on making use of nature to an extent that nature can no longer support."
Helga Kromp-Kolb

To achieve sustainable development in today's industrialized world, we need to produce and consume less—fewer material things, less energy, fewer resources, but this can also lead to greater satisfaction and happiness, which affects all aspects of life, including urban life and all planning aspects.

Finally, an important step in changing not only our cultural practices but also our way of thinking, and here all panelists agree with each other, is to empower the local people and involve them in urban transformation processes. We as planners can do so by creating places where we can co-create ideas and visions for a resilient, integrated, and sustainable landscape on the metropolitan scale *"as the scale we should talk about"* (Herbert Bartik). An important condition for this is to think outside the box, not only in a mental but also geographical sense, because, as Christaina Stockinger says;

"We shouldn't focus on administrative borders, they don't reflect people's worlds."
Christina Stockinger

Herbert Bartik
Future Cities,
Urban Innovation Vienna

Christina Stockinger
Regionalpark DreiAnger,
MA 18 - City of Vienna

Helga Kromp-Kolb
Climate Change Centre Austria,
University of Natural Resources
and Applied Life Sciences Vienna

Andreas Gugumuck
Future Farm

Anna Detzlhofer
DnD Landschaftsplanung

Scan to watch the documentation of the International Lectures and the Forum Discussion!

KEY FINDINGS ON CREATING RESILIENT LANDSCAPES

1. THE ZERO CARBON CITY REGION AS AN ULTIMATE GOAL

As cities and urban agglomerations are currently the largest emitters of greenhouse gases, there is a great sense of urgency to take responsibility for reducing CO2 emissions. Due to strong urban-rural linkages in terms of ecology, climate, and energy, the metropolitan area is the appropriate framework for developing and effectively implementing climate change mitigation and adaptation strategies. Transforming existing structures in terms of a holistic transition to a carbon-free urban region means, among others, promoting the development of low-emission and climate-friendly settlement structures and creating energy-efficient building and infrastructure systems. Moreover, climate goals can only be achieved with an energy transition away from fossil fuels and towards renewable energy sources. Ultimately, action must be taken now to achieve the 1.5-degree-target of the *Paris Climate Agreement* and become climate neutral.

2. CIRCULAR ECONOMY AT ALL LEVELS AS A PREREQUESITE FOR RESILIENCE

Circular value chain measures are needed to improve the resilience of metropolitan areas. The concept of the circular economy, which aims to close material and energy loops through durable design, maintenance, repair, reuse, remanufacturing, refurbishment and recycling, is an important component of our future carbon- and climate-neutral economy. It implies rethinking our usual way of producing and consuming and supports the idea of the sharing economy.

Now it is time to take the model of the circular economy, which is already being practiced in civic society led initiatives (e.g. in urban agriculture), to the next level. Experiments at the neighborhood level need to be scaled up to the metropolitan level where, for example, recycling building materials can bring about real change. However, since almost every transformation requires energy and generates a certain amount of waste, the concept of the circular economy cannot stand alone.

3. LOCAL AND REGIONAL POTENTIAL MUST BE STRENGTHENED IN THE SENSE OF SELF-SUFFICIENCY

Based on the idea of the climate-neutral city region following the model of the circular economy, metropolitan areas must activate and strengthen their own local and regional potential and focus on existing resources in terms of energy efficiency, renewable energy systems and local and sustainable food production. However, this transformation towards a self-sufficient metropolitan area is only possible if there are appropriate spatial concepts for it. To establish a largely independent energy supply, it is necessary, for example, to provide land for the expansion of renewable energy infrastructure. Urban agriculture and innovative forms of (vertical) farming also require space to grow food in a sustainable way within the city region. Therefore, local land resources should be identified and qualified —not only in the interest of self-sufficiency, but also of biodiversity.

4. BIODIVERSITY AND LAND MANAGEMENT ARE THE KEYS TO CREATING RESILIENT LANDSCAPES

Besides climate change, the loss of biodiversity is another fundamental crisis of this century. The protection of functioning ecosystems and their integration into urban development concepts and strategies, which are not only related to the municipal, but also to the metropolitan level, is a major challenge and places high demands on land management. As there is no specific agency for dedicating land for biodiversity (as there is for securing affordable housing, for example), new planning instruments are needed.

In view of increasing land consumption, soil sealing and urban sprawl, urban development and planning are strongly challenged to ensure and strengthen the diversity and quality of open spaces and green and blue infrastructures that contribute to the ecological balance of the living environment. In addition to strategically planned green networks, innovative strategies are needed to create and protect fertile soils that serve as arable land. In this respect, zoning also plays a significant role.

5. A RADICAL CHANGE IN THINKING IS NECESSARY TO CREATE RESILIENT LANDSCAPES

There needs to be a fundamental rethinking of the way we live and work together, which implies a general change in values in our social and economic system. Since unsustainable lifestyles are deeply embedded in economic, social and cultural practices (e.g. intensive use of motorized transport, or occupying too much living space per person), these need to be renegotiated with the help of raising awareness. In order to prevent action only being taken when the pressure of suffering (e.g. due to the increase of heat islands) becomes too great, it is enormously important to empower the local population. Accordingly, one of the key challenges is to contribute to problem-solving competence by raising general awareness of problematic urban transformation processes. Finally, creating resilient urban landscapes requires not only a variety of measures through climate-sensitive planning (adaptation to climate change, preservation of biodiversity or reuse of existing resources), but also the involvement of people and their local creativity and knowledge. The real hotspots of transformation are our minds. ▪

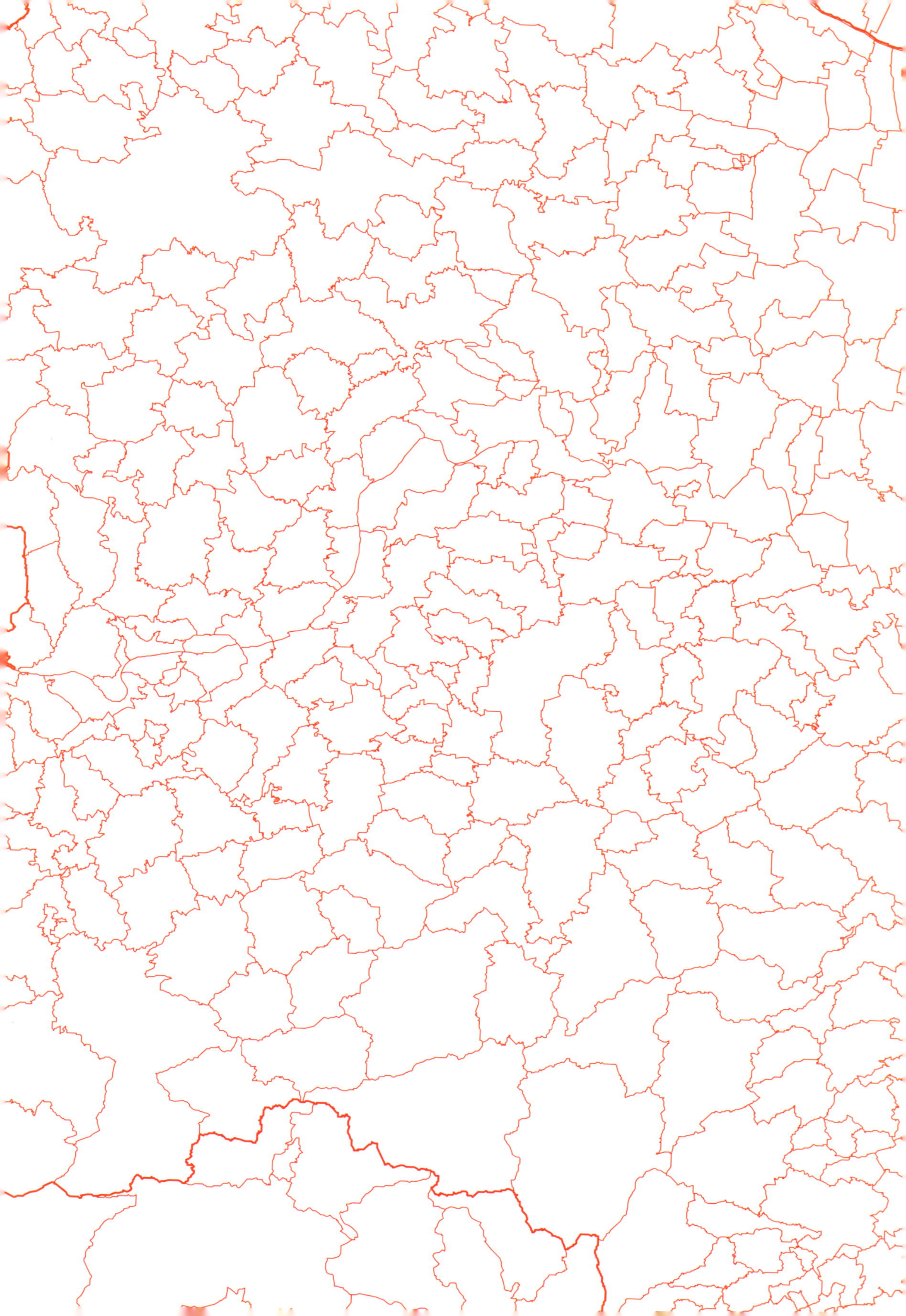

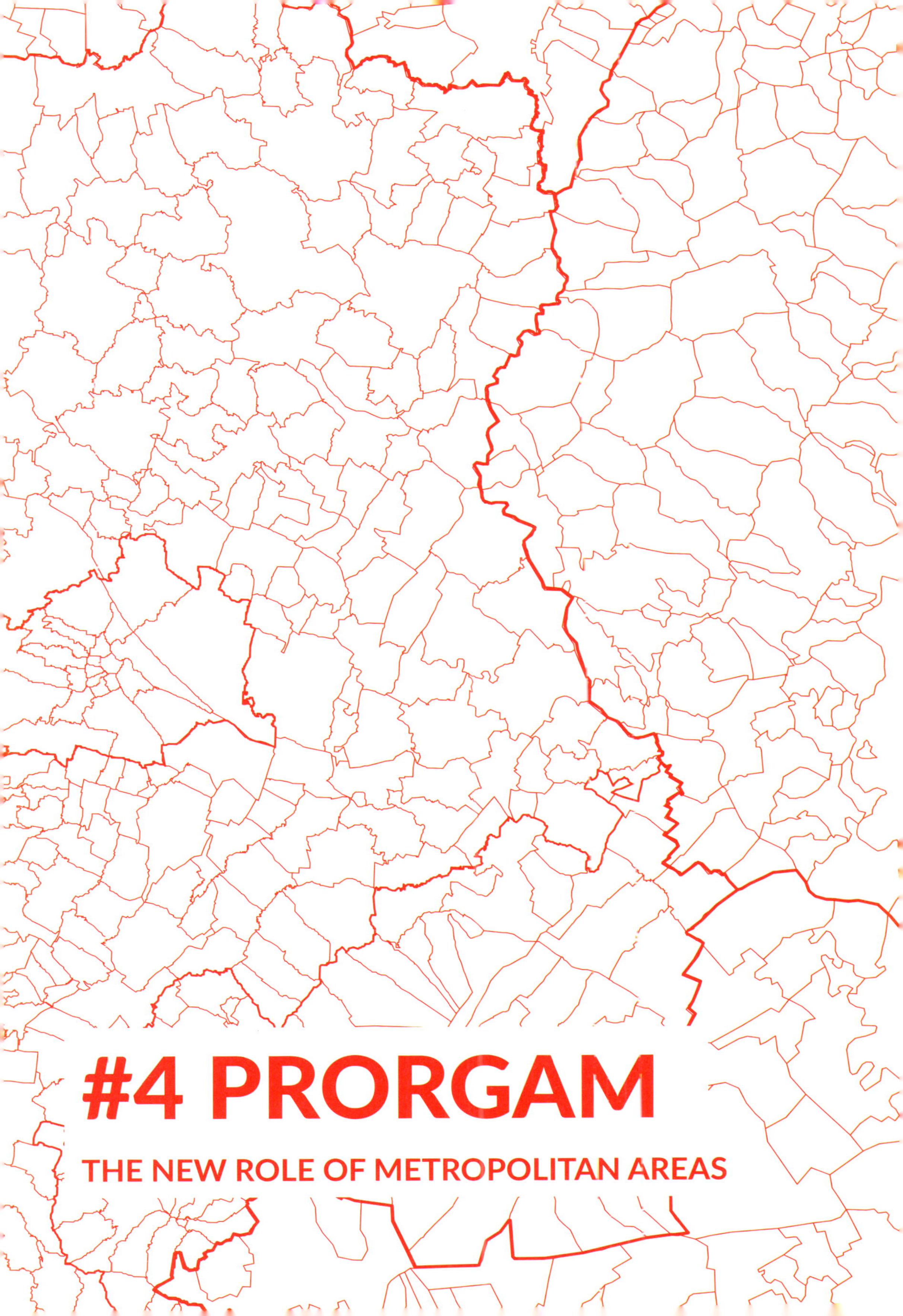

#4 PRORGAM

THE NEW ROLE OF METROPOLITAN AREAS

Flyer MetroLab Forum #4 PROGRAM

What is the new role of metropolitan areas?

Metropolitan areas consist of functionally connected heterogeneous environments that cross administrative boundaries and different spheres of competence. On the one hand, the great challenge is to sharpen a common identity of the metropolitan region. On the other hand, cross-border cooperation needs to be established within a well programmed polycentric network, shaped by the potential and role of all places. Multi-level governance structures as well as inter-municipal cooperation mechanisms are necessary in order to establish intra-regional synergies, ensure a coherent approach and thus, meet the challenges of sustainable metropolitan development. By exchanging knowledge and experience between different metropolitan areas, we discussed how to improve the attractiveness, competitiveness and integration of the Vienna Metropolis.

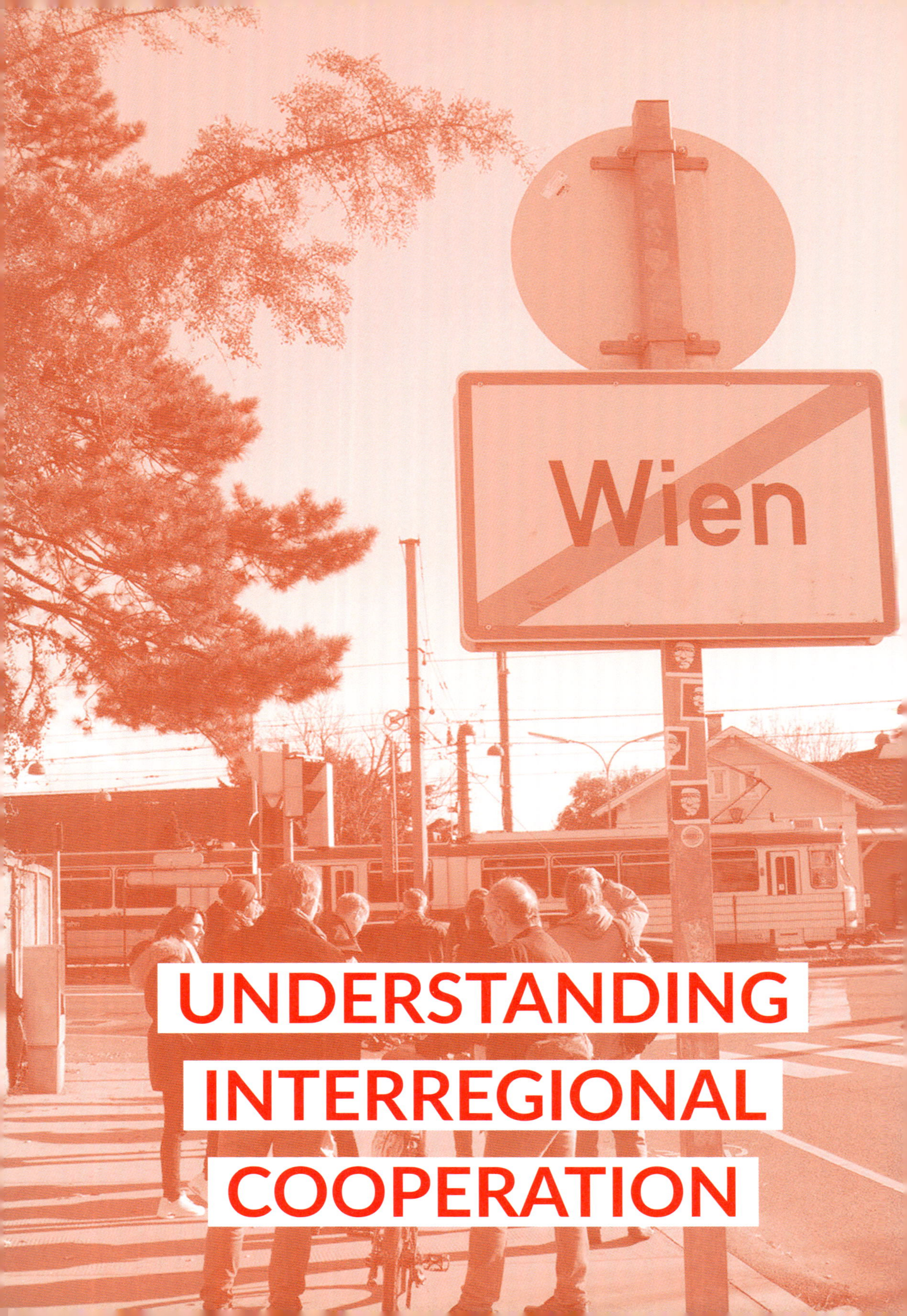

UNDERSTANDING INTERREGIONAL COOPERATION

In the transition from suburbanity to urbanity

Metropolitan Walkshop through Siebenhirten and Vösendorf

Volkmar Pamer—City of Vienna

Density should not be a bad word. The southern fringe of Vienna contains many challenges and has the potential to be a laboratory for cross-border planning. Like many other cities in the world, Vienna has to deal with the growth of the city and this growth should not end in urban sprawl which is quite often characterized by an amorphous structure, the lack of a identity, poor public transport and many other negative factors. Liesing, the southernmost district of Vienna, has undergone a remarkable transformation in the last 15 years. It has systematically and very structurally changed from suburbanity to urbanity: The re-structuring of Vienna's oldest and biggest industrial area, the renewal of an important old village core and the construction of about 13.000 new apartments. This dramatic conversion of the local urban fabric is a good example of how to deal with growth. The basis for such development is a clear vision of what is necessary to lead the change into the right direction. This works quite well within Vienna's city boundaries, but across the border in the neighbouring federal state of Lower Austria, it all becomes difficult—sometimes impossible. The reason has a constitutional background: Austria is a small country in the heart of Europe with about nine million inhabitants living on approximately 84.000 km^2. This small country is further divided into nine federal states. Each federal state has its own laws, regulations, structures, planning approaches—an anachronistic structure which greatly hinders urban development on a bigger scale.

Sustainable urban development is based on density and quality. Density is the basis for a critical mass of people to serve a certain function on one hand and an affordable infrastructural grid on the other hand. Every meter of water supply and sewage system, of public transport, roads etc. costs a lot of money, energy and resources. Compact cities are cheaper to run and far more sustainable. Denser structures reduce land grabbing and soil sealing and leave land for vegetation, water retention etc. This is one crucial factor to stop urban sprawl. But for most of the people living in suburban areas, "density" is a bad word because it evokes negative associations.

Austria is 'European champion' in land use although it is quite small and about one third of the country is mountainous. There is still no awareness—no matter on which level—of the need to use land sparingly. This means that the biggest challenge is not what planning in the fringe must look like, but how to convince the local people that densification is the necessary condition. As long as there is no answer to this question, all efforts will be in vain.

Of course, decision makers in these areas cannot solve all requirements with this issue on their own or on a local political level, even if they are willing to work together. The basis for cross-border cooperation in Austria must be developed at a higher level. There is no binding legal standard forcing cooperation on a bigger scale. A compulsion is necessary. Voluntariness will not lead to a satisfying result. ▸

People have to realize that in order to build livable and sustainable cities a certain density is not only needed, but it is actually a good thing. Support for local politicians has to go hand in hand with the paradigm shift that suburbs will have to remain suburbs. The reckless use of land must be considered as obscene as dumping old fridges into clear mountain streams—which it is, or even more so. ▪

Scan to watch the video documentation of the Metropolitan Walkshop!

www.skerget.si

The focus is on cooperation and what we can achieve together economically

Interview with **Raphaela Graf**—VIENNA REGION Marketing GmbH

MetroLab: The *VIENNA REGION Marketing GmbH* is a joint initiative of the *Vienna Business Agency, ecoplus, the Business Agency of Lower Austria*, and the *Business Agency Burgenland*. What overarching goals does it pursue as a marketing association?

Raphaela Graf: The *VIENNA REGION* was founded in 2008 with the aim of promoting the Vienna city region internationally as a business location and attracting companies interested in settling here. It is important to emphasize that the main focus of the *VIENNA REGION* is not lead generation in the target markets—i.e. it deliberately does not focus on the target markets of the mothers' agencies and thus avoids the idea of competition —but focuses on the Baltic countries Sweden and Finland. The marketing association always makes decisions together and speaks with one voice.

Our motto is "The Symphony of Opportunities", by which we mean that the *VIENNA REGION* is a place of inspiration in many respects. On the one hand, the Vienna metropolitan area offers not only tradition, culture and music, but also modernity and innovation, attracting many international companies. On the other hand, here one can find affordable, peaceful, and quiet spaces with a high quality of living. This dynamic business environment allows the companies of the future to benefit from the region. In this context, we offer, among other things, wide-ranging support and funding opportunities by creating collaborations with research, technology and development institutions. We want to make visible that there are many advantages for entrepreneurs to come here, to be creative here and to lead their company to success.

"On the one hand, the Vienna metropolitan area offers not only tradition, culture and music, but also modernity and innovation, attracting many international companies. On the other hand, here one can find affordable, peaceful, and quiet spaces with a high quality of living."

Like the concept of the *SuperWien Metropole*, the *VIENNA REGION* also emphasizes the special geographical location as well as the multifaceted nature of the city region. How do you evaluate these aspects from an economic perspective, especially since it is a very heterogeneous area that is marketed as an integrated region?

First and of all, the Vienna city region is the perfect location as a gateway to Eastern and Western Europe, which means that there is particularly strong interest from companies in entering the market here. In addition, there is the exceptionally high standard of living compared to other European metropolises, and many talented and highly qualified employees can be found here. I think that this heterogeneity on the one hand and the integrity of the region on the other go well together, because the Vienna city region consists of three federal states that complement each other well.
Despite existing demographic and political differences and administrative borders, each federal state offers an incredible range of opportunities in its own way. As a marketing association the *VIENNA REGION* offers an all-round package that each individual federal state cannot provide on its own. For example, the City of Vienna attracts international companies but does not have as much space for company buildings as the surrounding federal states. Therefore, it is necessary to coordinate the settlement of new companies and production facilities with Burgenland or Lower Austria and this is the great advantage of the *VIENNA REGION*. Its all-round package and the great combination of the City of Vienna as a mobility hub and headquarter of international companies and multilateral organizations such as the *UN* with the good transport links to the surrounding area are the reason for our strong belief that this is the best business location in Europe.

"I think that this heterogeneity on the one hand and the integrity of the region on the other go well together, because the Vienna city region consists of three federal states that complement each other well."

The *VIENNA REGION* draws on a common pool of resources, including financial resources, and then invests, for example, in a local business settlement. How does this work so that the entire region can benefit from targeted local funding?

The municipalities and the respective economic agencies work this out among themselves. However, the marketing association *VIENNA REGION* has nothing to do with this. There is a clear demarcation where the lead generation begins. If someone knocks on our door and says they would like to expand here, we coordinate the process: we first filter, report back to the individual business agencies, ask for an offer and then match the right stakeholders. In this way, we want to avoid competition among the business agencies and in no way take away the main tasks from the business location departments in the respective agencies. ▸

In other words, the *VIENNA REGION* takes on the role of a mediator and has recognized that a joint integrated positioning is more lucrative in an economic sense than an isolated positioning of these three federal provinces?

As representative of Burgenland within the *VIENNA REGION* marketing association, I see it as an absolute advantage to be part of a metropolitan region. This makes it easier for us to build a broad stakeholder network and to draw attention to ourselves internationally. We would not have this power on our own. There are also many examples of companies that outsource their production to Burgenland or Lower Austria, while at the same time wanting to offer their employees a stable environment with a high quality of life near a metropolis. This is only possible if we cooperate with each other across administrative borders.

"I see it as an absolute advantage to be part of a metropolitan region. This makes it easier for us to build a broad stakeholder network and to draw attention to ourselves internationally. We would not have this power on our own."

Do you feel that the metropolitan area across the federal states is perceived as a common economic space?

All three federal states together have 17 universities and 19 leading educational institutions. We are talking about 220.000 students here, and not just in Vienna. So, each federal state with its local talents plays a big part in making the *VIENNA REGION* as successful as it is today. Moreover, in addition to these large universities, we have many small niche areas that make their contribution to strengthen industry, research and drive innovation. That is why I believe that in the perception of the common economic space we do not stand in each other's way, but rather we see ourselves as a common big whole.

As the regional dialogues conducted by *MetroLab* in Lower Austrian municipalities have shown, the surrounding area is not only dependent on the city, but the city also depends on the surrounding area, as can be seen, for example, in the area of tourism and leisure. How do you experience this in your work context?

Attracting companies is not only about the business location, but also about destination and tourism marketing. Therefore, we must take advantage of regional assets. The heterogeneity of the region is also reflected in the fact that someone living in the inner city can benefit from centrality and travel to the countryside for leisure. This also works the other way round, someone who appreciates rural life can still travel from there to the city to work. It's a matter of giving and taking on both sides.

Finally, one could say that the common image of the Vienna city region is a heterogeneous space made up of many individual puzzle pieces. But what is the smallest common denominator of this puzzle that spans three federal provinces? Is there a common vision for the future?

In terms of content, not necessarily. For example, the *Business Agency Burgenland* is particularly active in niche technologies in the field of certain industrial and technological areas such as high-performance transmission systems for helicopters or high procession producers of laser source related components. This means that we focus on something different than other regions and that is a distinguishing feature. I think this heterogeneity is not a contradiction when it comes to the vision for the future. Our common denominator and predominant in our work are the synergies that exist between the three federal states. We are grateful for these, we hold on to them and we want to expand them further. The focus is on cooperation and what we can achieve together economically for the entire region. To act together, we look beyond political borders with the aim of continuing to grow together in the future. ▪

"The focus is on cooperation and what we can achieve together economically for the entire region. To act together, we look beyond political borders with the aim of continuing to grow together in the future."

It is important to make municipalities more aware of their city-regional role

Interview with **Peter Görgl**—Department of Geography and Regional Research at the University of Vienna, Modul5 GmbH

MetroLab: As a geographer at the *University of Vienna* and in your office *Modul5 GmbH*, you work, among others, on topics of urban-regional development and management and identify planning problems and challenges in the Vienna city region. How exactly do you approach your various projects?

Peter Görgl: Our research projects range from regional governance and statistical spatial analysis to regional master planning and the monitoring of spatial developments. When working on municipal development concepts our claim always is to think about the urban-regional and intermunicipal context. In this way, we get to the bottom of the question of what one municipality must do on its own and where it makes sense to create functional and socio-spatial synergies through cooperation with neighboring municipalities. In general, it is also a matter of increasing city-regional sensitivity, because every territorial authority, including the capital Vienna, should not develop alone today. At least that is not the sustainable way to ensure a future-proof city region.

"We get to the bottom of the question of what one municipality must do on its own and where it makes sense to create functional and socio-spatial synergies through cooperation with neighboring municipalities."

If we understand the city region as an agglomeration of spatial units that are developing at different speeds and dynamics, what are the common issues and challenges?

A classic topic of the Vienna city region, for example, is suburbanization on the one hand and a stronger influx towards the capital on the other. So, a positive migration balance, but also a socio-economic exchange that takes place. Related to this is the issue of growth management, as we often call it. Demographic phenomena such as the ageing of the population, the challenges posed by high traffic congestion and land use problems, are especially problematic as well as the management of extreme housing demand, which are cross-border issues. Landscape and open spaces are of course also important in joint urban and regional development.

In the regional expert dialogues, we held in various municipalities in Lower Austria, we came across the desire to remain a village and become a city at the same time. Isn't that contradictory? How can the challenges of the future be tackled with this attitude?

"Ideally, the next step in raising a municipality's awareness is to show that neighboring communities face the same challenges, which can be better solved together."

It is very important to question the self-image of these communities, to show them who they really are and to make them more aware of their city-regional role. This is the first step in developing a different attitude towards settlement development and their own future, because "village" is definitely the wrong term for the vast majority of the surrounding communities. Ideally, the next step in raising a municipality's awareness is to show that neighboring communities face the same challenges, which can be better solved together. These are tiny but extremely important steps on the way to city-regional governance.

In 2011, the strategy paper on *Stadtregion+* was published with many interesting approaches. What value does this ten-year-old strategy still have today?

The basic challenges already mentioned have not changed. City-regional development has a long tradition, so there's nothing wrong with ten-year-old strategies: the big topic of inner development versus outer development or measures against urban sprawl are still of great relevance. So, the strategy offers good and solid ground to build on and small steps have already been taken, all pointing in the right direction. For example, in all three federal states, Vienna, Lower Austria and Burgenland, a strong awareness of cross-border cooperation issues has developed at the departmental level.

What is the value of central institutions, such as the *Planungsgemeinschaft Ost (PGO)* or the *Stadt-Umland-Management (SUM)*, when it comes to cross-border collaboration? In your opinion, are additional institutions needed to fulfil this demanding task?

In this context, the *PGO* is more or less a think tank that commissions the analyses and actually works more at the strategic and mission-related level. And the *SUM* is very active at the operational level. Its two managers are actually the ones who work on site, who communicate with the municipalities and their stakeholders. And finally, they contribute to the implementation of existing guiding principles through concrete realizations. From that point of view, I believe that this is actually a very good system to build on. Because this relationship of trust that the *SUM* has built up with the municipalities over many years is enormously important for the communities to participate in the discourse on regional development in the first place. Maintaining this continuity is certainly a challenge. Therefore, I would argue in favor of expanding the existing institutions before creating new ones. ▸

"I would argue in favor of expanding the existing institutions before creating new ones."

Does project-based planning have the power to set impulses for a holistic development? Can positively perceived topics such as green and open space development serve as a starting point?

I think the best way would be to always have a strategic overall concept in mind and from there develop very tangible or, above all, informally organized projects. But not with the aim of creating a special-purpose association or institutionalized organizational forms out of it, in which the municipalities have to participate. The more informal intermunicipal cooperation is—although informal does not mean that it is not serious—and the softer the structures are, the more likely it is to actually work. Informal projects are also a great way to get to know each other and have fun, which boosts motivation. This emotional work is the way to generate a willingness that lasts longer and is more sustainably rooted in people's minds. In this way, it is then possible to work together on much tougher issues in the long term.

What potential do you ascribe to informally structured organizations, which are more firmly anchored in social life per se, compared to politically legitimized institutions?

On the one hand, I think we have already come to the conclusion that highly formalized forms of organization would not work for the Vienna city region at the moment. The legal basis does not speak for it. And when I start to formalize something, I also have to finally delimit the Vienna city region and define the area of responsibility. And that's where you run into difficulties. On the other hand, in informal approaches, you can tailor the project to the space (and vice versa) as it suits. I am convinced that the informal and project-based approach is the best way to establish cooperation. First and foremost, it is all about implementation successes and shared learning in very informal, hands-on projects.

What is your vision of the city region in the future?

Well, it is definitely a positive vision: That at some point there will be a strongly staffed city-regional management that thinks long-term. I envision a great city-region in which there is no single governing body, but a strong shared sense of cooperation. So that projects which are special now, like the *Regionalpark DreiAnger*, are then on the agenda as a matter of fact. From a future perspective, I imagine that the municipal perspective has also changed, and that stakeholders no longer exclusively develop solutions for their own challenges, but that they rather include all points of view. I also imagine that one has developed a neutral discussion platform which encourages an informal exchange about topics relevant to the city region. And in my "super-vision", this even leads to the fact that it no longer matters whether a new business park is located in the municipality X or Y or in the middle of the city, but that it is simply agreed on that the location is organized inter-communally and that one can participate proportionately. And finally, I imagine that it is simply a political and planning-strategic consensus that you meet at eye level. And everything else becomes almost utopian. ▪

> *"I envision a great city-region in which there is no single governing body, but a strong shared sense of cooperation."*

We need to focus on new strategies for medium-sized cities to control their growth and provide efficient transport

Interview with **Michel Duchène**—Bordeaux Métropole, Author

MetroLab: Since the *MetroLab* has set itself the goal of reporting on inspiring international examples of metropolitan planning, we are particularly interested in your approach to the use of governance tools regarding the Bordeaux metropolitan area. What specific instruments were used to facilitate the project of *Bordeaux Métropole*, which comprises 28 municipalities?

Michel Duchène: First of all, such a project relies on a committed political group that supports the mayor and provides political coherence and momentum. Structuredness, intelligence and thoughtfulness as well as the big vision for the overall project are key factors. This vision of the city and its future is crucial and can be initiated, for example, with a tram project. It's impossible to succeed without it! It is also important to be balanced enough to accept failure, to take steps backwards but keep the essential perspective to then take a big leap forward and complete the project.

Secondly, a project of this type must be based on a strong, organized, structured and, above all, well-trained administration. Therefore, we have tried to change the administrative culture of the urban community and embed it in a framework of urban ecology and sustainable development. What has taken us time in this process is to train the private sector in this area, to convince our promoters to attend trainings to train them in ecology, transport, cleanliness issues and others. This was the only way we could move this project forward together and to face the challenges of limited financial resources. In conclusion, I believe that a stable city and municipal administration that stands by its word is essential. Relying on the residents is also fundamental. ▸

"A project of this type must be based on a strong, organized, structured and, above all, well-trained administration."

The community of the *Bordeaux Métropole* emerged at the end of the 1960s. What preconditions does such a project need so that a real metropolitan vision can be developed over the years?

"The question is simple: Are politicians brave and willing enough to go beyond particular interests and lead a global policy with a long-term strategy?"

The strength and power of the urban community, especially in times of metropolization, lies in the major strategic areas such as housing, transport, the environment. Although the municipalities cooperate with the urban community, the latter has a very great weight. The municipalities have been disempowered, so to speak. This fueled the anger of the mayors who blamed metropolization. As a result, large departments were abolished. I will give you a very simple example: Why, for example, was the tramway project in Bordeaux carried out at a very reasonable price and with so much consistency? Because a special team was set up for it, which implemented the project perfectly. There will always be mayors who want bicycles, and mayors who don't want bicycles, and mayors who want trams, or don't want trams. And although the politically elected representatives in the municipalities want to have more to say, it is essential not to deprive the metropolises of their power. After all, they have a financial power and an urban power that allows them to pursue major strategies that counteract problems such as global warming. The question is simple: Are politicians brave and willing enough to go beyond particular interests and lead a global policy with a long-term strategy?

Apart from the main tramway strategy you mentioned, what other missions were in the foreground?

For a long time, one of the main tasks has been the reorganization of the municipalities, everything that concerns the rehabilitation of the roads, the tramway or other sectors. So, there is a wide range of tasks and measures that are very broad and diverse and related, for example, to sustainable development, energy, etc., and which, as long as the central political power is not questioned, are also supported by the municipalities.

Now that we have talked about the successes, were there also failures? What are the current challenges the *Bordeaux Métropole* is facing?

"If we set limits to the metropolitan area, we can negotiate with other urban centres [...] to develop their urbanity, in a way that welcomes new inhabitants without causing urban sprawl."

One of the biggest challenges is the return of people to the city and at the same time the urban sprawl. The population in the city has increased at a catastrophic rate, which has provoked an interesting debate between architects and urban planners. I have always defended the idea of a dense metropolis that remains self-contained. If we set limits to the metropolitan area, we can negotiate

with other urban centres—which can be small towns, medium-sized towns, villages or cities—to develop their urbanity in a way that welcomes new inhabitants without causing urban sprawl. And in the midst of these urban spaces, there must be large areas of vegetation—agricultural land, open green spaces, forests, etc.—but unfortunately that is not what is happening in France at the moment, nor in Europe. So, we need to question demographic change in order to deal with current developments.
Another failure is the transmission of an urban culture. What I regret very much is that very often political changes, changes of teams and administrations interrupt the continuity of the urban project and the continuity of the policies implemented. It's a bit of a rollercoaster ride. Despite new concepts of resilience, sustainable development and ecology, there will always be those politicians who are pro-car and anti-density city. Perhaps one of the failures is that we have not sufficiently educated and instructed the elected representatives, politicians, administrators, engineers, developers and others.

"Perhaps one of the failures is that we have not sufficiently educated and instructed the elected representatives, politicians, administrators, engineers, developers and others."

What are the personal lessons you take away from this experience?

From this central perspective you sometimes end up saying things in a rather authoritarian way—they seem inevitable—and you come across people who don't believe in them and who therefore start having arguments that create friction. Some people's happiness today is to live in a private house with a garden and a swimming pool. And what right do we have to forbid them? But it is our right to say that we are obviously heading towards a disaster if we continue like this. For me, urban sprawl is a failure. I thought that by re-circling Bordeaux and making the metropolis attractive, we would curb urban sprawl. Unfortunately, we have not yet succeeded. We need to focus on new strategies for medium-sized cities to control their growth and provide efficient transport because the car is not the solution.

"We need to focus on new strategies for medium-sized cities to control their growth and provide efficient transport, because the car is not the solution."

So, what does the metropolis of tomorrow look like in your opinion? Is it a polycentric metropolitan area?

Yes. While I believe that a certain centrality must be maintained, I also believe that the metropolis has reached the limits of its power and so must allow other centralities to emerge. What we need to clarify for ourselves is: What kind of city do we want? What kind of agricultural and natural space do we want? How will we build in the future and what is needed in terms of public transport? In my opinion, it is a worrying development that natural landscapes, for example, are disappearing more and more. ▪

"The metropolis has reached the limits of its power and so must allow other centralities to emerge."

LEARNING FROM INTERNATIONAL APPROACHES

Metropolitan governance in France. Solving problems and creating new ones

Gilles Pinson—Institute of Political Science at Sciences Po Bordeaux

Since a series of laws were passed during the 2010 decade, most major French cities have been governed by so-called metropolitan governments. A total of 22 "metropolises" were created during this period. What weight do these institutions actually have in the governance of French cities?

When we look at the functions performed by these metropolises, we can only be impressed. In fact, almost all functions related to urban planning, transport, network services, economic development, housing, urban regeneration, or the environment, which were previously exercised by the municipalities are now in the hands of the metropolises.

Today, the metropolises also have clear budgetary authority. This can be seen by comparing, for example, the budgets of the *City of Lyon*, the *Métropole de Lyon* and the *Auvergne-Rhône-Alpes Region*, of which Lyon is the capital. For 2021, these budgets were respectively 0.690€ billion (for 518 635 inhabitants, i.e. 1 330 € per inhabitant), 3 970€ billion (for 1. 398 892 inhabitants, i.e. 2 837€ per inhabitant) and 3 943€ billion (for 7. 994 459 inhabitants, i.e. 493€ per inhabitant). The same situation can be found in most other metropolitan configurations. The metropolis has become, at least in terms of functions and resources, the most powerful level of local government in France. However, if we take a closer look at the actual functioning of these French metropolises, we are quickly confronted with several surprises. Firstly, there is a great diversity of local situations in terms of the effective political capacity of metropolises. While some metropolises, such as Lyon, Nantes or Rennes, are recognized as having become the major players and spaces for shaping territorial policies, in other cities, such as Lille, Bordeaux or Marseille, the metropolis struggles to impose itself on municipalities and mayors. The balance of power between metropolitan and municipal interests depends on various factors: the demographic weight and attractiveness of the central city in relation to the peripheries, the degree of municipal fragmentation, or the presence or absence of partisan hegemony at the metropolitan level.

Secondly, it is further surprising that in the case of metropolises we are far from the model of "metropolitan government" identified by Christian Lefèvre (1998). This is because the metropolis is far from erasing, marginalizing or even abolishing municipalities and mayors. Indeed, it must be emphasized that metropolitan councils are still composed of municipal representatives. Electoral legitimacy remains with these municipal elected officials and, in particular, with the mayors, who generally closely control the composition of the lists for the municipal elections.

In the end, the effective political functioning of metropolises is more a matter of the metropolitan governance model than of the metropolitan "big government". Metropolitan policies are the result of negotiations and intergovernmental balances. Every effort is made to avoid infringing on municipal sovereignty. Sometimes these negotiations can result in ambitious policies and a real empowerment of policy-making and regulation at the metropolitan level. Sometimes, municipal self-interest prevails against the back-drop of a lack of vision and a metropolitan territorial project. ▸

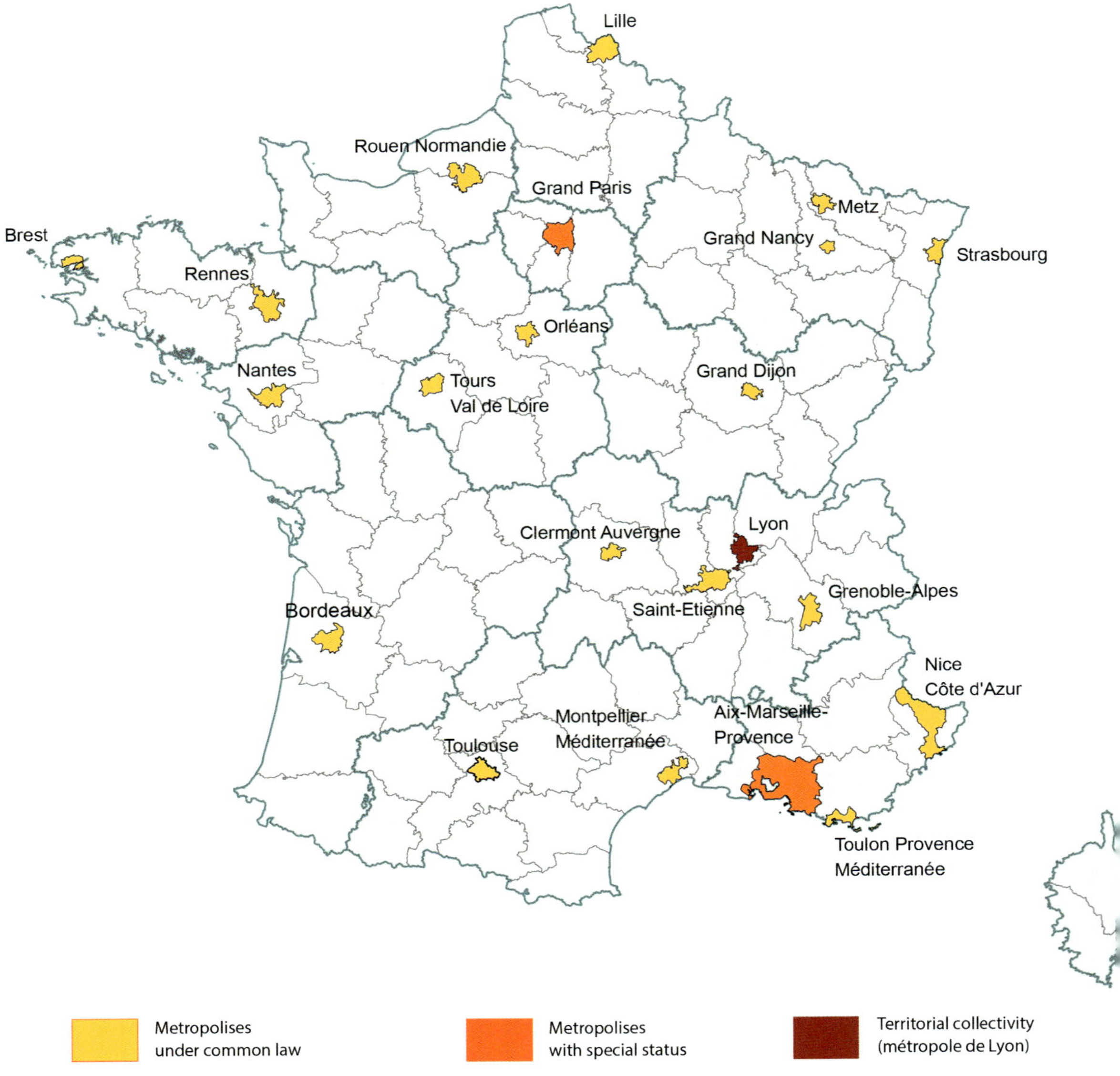

Figure 1: Map of the 22 French Metropolis

In short, although the French metropolises are powerful on paper, their actual capacity to supervise metropolitan development and regulate socio-spatial inequalities varies greatly in practice.

How did we get into this situation? There is an "original sin" underlying the metropolitan structure in France. France has historically been characterized by a high degree of municipal fragmentation. In 2021, there are 34.965 communes in the country. The average population of municipalities is 1 908; in Austria, it is almost exactly twice as high (3.834). While most European countries "rationalized" their municipal codes in the 1960s and 1970s, France was unable to do so, mainly because of the political weight of local elected representatives and the practice of holding multiple offices, which allowed a mayor to be both a member of parliament and sometimes a minister. The relationship between the state and local governments has long been based on the paradox that local governments have little functions and opportunities to act but are led by local elected officials who have always been and continue to be important political figures capable of exerting pressure on state authorities the central and local levels (Pinson 2010). This weight of local elected officials was reflected in the resounding failure of a law promoting municipal mergers in 1971. So-called "inter-municipal cooperation", the most recent expression of which are metropolitan areas, is therefore an alternative solution that has been experimented with and then institutionalized to organize the governance of large territories.

French metropolises today face three types of political challenges. The first is the risk of implosion. The more they gain in functions and the more they accumulate financial and technical resources, the more metropolises become the object for political rivalries. Sometimes these rivalries are played by the assertion of political hegemony by one leader or a party, sometimes by inter-party arrangements. But sometimes there is political gridlock, or even the threat of secession of certain communities, as we are currently witnessing in Lyon. Perhaps it is time to change the system and introduce direct universal suffrage for metropolitan councils to create a true majority logic in metropolitan areas that ensures political clarity and policymaking capacity.

The second political challenge is the relationship between the metropolises and their territorial environment. The rise in power of these institutions is causing more and more tensions in their immediate surroundings. In the peri-urban and rural areas adjacent to the metropolises, so-called "defensive" inter-municipal cooperation bodies have been created, with which the metropolises find it difficult to develop cooperation, even though the interdependencies between these areas are becoming increasingly evident.

This is one of the challenges that metropolitan areas will have to face in the coming years. Finally, metropolises are facing with the emergence of a "metrosceptic" mood in public opinion. Various types of discontent seem to be directed against them, of which the *Yellow Vests* movement is one of the most spectacular manifestations. The metropolises are accused of pursuing policies of growth, attractiveness and competitiveness that leads to exclusion, of being beneficiaries of state policies that are accused of abandoning rural areas and medium-sized cities, and of being undemocratic spaces. Faced with these challenges, the French metropolises must thoroughly rethink their political functioning. However, this can only be done by changing legislation over which they have no control. Moreover, they must no longer limit their agenda to infrastructure, planning and development issues. They must also address social issues. The welfare metropolis must be invented today! ▪

Form & function. Metropolitan development against the grain

Review of the lecture of **Paul Gerretsen**—Deltametropolis Association Rotterdam

Paul Gerretsen introduces his lecture with a brief introduction of the *Deltametropolis Association*, of which he has been the director since 2008. The association was founded as an independent network for metropolitan development. It functions as a platform for decision makers as well as a laboratory for innovative projects on the other. The association's aim is to ensure a resilient and futuristic positioning of the Netherlands worldwide.

URGENCIES FOR GOVERNMENT AND GOVERNANCE

The Netherlands has four levels of government: the national government, the provinces, the municipalities, and a fourth special level of government—the water boards, which deal only with water issues that are important throughout the country. There is also a highly centralized national tax system: Citizens pay almost all taxes to the national level, which then decides on the distribution of the budget to the municipalities. This often results in municipalities having no rights in how the budget is spent and makes it very different to govern. In recent decades, there have been many attempts to find new forms of governance for a more interconnected and regional government. So far, however, all have failed.

In his lecture, Paul Gerretsen argues that there is an urgent need to think about the Netherlands as a whole. This is necessary in many ways, for example, to connect cities effectively by public transport such as high-speed trains. Additionally, there are very serious problems in the Netherlands that can only be solved together at the national level, such as very high nitrate emissions or the dramatic loss of biodiversity, as well as the energy transition that is progressing too slowly.

When looking at possible ways out of the challenges mentioned above, there are promising approaches. For example, a project has been initiated that looks at the river system and waterways in the Netherlands and how to deal with floods. Thereby a concept was developed that combines the national need for change in this river system with very a local and regional, quality-oriented project. The concept involved digging a wide completely new river next to the natural one that would be needed only during floods, i.e., a dam of a certain height that would be flooded when needed.

This kind of interaction between the national goal and a new regional quality could be a solution. These new approaches could also be applied to the energy transition sector. Together with other offices, the *Deltametropolis Association* created a national perspective for the year 2050 showing that—if one really wanted to—all the energy needed for the Netherlands could be produced within its own borders. Following that, they presented how this national perspective could interact with regional specific proposals that actually bring various qualities to many different regional perspectives. Finally, Paul Gerretsen summarizes: *"Unfortunately, in the metropolitan development of the Netherlands, form does not equal function. However, these functional units will become more and more important in the coming decade."* This, he concludes, will be one of the most fundamental challenges of the coming decades. ▪

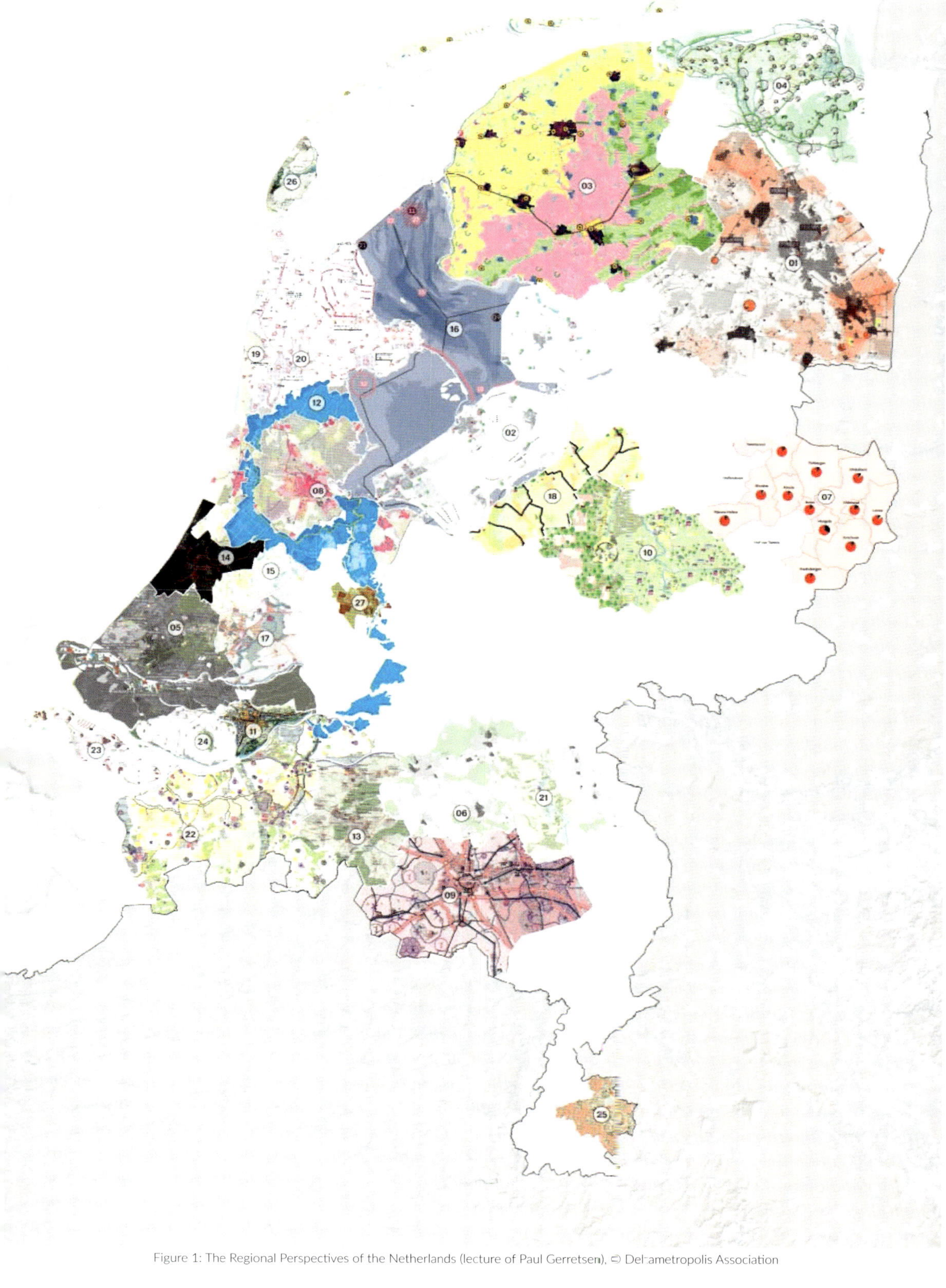

Figure 1: The Regional Perspectives of the Netherlands (lecture of Paul Gerretsen), © Deltametropolis Association

Avinguda del Vallès—a co-creation process

Judith Recio Heredia & Anna Majoral Pelfort—URBACT-RiConnect, Àrea Metropolitana de Barcelona (AMB)

The *Barcelona Metropolitan Area (AMB)* with the participation and involvement of all stakeholders is drafting an Integrated Action Plan. This plan will define the actions required to transform the national road *N-150* into a metropolitan avenue.

This project is being developed within the European programme *URBACT*, a programme of territorial cooperation aiming to foster sustainable integrated urban development. The *AMB* is leading the *RiConnect* network, composed by eight metropolitan areas, and which aims to rethink, transform, and integrate mobility infrastructures to reconnect people, neighbourhoods, cities, and natural spaces (Rull, Caba et al 2019). The main output of each partner is to draft an Integrated Action Plan, a plan which has to define the future vision and goals for the project area and propose the necessary actions to achieve it.

The *AMB* is also drafting the *Metropolitan Urban Master Plan (PDU)* which will define the urban development model of the metropolis for the next decades, integrating the current diversity into a common project. One of the main goals of the plan is fostering sustainable mobility, and to do so it proposes a network of "metropolitan avenues" that structure and connect the territory for people. As backbone of this network, the metropolitan avenues will be the reference axis that connect the city centres and must support sustainable mobility, guarantee high quality public spaces and a great intensity of uses (PDU 2019).

One of the main challenges that we face to develop the metropolitan avenues is the governance. As they pass through many municipalities, the property of the road changes from each municipality to another. In some cases, even the Catalan government or the central state are the owners of the infrastructure. In addition, almost all the proposed avenues are existing road infrastructures, which must be integrated to the surroundings diminishing their externalities, incorporate sustainable mobility and promote urban intensity and mixed uses around them. For that reason, the *URBACT* programme and the *RiConnect* network is a great opportunity to test how to transform a road infrastructure into a metropolitan avenue with an integrated approach.

To develop the Integrated Action Plan, we selected a section of the avenue that will connect Sabadell with the *Barcelona's Forum* harbour. The selected area is a six kilometers long section that goes through four municipalities: Barberà del Vallès, Cerdanyola del Vallès, Ripollet and Montcada i Reixac (see Figure 1). The project area concentrates many infrastructures (national road, *C-58* highway, railway, *Ripoll River*, *Sec River* and *Sant Cugat creek*) that divide the territory and generate externalities such as discontinuities, congestion, barrier effect, pollution, etc.

The national road, which will be the future metropolitan avenue, crosses many municipalities with a large population and activities, but the property of the road is of each municipality. Therefore, to achieve a common vision and an integrated project, it requires the cooperation of the different administrations involved, such as associations and citizens. ▸

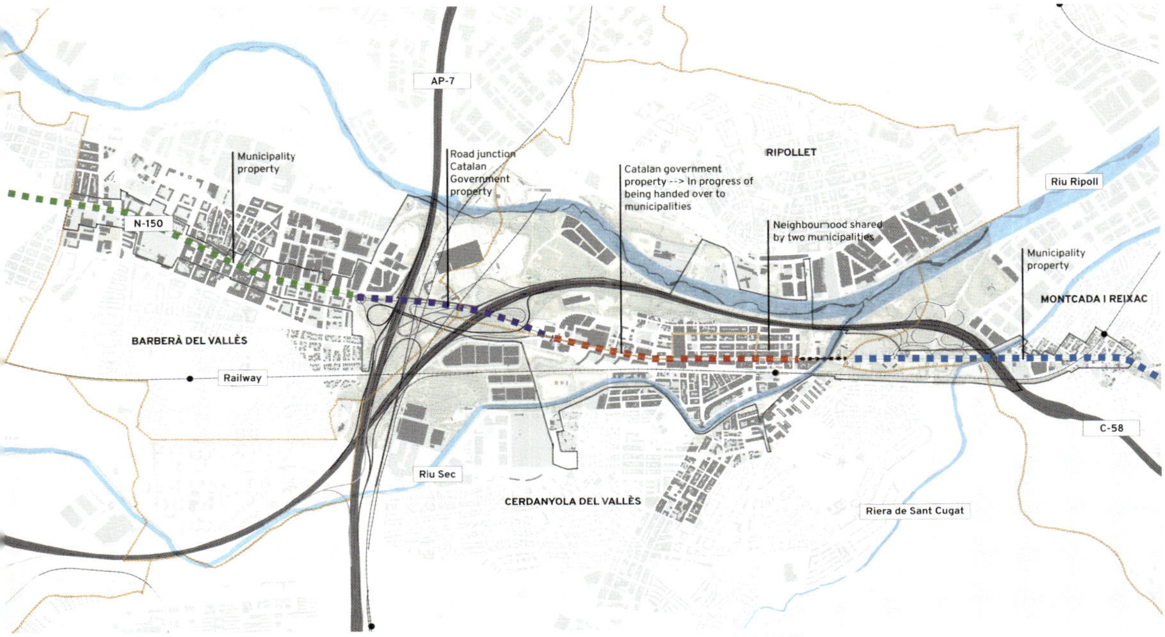

Figure 1: Area of the Integrated Action Plan, © Avinguda del Vallès

Figure 2: Co-creation sessions with differnet stakeholders, 2021

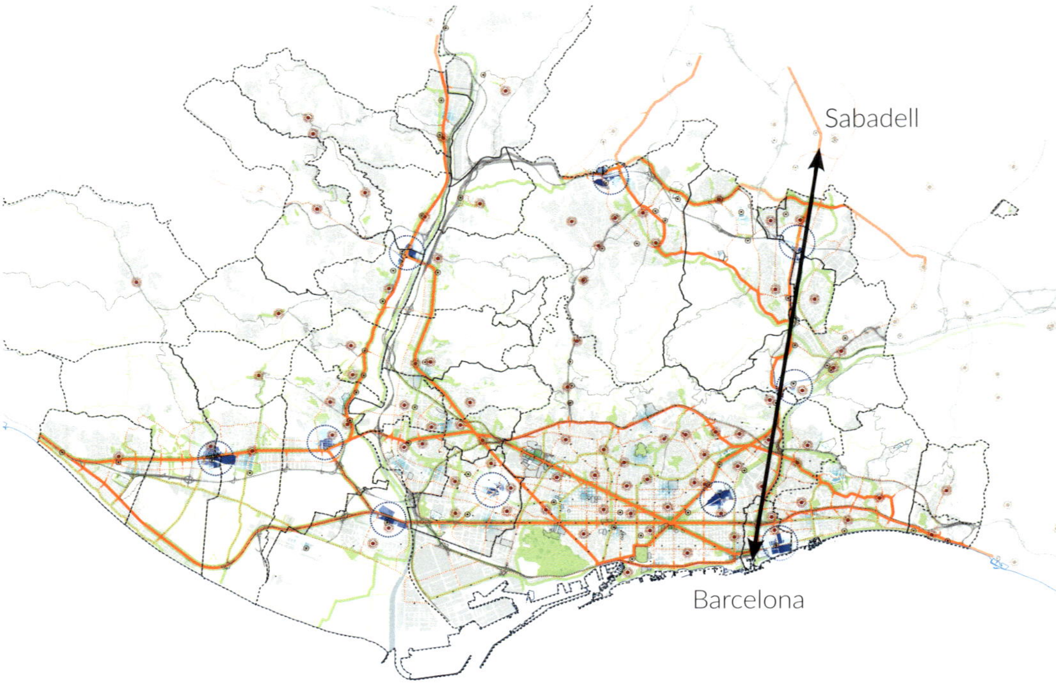

Figure 3: Metropolitan Avenues Network proposal, 2019 © Avinguda del Vallès

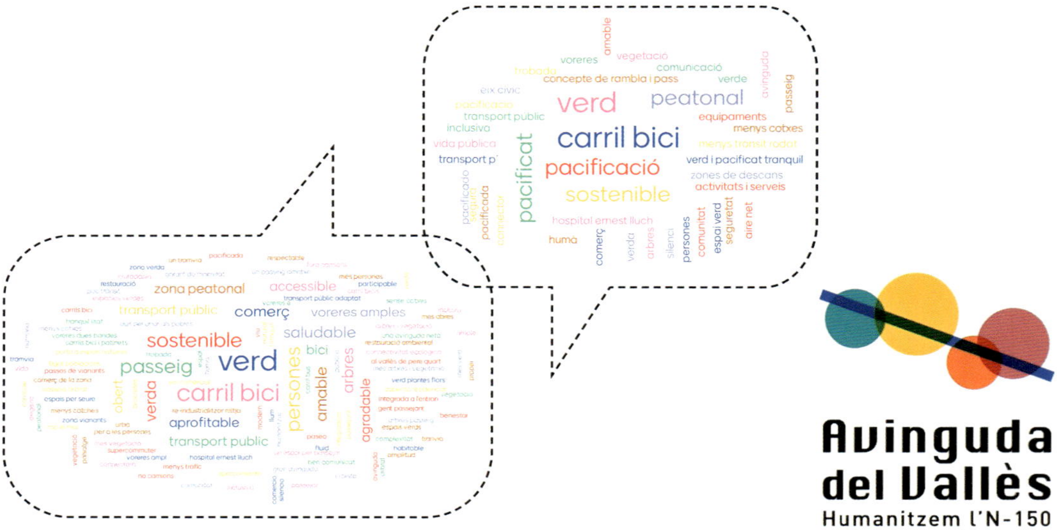

Figure 4: Word Cloud of the first co-creation session and citizenship session © Avinguda del Vallès

As a result, it is a very complex area, with a lot of administrations involved. Hence, it requires the participation of a broad range of stakeholders and an integrated multi-scalar approach.

To draft the Integrated Action Plan, we designed a co-creation process, identifying the different stakeholders of the area and grouping them into four groups with different responsibilities and levels of involvement: the core group, which designs the process; the co-creation group, which takes part in meetings and decides on actions; the commitment group, which ensures political support; and citizens, who are informed of the development of the process (see Figure 2). The design of the co-creation process, with the participation of the different groups, assures us that at the end of the process we will deliver an Integrated Action Plan where the views of many stakeholders are represented.

The process started in January 2021, with the launch of an online questionnaire open to the citizenship. There were more than 1.000 answers, which allowed us to better define the project area and to identify the emerging topics. After that first approach, we started with initial meetings to present the project to the commitment group and to the citizens.

Once we had presented the project, we started the co-creation process with the core and co-creation groups. During this year we have conducted seven co-creation sessions, and more than 15 sessions with the core group to co-organize the meetings and get technical support.

In the first co-creation session, which was held online due to the pandemic, the main goal was to develop a common vision, define the goals of the project and to develop a corporate image to easily identify the project and develop the communication strategy.

The main goals of the project are:

» Connecting avenue
» Kind and inclusive avenue
» Healthy and sustainable avenue
» Concerted avenue

After the introductory workshop, we conducted three diagnosis sessions, two online and the last one in presence, where we obtained an accurate diagnosis of the site, both from the technical point of view and from the citizens' perspective.

To respond to the different demands, we developed the urban strategy. This served as a starting point for the next co-creation phase, with three more workshops to discuss and deepen the proposals with the co-creation group, and review, enrich and prioritize actions. This phase will end with the delivery of the Draft Integrated Action Plan. However, before doing so, we will hold a Small-Scale Action, addressed to engage with all stakeholders and the citizenship. In this open activity we will address the different goals of the project with attractive activities, while showing and communicating the proposed actions and collecting new contributions from citizens.

Finally, next year we will focus on planning the implementation of the actions. It will be a challenging phase to address governance models of cooperation, transversal policies or working beyond the borders of the *AMB*.

To sum up, we expect that this process will allow us not only to rethink all together a better future for this stretch of the *N-150* road, but also to serve as a testbed for the *Metropolitan Avenues*. The *URBACT* methodology is helping us to establish successful dynamics for citizen engagement and institutional collaboration, which will be key for the implementation of the *Metropolitan Urban Master Plan* and will lead us to a better connected and more liveable metropolis. ▪

Governance models and development ideas for metropolitan areas

Iván Tosics—Metropolitan Research Institute Budapest

The term "metropolitan areas" is still quite a mystery for many decision makers. The idea that EU policies should acknowledge metropolitan areas and give them an important role as one of the terrirotial levels in policy making, usually falls on deaf ears in Brussels. The best reaction is that "we know that metropolitan relations are important but we do not know what these areas are and how they can be defined. And if such an area is incidentally delineated, where is its trustworthy leadership which could make democratic decisions at this level?"

Thus the official recognition of metropolitan areas is far behind their importance in real life —not only amongst Brussels decision makers but also in many of the member states. To fill this gap many efforts were taken in the last years by different organizations and experts. This article gives a brief account on some of these efforts, with the aim to draw a few conclusions for the case of Vienna.

METROPOLITAN AREAS: WHAT ARE THEY AND WHY ARE THEY IMPORTANT?

Urban areas face many different challenges: demographic, employment, environmental, social problems of development, which emerge simultaneously. For balanced urban development public policies have to be integrated, as policies tackling exclusively only one of the challenges create huge problems (externalities) regarding others (Tosics, 2013). Integration of the different aspects of urban development requires different types of co-ordination: across policy sectors (horizontal), across administrative areas (territorial) and across government levels (vertical coordination, multi-level governance). The territorial coordination challenge means that integrated policies need a territorial base which is large enough to deal with the externalities of each of the policy domains. For this reason there is a growing need for cooperation between municipalities beyond the administrative boundaries of the cities, as in most of the European cities the administrative borders are outdated, do not cover the territory of everyday links, e.g. the housing market or the commuting area (European Union, 2011).

The functional urban areas (metropolitan areas) of the cities are in most cases fulfilling this criteria (Rubbo, 2018). Strengthened collaboration and joint planning in such areas might lead to more integrated solutions—without necessarily creating any new form or level of universal public management or administration. However, "metropolitan cooperation" can frighten rural stakeholders who might think that cities will dominate them. In many cases, not even the residents of urban areas understand this from everyday perspective rather abstract idea. Moreover, in many cases, the well-established administrative regions are against metropolitan cooperation, protecting their own power against the joint power of the city and its surrounding settlements. In order to overcome this metropolitan governance challenge, strong citizen support would be required for metropolitan cooperation, but public awareness is quite limited and people are quite reluctant to see any new administrative units to develop.

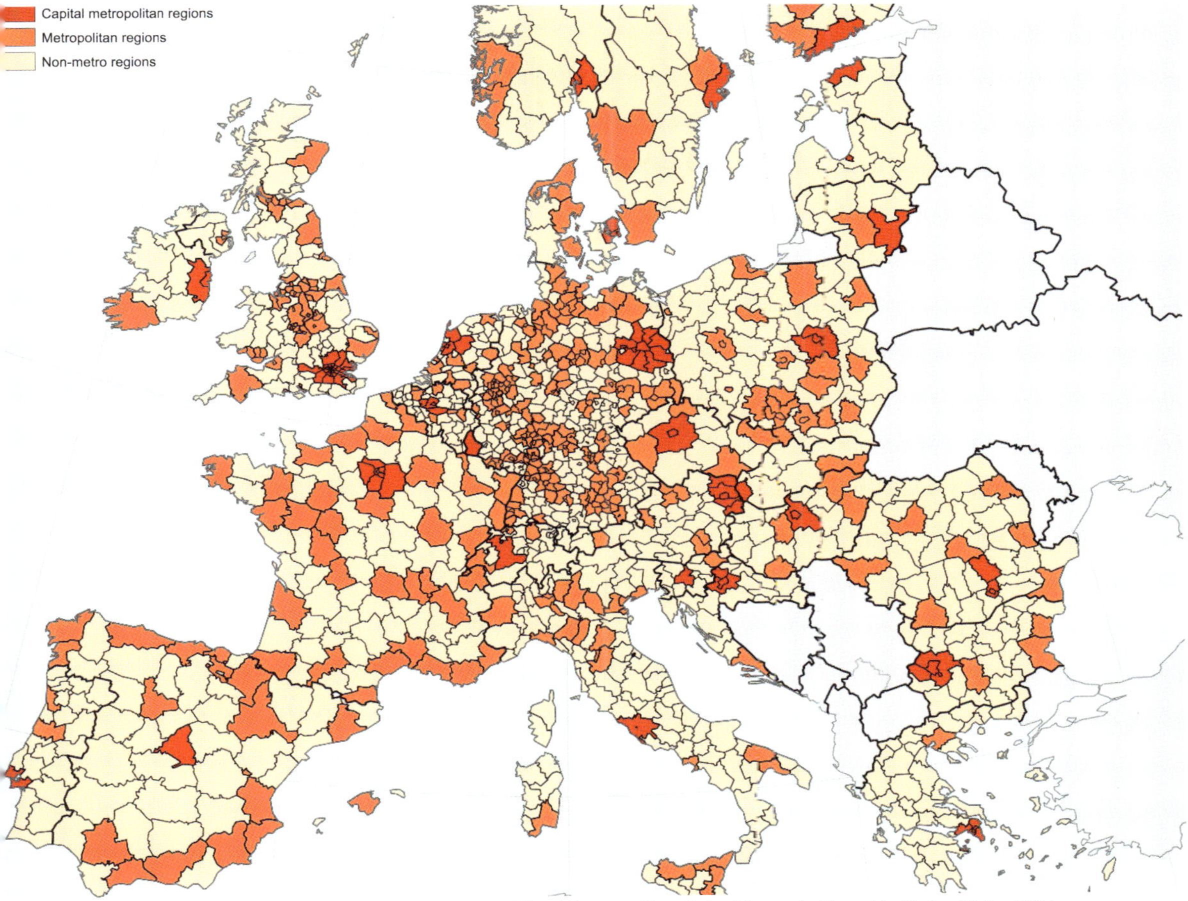

Figure 1: Typology of Metropolitan Regions © Eurostat, JRC and European Commission Directorate-General for Regional Policy, 2016

Thus, metropolitan cooperation is not at all a natural process, but to be developed by systemic and long-lasting efforts, led by public actors.

As already mentioned, there is no uniformly accepted definition and delineation of the metropolitan areas in Europe. For the spatial localization there are different databases regarding the functional urban areas (FUA): the *ESPON* research (2007) and the *OECD* (2013) attempt to determine metropolitan (FUA) areas around larger cities in the *OECD* countries. These delineations do not perfectly match, as for some cities the *ESPON* and *OECD* definitions of the *FUA* are different.Regarding the definition and delineation of metropolitan areas *Eurostat* made pinoeer work, coming up with maps about such areas (see Figure 1). In their definition metropolitan regions are approximations of functional urban areas (cities and their commuting zones) of 250 thousand or more inhabitants consisting of one or more *NUTS* level 3 regions. *Eurostat* data show that almost 300 million people are living in the EU's metropolitan regions, i.e. almost three out of five EU inhabitants. Countries with ▸

Size of the collaboration	1. Statistical unit	2. Networking, weak strategic planning	3. Single function	4. Multiple functions	5. Strong strategic, spatial planning of binding nature
A) Smaller than FUA	Budapest, Brussels	**Ghent**, **Malmö**, Vienna, Zurich.	**Frankfurt**, Helsinki[1] , **Katowice**, Warsaw	**Amsterdam**, **Rotterdam**	**Lille**[2], **Lyon**, **Rennes**, **Strasbourg** **Milan (metropolitan city)**
B) FUA	Berlin, Budapest, Ghent, Linköping, **Lisbon**, **Strasbourg**, Vienna, Warsaw	**Amsterdam**, Birmingham LEP, **Bratislava (region)**, Brno, Brussels, **Gothenburg**, Katowice, **Lyon**[3], **Malmö**, Sofia[4], Terrassa		Helsinki[5] , **Madrid (region)**, **Munich**, Manchester, **Oslo**, Preston, **Stockholm (county)**, **Tampere (region)**	
C) Somewhat larger than FUA	Sofia	BrabantStad, **Zurich**	Brussels	**The Hague**, **Torino (province)**, **Helsinki (region)**	**Stuttgart**, **Torino (metropolitan city)**
D) Much larger than FUA (larger economic zone)	Birmingham, Budapest	Amsterdam, Bratislava, Frankfurt, Ghent, Gothenburg, Hamburg, Katowice, Lille, Linköping, Lyon, Malmö, Oslo, Rennes, Stockholm, Strasbourg, Stuttgart, Tampere, Vienna, Zurich	Rotterdam—The Hague	Katowice (region), Lisbon (region),	Berlin, Malmö (region)

Table 1: Classification of cities based on the size and functions of the different collaboration territories

Cities in bold: some type of metropolitan organization exists. As many cities did not supply enough detailed information, this table can only be regarded as a hypothesis. Polycentric FUAs are more complex and are in most cases part of the C or D categories: Frankfurt, Lille, Katowice, Brussels, Lyon, Rotterdam—The Hague, Malmö, BrabantStad and Zurich—at least—are fitting within this category.

[1]There are two different levels smaller than the FUA around Helsinki: a common Environmental Service Authority for 4 municipalities and a common transportation authority for 7 municipalities.

[2]Lille has two levels that are smaller than the FUA and they operate several common services—for 85 municipalities—and a SCOT system for 124 municipalities. (The FUA would involve about 150 municipalities.)

[3]The Metropolitan Cooperation around Lyon consists of 4 metropolitan areas that are not connected directly (so this area is not exactly a FUA). They promote common policy development.

[4]Sofia agglomeration was defined in the Operational Programme Regional Development (2007-2013) as an area for strategic planning.

[5]In the Greater Helsinki area not really common services were organised, rather special contracts with well-defined targets in the area of social housing, homelessness services and employment programmes.

the largest share of the population in metropolitan regions are Spain (69.2 %), Denmark (69.0 %), Germany (67.5 %), the UK (66.2 %) and France (65.6 %)—predominantly the western part of the EU. (Eurostat 2018 quoted according to EPRS 2019)

How are such metropolitan areas governed? The *OECD Metropolitan Governance Survey*, conducted in 2014 across the globe in *OECD* countries in 263 metropolitan areas with more than 500 thousand inhabitants, explored three categories: metro areas with strong coordination by inter-municipal authorities, supra-municipal authorities or metropolitan cities; with weak informal/soft coordination; or with no coordination at all. The results show that these categories have roughly equal 1/3 share in *OECD* countries. (OECD 2014)

RESEARCH RESULTS ABOUT METROPOLITAN AREAS

Regarding the functional aspects of cooperation, very different types of links can be observed between the core city and its neighbouring municipalities. European cities differ substantially in this regard, as the following research results show.

In 2012, the *Eurocities Metropolitan Areas Working Group* collected information about the different territorial collaboration forms around 40 European cities. The *Metropolitan Areas in Action* survey has shown that in the majority of cities there are no institutions or strong collaborations existing in the spatial level of the functional urban area (row B in Table 1). In those, roughly one third, of the cities which came close to have some metropolitan cooperation (columns 4-5 in Table 1), two types of mismatch have been identified: cities where the metropolitan areas have governance structures but miss the strongest functions (cell B-4); and cities, which have strong strategic territorial cooperation but this does not cover the whole territory of the functional area (cell A-5). To handle these problems, cities in the position of B-4 need to achieve 'functional expansion', while cities in the position of A-5 need to achieve a "territorial adjustment". In order to achieve such steps, bold and conscious public policies are needed, which can hardly be achieved without the support of the regional and national level. (EUROCITIES 2013)

In 2018, the *Metropolitan Research Institute Budapest* carried out a systematic analysis of the governance systems of six innovative European metropolitan areas for the *Àrea Metropolitana Barcelona* (Gerőházi-Tosics 2018). The cases of Barcelona, Manchester and Stuttgart have shown that metropolitan level coordination might be achieved one the one hand by institutionalization, by establishing a metropolitan organization with independent functions and competencies, either as a new territorial government level or in the form of a strong institutional setting, on a fixed territorial basis with a sufficiently large range of competences. Another approach, illustrated by the cases of Amsterdam, Copenhagen and Zurich is procedural approach, building on collaboration and planning processes and agreements, which allow for coordinated activities within a sufficiently large metropolitan territory, although not necessarily in fixed territorial constellations. This second model is similar to the perception of *New Regionalism* (Kunc et al. 2021), focusing on voluntary cooperation, informal networking, and integration—for more details see e.g. the *ESPON SPIMA* project (ESPON 2018).

These two approaches are very different but not mutually exclusive, and elements of the other appear in both approaches. For example, the key element of the procedural approach is strategic and spatial planning, which is also an important aspect in the institutional approach, and vice versa: even though the existence of a strong institutional structure on the metropolitan level is specific to the institutional approach, the functional approach also strives for some forms of institutions, although in a much more flexible way. ▸

Procedural metropolitan coordination			Institutionalized metropolitan coordination		
Amsterdam	**Copenhagen**	**Zurich**	**Greater Manchester**	**Stuttgart**	**Barcelona**
2.4 million inhabitants, 33 municipalities (2015)	2 million inhabitants, 34 municipalities one third of the national population	1.9 million inhabitants (2006), 238 municipalities one fifth of the national population	2.7 million inhabitants (2011), 10 boroughs	2.7 million inhabitants, 179 municipalities one quarter of the population of Baden-Württemberg	3.2 million inhabitants, 36 municipalities (AMB) 43% of the population of Catalonia
Informal, no representation worked out	No organisation	Each municipality + 8 cantons at the Metropolitan Conference, 8 representatives by the cantons and 8 by the municipalities: Metropolitan Council	Greater Manchester Combined Authority Councillors of the 10 boroughs are the council members + directly elected mayor	Region Stuttgart Directly elected members of the Assembly (election based on party lists)	AMB Àrea Metropolitana de Barcelona Metropolitan Council with 90 metropolitan councillors (weighted representation)
Forum for bi- and multi-lateral negotiations	Strong spatial plan (Finger Plan) elaborated on national level	Spatial planning. Lobbying towards the central government. Pilot projects with metropolitan relevance	Public transport and highways, spatial planning, economic development, police, waste management, health care coordination, funds in social and housing topics	Public transport. Spatial planning. Economic development. Branding	Public transport, territorial planning, urban planning. Common services: water, waste, environment, slightly social and hosuing issues
No budget	No budget	Appr. 0.9 million EUR	Appr. 340 million EUR with direct competencies, about 2,2 billion EUR with all common services (in addition controls different funds and national sources)	Appr. 350 million EUR	P684 million EUR for the metropolitan administration (AMB); 1,7 billion EUR with all the metropolitan companies and institutions

Table 2: Main information about metropolitan areas of six European cities: population, governance system, functions and budget

In an abstract form, the dynamism of metropolitan development in growing urban areas can be outlined as follows. Collaborations develop in procedural way beyond the border of the administrative city through networking, and common activities like planning and marketing. After a time these collaborations achieve a form of institutionalization, covering a certain metropolitan area with new competences devolved to the new institution, mostly by national legislation. After a while the area of the new institutional arrangements proves again to be too small compared to real economic processes and a new process of procedural collaboration building starts on a new and enlarged metropolitan scale (sometimes, as in case of Amsterdam and Copenhagen, with the parallel "downgrading" of the former competencies in the former metropolitan area). This might again lead to an act of institutionalization on the larger territorial level—and these steps follow until metropolitan expansion is feasible, or the enlarged area would cover too large a share of the upper governmental level (usually the administrative region).

Thus, the results of the study indicate that these two approaches, although being very different, are not exclusionary and might even follow each other in time in the development of metropolitan relations of given cities. Moreover, tackling the problems of a metropolitan area might require a combination of the institutional and the procedural approaches and the application of different tools at the same time. Two recent *ESPON* studies also dealt with the topic of metropolitan areas. *ESPON SPIMA* (2016-17) explored the spatial dynamics and strategic planning in metropolitan areas, while *ESPON MISTA* (2019-20) tackled the relationship between industry and the city. Vienna was part of both projects as one of the stakeholder cities that initiated the research work.

METROPOLITAN EXAMPLES—COMPARABLE TO THE VIENNA SITUATION

When looking for comparative city examples, which can be relevant for Vienna, the most important characteristic of the city has to be taken into account. This is—besides being a large, monofunctional urban area—its administrative status: Vienna is a local muncipality and state at the same time. This is a quite special situation, with some advantages but also disadvantages. In such cases, cities have strong functions because they are also states/regions/provinces/cantons. On the other hand these cities have usually very limited possibilities for procedural cooperation beyond their borders, as this would need cross-regional agreements with the other municipalities.

From the earlier mentioned research projects the cities which can be considered as comparative cases to Vienna are Berlin (city and state), Zurich (city and canton), Turin (city and province), Prague (city and region). All these cities constitute monofunctional urban areas and their "metropolitan stories" carry important messages for Vienna.

Berlin: Although in 1996 a popular referendum rejected the idea to merge Berlin with the surrounding Brandenburg, as a remnant of the unification efforts there is a joint planning authority existing for the two states. Also a common spatial development plan covers the entire area of the two states, although creating only a vague framework for manufacturing land use and locations. At a more local level a municipal neighbourhood forum exists with 4 informal working groups (North, South, East, West). They comprise the boroughs of Berlin and their bordering municipalities, having no formal power They meet three times a year ▸

and in addition hold an annual conference where a specific topic is discussed in depth. So far the municipal neighbourhood forums have been paid exclusively by Berlin, while now there is a plan to turn these institutions into a registered non-profit organization and to require all its members to pay a small membership fee (of € 0,1 per inhabitant). This step would increase the stability of the organisation as it would then have a legal basis and formal statute, and the commitment of the involved partners would increase.

Zurich: The cooperation between the cities and the surrounding areas was very problematic in Switzerland and urban sprawl was an increasing problem. To fight this problem, the Swiss government defined metropolitan areas of the country and prescribed mandatory cooperation within them. One of these areas is the *Zurich Metropolitan Association*, including 1,9 million people in 8 cantoons and 122 settlements, with Zurich (415.000 people) being the center. It took 7 years to build up the cooperation, which includes agreement on the regulation of growth and how to compensate those areas whose growth is limited. The agreement was achieved on the informal level of the planning conference of the 8 cantons, whose resolution is not binding, but will be gradually adopted by the 8 cantons which make binding decisions. Those cantons that do not implement the resolutions of the planning conference risk having their cantonal plan approved by the federal government. In this way, strategic spatial planning initiated by the national is used as meta-governance tool.

Turin: The Italian government established 14 Metropolitan Cities by a National Act in 2014, by merging the cities with their surrounding provinces. Turin Metropolitan City thus comprises 316 municipalities. It is the most unbalanced among all metropolitan cities, as it has a large mountainous area with no links to the city. The metropolitan strategic plan sets the guidelines for metropolitan development in the entirw territory. It is mandatory, has a duration of three years, but is updated annually. It has to be approved by the Metropolitan Council and the Mayors Assembly of the 11 homogeneous zones of the metropolitan city. The 316 municipalities are developing their General Urban Plans, which must be in compliance with the metropolitan plans. These plans are a key instrument in Italy, allowing municipalities to designate land-uses for a ten-year period.

Prague: The city is a *NUTS3* region, surrounded by the Central Moravian region. The cooperation across the city border has always been a huge problem. For the 2014-2020 European funding programme, the Czech Republic has chosen to use the *Integrated Territorial Investment (ITI)* funding instrument on a metropolitan level. A national proposal for the delienation of the seven largest metropolitan areas and six smaller urban areas was elaborated. This national *ITI* framework provides a guideline for the development of the *ITI* programming documents, the operation of the managing authority and the secretariat, and on the calls for proposals. The Prague delineation of the *ITI*-based metropolitan covers 515 settlements (315 as inner ring, 199 as outer ring). A strategy has been prepared for this area, containing only those issues that can be covered by EU funds both in Prague (a "more developed region" in EU cohesion terms) and Central Bohemia ("a less developed region"). Consequently, the strategy focuses on three topics: transport and mobility, environment and the regional education system. Prague *ITI* has a funding of €145 million and 85% of the *ITI* funds must be used outside of the capital, in the less developed areas. The working group, which participated in the preparation of the *ITI* and takes part in preparing the calls for proposals and the evaluation processes, consists of representatives of both Prague and the region.

Of the four cities discussed, Turin can be considered as belonging to the institutional model, Zurich to the procedual model, while Berlin and Prague are mixed cases, with only partial metropolitan institutions. In each of them some kind of metropolitan coordination can be observed, although such cooperation has to be establised not only across the city border but also across regional borders. To overcome this difficulty, some kind of intervention of the national government was needed in each case.

CONCLUSION: THE IMPORTANCE OF METROPOLITAN COOPERATION AND THE CASE OF VIENNA

In view of the growing challenges and threats (such as climate change, demographic change, and the recent sudden crises such as the pandemic and the energy crisis), territorial cooperation in large urban areas is more important than ever to ensure sustainability and resilience of future development. Besides efforts from below, democratic and inclusive national policies are needed, led by progressive national governments that consider the cities as allies, not enemies, in the steering of future development.

The city examples discussed suggest that Vienna might develop different ideas for metropolitan cooperation. It could aim at strengthening the neighbourhood forums and trying to initiate a joint planning body (as in the Berlin example). It could pursue a joint planning conference with the surrounding region (as in the Zurich example). It could seek an *ITI*-type coordinated development with the functional urban area (as in the Prague example). The Turin example is probably the least relevant, as it would need a decision by the central government to merge the surrounding administrative units with the city.

It is a fact that the federal structure of Austria is very strong, which means that all these options for cooperation within the Vienna metropolitan area would need a strong support, even an initiative of the central government, directly or indirectly enforcing the cooperation between Vienna and Lower Austria regarding the metropolitan area. At the moment, however, there is no indication that the Austrian government would take steps to support metropolitan cooperations across the regional borders.

So is it totally hopeless for Vienna to come up with metropolitan ideas along the lines of the European examples discussed? Probably not, as the urgency to become carbon neutral and the recent EU efforts to reach the ambitious goals of the *Green New Deal*, the *Fit for 55* and the *Farm to Fork* strategies (just to name a few) would all require stronger collaborations across metropolitan areas. This might also lead to a change in the Austrian national position, which could in turn create better opportunities for metropolitan cooperation in the Vienna metropolitan area.

Until this change happens, Vienna has to strive for "cooperation from below", aiming to strengthen the functional, procedural links to the neighbouring municipalities. The city examples analysed in this article might provide a good basis for such efforts.▪

Cross-border spatial development. Informal planning strategies between Maas and Rhine

Christa Reicher—Department of Urban Planning and Design at RWTH Aachen University

Cities and regions worldwide are facing comprehensive transformation processes: social and demographic change, climate change, digitization or new technologies are the major challenges. If we want to shape transformation in a sustainable way, we need to "consume" significantly less land, develop smart concepts for spatial development on a regional scale, and overcome the boundaries between municipalities and states—in other words, transcend existing boundaries at all levels.

Formal planning with its instruments will no longer be able to answer these challenges in the future. In some cases, it is not dynamic enough and does not provide the vivid images needed to communicate with local people. Against this background, informal planning concepts and strategies, such as those we are testing between the Rhine and the Meuse, are of central importance.

THE AGGLOMERATION CONCEPT OF THE COLOGNE/BONN METROPOLITAN REGION

The agglomeration concept of the *Cologne/Bonn Metropolitan Region* has created a common spatial image of the region until 2040. The region is currently facing a variety of challenges in spatial development and will continue to do so in the coming years.

The demands for use arising from demographic developments, a shortage of development areas, mobility problems, and the demands of the energy transition and climate change, which come together in a confined space, interact with each other and, in some cases, compete with each other.

In an intensive dialogue with the stakeholders in the region, a spatial image has been developed that shows a balanced spatial condition. Building on a strong open space framework, the settlement and mobility structure forms the starting point for sustainable spatial development. Residential and commercial areas are developed along future rail lines. The principle of polycentricity in the form of a division of functions and tasks in the region forms the basis for the perspective spatial development of the agglomeration.

INTEGRATED SPATIAL STRATEGY PROCESS 2038+ IN RHENISH MINING DISTRICT

With the political decision to phase out lignite mining at an early stage by 2038 at the latest, the transformation region of western Germany, the Rhenish mining area in the triangle of cities between Aachen, Mönchengladbach, Düsseldorf and Cologne, is facing enormous social, economic and design challenges. The "largest landscape construction site in Europe" is to become—according to the claim and the objective—the first climate-neutral model region in Europe.

A total of 2.4 million people live in the Rhenish mining region and are affected to varying degrees by structural change. In order to organize this structural change, the *Zukunftsagentur Rheinisches Revier (ZRR)* was founded as a joint platform and pioneer for the transformation process. The state of North Rhine-Westphalia has given the *Future Agency* the task of managing the process of structural change. The *Revierknoten* with their respective chairmen accompany and shape the future issues. In a first step, the district node chairmen and their teams played a key role in drafting the economic and structural program and thus provided the guidelines for the operational implementation of structural change. Structural change does not start from zero. In recent years, many initiatives and projects have already been initiated that show new perspectives for regional value creation and also innovative approaches to a possible spatial future.

In the medium to long term, the combination of the three opencast mines—Inden, Hambach and Garzweiler—will create a Rhenish lake landscape. The *Integrated Spatial Strategy 2038+*, which was launched in an intensive regional discourse, takes up the development potentials and talents of the region and derives spatial future paths from them. The spatial strategy is thus a central building block for mastering this "structural change task of the century".

The spatial strategy process is divided into three stages: In stage 1, the most urgent requirements for action and issues are identified and a spatial description of the initial situation and interdependencies in the region is drawn up. On this basis, interdisciplinary planning teams will develop visions for the spatial development of the Rhenish mining area in stage 2. The aim is to present the broadest possible spectrum of solutions, projects, scenarios and necessary actions and to discuss these with regional stakeholders.

Finally, in stage 3, the results from the previous work phases, the existing preliminary work and the discourse with the region will be brought together in an integrated manner in the *Integrated Spatial Strategy 1.0*. In addition, this process design must be cleverly linked with the stakeholders involved—municipalities, associations, initiations, people—on the one hand and with formal planning, regional planning, on the other.

ZL'EU—SPATIAL STRATEGY ZUID-LIMBURG IN THE EUREGIONAL CONTEXT

The challenges of spatial development are similar beyond the borders. The Netherlands and Germany are facing urgent tasks that play an important role locally, nationally and globally. The tasks concern climate change, the energy transition, the circular economy, infrastructure, mobility, health and housing.

With the cross-border spatial strategy, the *ZL'EU* project forms a basis for cooperation between the *Regio Parkstad Limburg* and the *Städteregion Aachen*. It helps to exploit opportunities and remove obstacles that citizens and businesses face when it comes to living, working, redesigning and experiencing culture across borders. The project also aims to strengthen the euregional mindset of citizens and businesses by organizing and supporting accessible, cross-border participation formats around integrated planning.

PRELIMINARY INSIGHTS

» Successful management of structural change can only succeed if there is a vision of the new.
» A successful transformation process will be measured by how economic performance and a high quality of life and space are intertwined and what synergy effects they will generate.
» If the region is to make a real quantum leap, every single project must meet at least two requirements: pursue the highest design ambitions and generate impulse effects.
» The region can only develop into a model region with international perception and appeal if it has the courage to test and implement innovative solutions. ▪

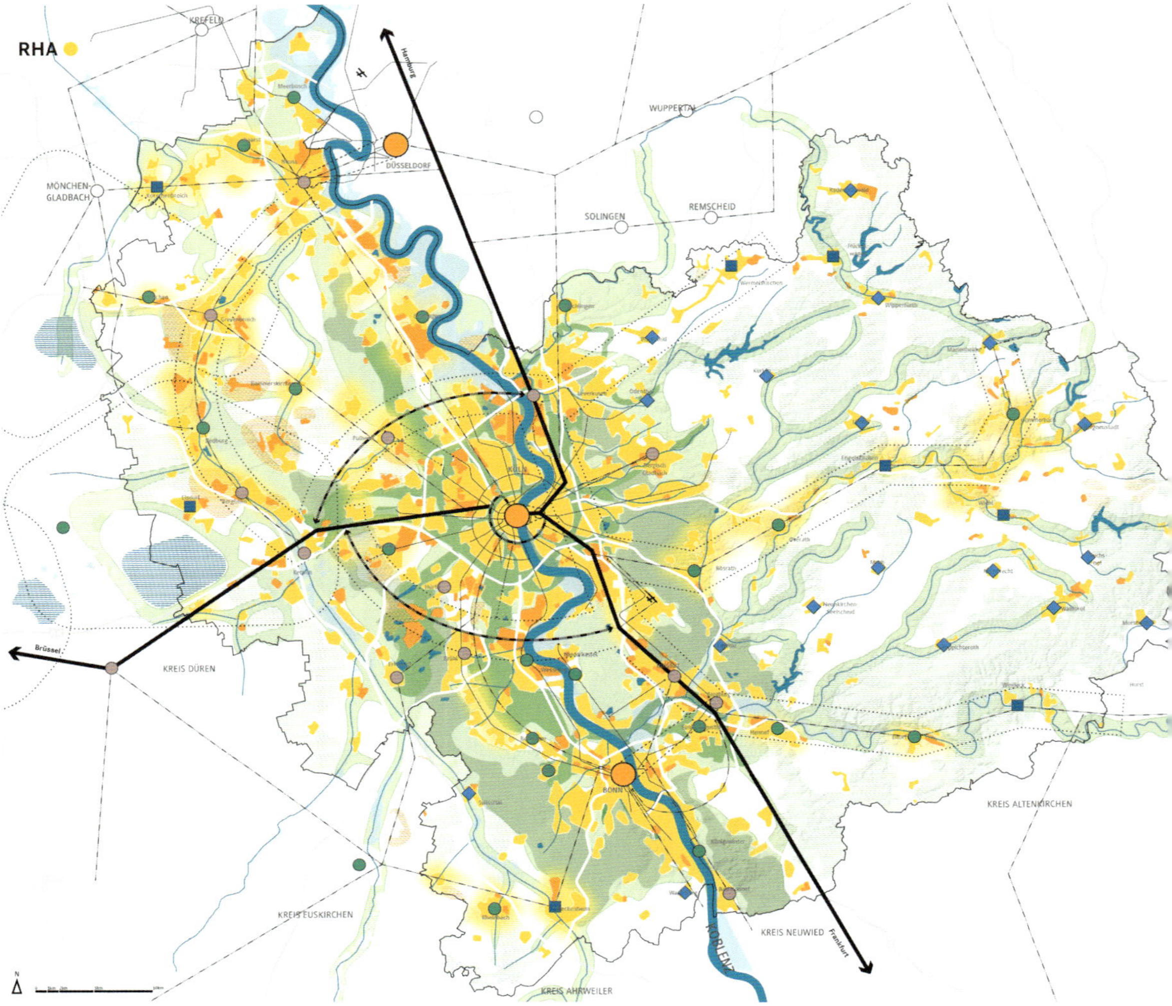

Figure 1: Preliminary Draft of the Regional Structure Plan 2040+ of the Cologne/Bonn Region, © RHA REICHER HAASE ASSOCIATE, Aachen

Legend

- Regional Open Space Network
- Open Space System Rhine Rail (*Rheinschiene*)
- Forest Corridor
- Unfragmented Spaces
- Regional Water Network
- Lakeland
- Settlement Area
- Search Area Settlement Development
- Commercial & Industrial Areas
- Search Area Commercial & Industrial Areas
- Regional Development Areas
- Highway
- Regional Rail Network
- City Rail Network
- Main Traffic Axis (supraregional)
- Metropolitan Cores
- Urban Centers
- Urban Candidates
- Regional Centers of Gravity
- Development Anchors

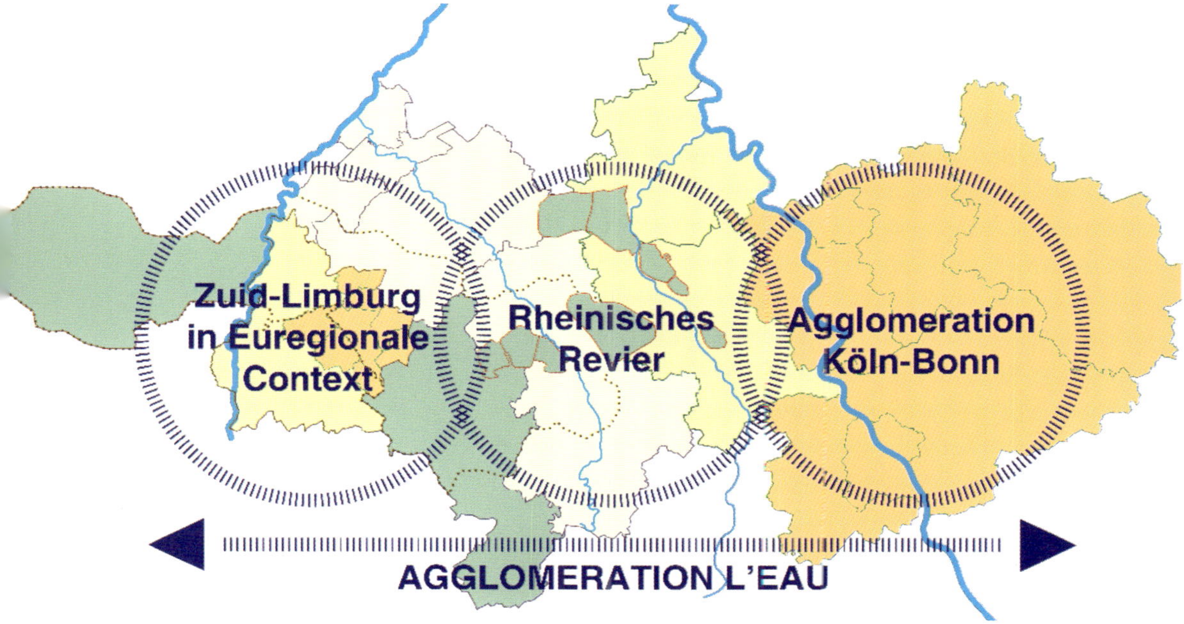

Figure 2: Spatial Overview of the three Regions between Rhine and Meuse, © Department of Urban Design /RWTH Aachen

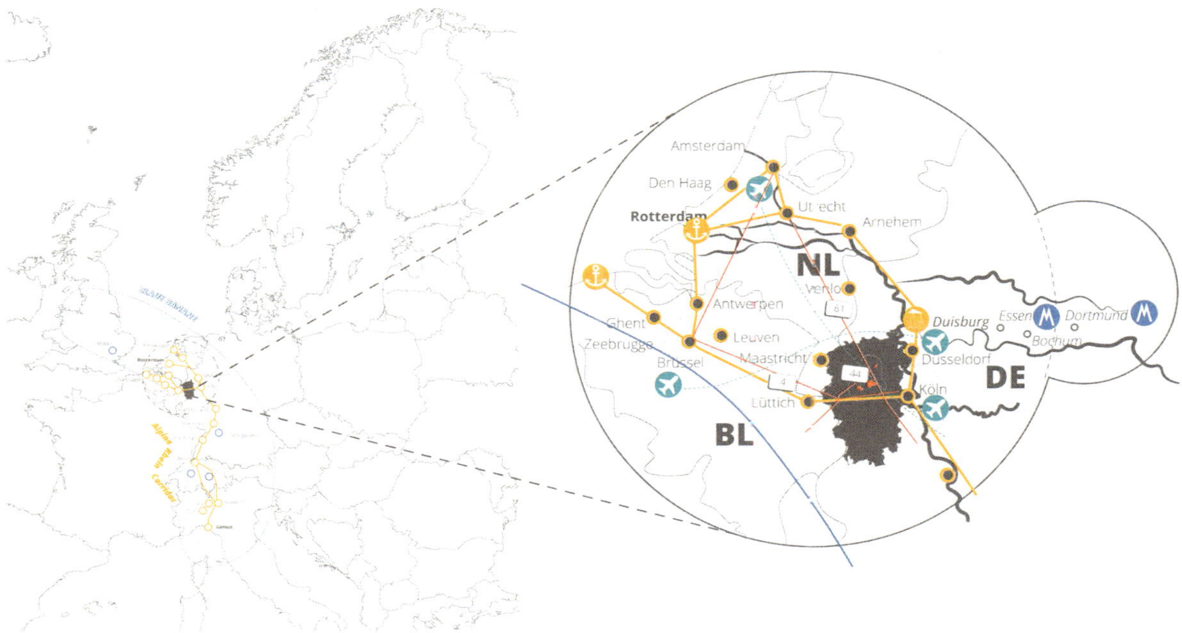

Figure 3: The Region in Context, © Department of Urban Design /RWTH Aachen

Iván Tosics,
Metropolitan Research
Institute, Budapest

Paul Gerretsen
Deltametropolis
Association, Rotterdam

Judith Recio Heredia,
URBACT-RiConnect,
Àrea Metropolitana de Barcelona

Gilles Pinson
Institute of Political Science
at Science Po Bordeaux

Christa Reicher
Institute for Urban Design
at RWTH Aachen

DISCUSSING THE NEW ROLE OF METROPOLITAN AREAS

We should focus more on a common narrative about what we are as a metropolis

Forum Discussion

In the face of rapid urbanization, which poses administrative, socio-economic and environmental challenges to all city-regions of the world, the panel discussion on the new role of metropolitan areas looked at what makes a integrated and well-programmed metropolis. For example, to what extent should its development and organization be institutionalized, and which key thematic areas require cross-border management through interregional cooperation? In this context, what co-creative potential can be mobilized in metropolitan planning and what does this consequently mean for metropolitan governance?

In the Vienna metropolitan area, especially in the economic field, it has proven successful to tackle new challenges from different angles and to join forces in the process, Eva Czernohorszky reflects regarding the international examples presented. As director of *Technology Services of the Vienna Business Agency*, she positively highlights the dynamic development of the innovation ecosystem, which is largely due to Vienna's economic strategy, which she helped to shape:

> *"I appreciated that the idea was not to write a smart paper that is taken as a reference for decisions, but to establish routines for collaboration and coordination."*
> *Eva Czernohorszky*

This approach has resulted in 70 multi-stakeholder lighthouse projects which serve as good practices in economic metropolitan development.

In other sectors however, the collaborative spirit seems to be less prominent. While, for example, in the manufacturing industry, cooperation across federal state borders in the search for the optimal location for a business has become quite common, the way housing is dealt with varies greatly from one administrative unit to another. According to Bernhard Steger, the *City of Vienna* represents a city with a very high level of competence, but little experience in inter-municipal cooperation. Therefore, the *Head of Department for District Planning and Land Use Central-Southwest* emphasizes that,

> *"We should focus more on a common narrative about what we are as a metropolis and what we want to stand for on a national and international level."*
> *Bernhard Steger*

Even though cross-border visions have become indispensable in individual sectors, for example in the area of economic and location development or transport, there is no general understanding of why an overall metropolitan approach might be necessary in the Vienna region, says Johannes Suitner, who represents the *Research Unit of Urban and Regional Studies at the Institute of Spatial Planning* at *TU Wien*:

> *"I think there is a lack of problematization of why this territorial scale necessitates some kind of common action."*
> *Johannes Suitner*

From a scientific point of view, it is not least the sustainability transformation of the Vienna city region that makes a stronger focus on the metropolitan scale indispensable, he argues. Against the background of his recent research, which focuses not only on strategic agency in the field of energy transition and climate adaptation, but also on the role of experimental approaches and social innovation for urban development, he emphasizes the importance of narratives of change and imaginaries of sustainable urban futures. These can, for example, encourage the development of experimental governance projects that position themselves at the intersection of typical bureaucratic planning and radical artistic projects. Bernhard Steger agrees that the right balance has to be found between the pragmatic formalized approach of the city administration and informal, co-creative ways of working together. They do not have to be mutually exclusive, because, as Suitner points out: *"It's not about either or. I think you can take a procedural approach as a planner with resources we have in the Business Agency, the administration and all the intermediary bodies and still be successful in co-creating the metro-region."* Andreas Hacker, manager of the *Stadt-Umland-Management (SUM) Vienna/Lower Austria*, has a clear position on the question of whether cooperation within the metropolitan area should be institutionalized. Even though he highlights best-practice examples of city-regional cooperation, such as in Hanover, he nevertheless criticizes the lack of space for creativity and innovation. Compared to other Austrian institutions, such as the *Verkehrsverbund Ostregion*, as an important association for city-regional public transport, the marketing association *VIENNA REGION* or the *Planungsgemeinschaft Ost (PGO)* with its special treaty between Vienna, Lower Austria and Burgenland, he and his long-time colleague Renate Zuckerstätter have always been quite free in shaping their daily work. Even though they only have a modest budget at their disposal, the *SUM* has had a lasting impact on the development of the city region over the past decades. As the composition of the stakeholders and the focus topics of the region have constantly changed, their job description has been adapted accordingly, Andreas Hacker says:

> ***"Our job is that of a networker or mediator, we offer a platform for communication."***
> *Andreas Hacker*

Therefore, being in contact with so many different stakeholders and partners, credibility is a very important point, he emphasizes. It is also of utmost importance to be able to communicate on different levels, because when talking to mayors and citizens, it is not only technical language that is needed.

Finally, in a concluding round, his colleague Renate Zuckerstätter argues: *"When we talk about an institution, we must first ask what it is supposed to be good for. What is the function of this institution, which is then followed by a certain form?"* Regardless of what form a metropolitan organization might take, the panelists agreed that such an institution should address not only issues of economic development, attractiveness, and innovation, but also issues of social segregation and environmental inequalities. Furthermore, there was a broad consensus that joint projects, especially in "soft" thematic areas such as green space development, are a good way to initiate inter-municipal metropolitan cooperation processes and thus create a starting point for further projects. Nevertheless, especially when it comes to "hard" strategic issues such as large-scale industrial transformations or urban growth, it is crucial to create incentives for cooperation mechanisms between settlements and at the same time raise awareness among the population for integrated metropolitan development. This could be the starting point for metropolitan planning as a new discipline. ▪

Andreas Hacker
SUM South, Metropolitan
Area Management
Vienna/Lower Austria

Eva Czernohorszky
Technology Services,
Vienna Business Agency

Bernhard Steger
District Planning and Land Use,
MA 21 A, City of Vienna

Scan to watch the documentation of the International Lectures and the Forum Discussion!

Johannes Suitner
Institute of Spatial Planning,
TU Wien

KEY FINDINGS ON THE NEW ROLE OF METROPOLITAN AREAS

1. UNDERSTAND METROPOLITAN AREAS AS FUNCTIONAL UNITS

Raising the question of the new role of metropolitan areas means at the same time having to take a closer look at the functionality of these complex spaces. As cities increasingly spread beyond their political and administrative borders, leading to the emergence of functionally intertwined city-regions, the city-regional approach becomes key to providing integrated solutions to current spatial development challenges. Above all, the sustainability transformation of city regions worldwide makes a stronger focus on the metropolitan level indispensable. Whether economic or settlement development, landscape and nature conservation or major infrastructural concerns—a multitude of interests requires a supra-local perspective that acknowledges the metropolitan area as a functional unit. For example, water management, energy transition, shifting transportation to more sustainable modes, or even small-scale climate adaptation strategies address extensive functional interconnections and spatial relations and thus require intensive cooperation.

2. FINDING A COMMON SENSE IS THE KEY TO COLLABORATION

There is no doubt that excellent solutions are needed for cross-border cooperation and interregional collaboration in the sense of an integrated metropolitan area or smart city region, where the core city and its surrounding area are thought together. But there is often a lack of inter-sectoral, cross-border visions that could spark the imagination of decision-makers and citizens. It is therefore of utmost importance that as many stakeholders as possible develop a common sense to drive joint projects forward. This can be achieved, for example, by emphasizing narratives of change and imaginaries of sustainable urban futures that encourage the development of experimental (governance) projects which position themselves at the intersection of typic bureaucratic planning and radical artistic projects. Niche experiments can stimulate local creativity, which in turn promotes self-efficacy. Meaning that people and regions that have had the experience of being able to influence and shape their own future can contribute greatly to the resilience of metropolitan regions.

3. PROJECT-BASED PLANNING AND INFORMALITY ENABLE STRONG COOPERATIONS

Building niches and developing micro-utopias through actor-supportive planning is an essential element in co-creating change, e.g. by making metropolitan action visible and tangible. Once a common sense of purpose is found, procedural models of planning that use a variety of small steps to show a perspective path can be of great value. This favours project-based planning rather than large-scale programmes, as well as a certain informality of processes and the formation of project-based collaborations. Compared to "hard topics", such as large-scale infrastructural redesigns, "soft topics", such as green space development or ecosystem conservation can serve as a starting point for such cross-border cooperation. For example, by preserving natural recreational areas and their biodiversity, or by promoting the circular economy, innovation can be made possible in the long term and endogenous potential can be mobilized. Moreover, project-based work is much easier if it is done in cooperation with people who trust each other and in an informal way, instead of institutionalizing it.

4. GOOD GOVERNANCE DEPENDS ON THE RIGHT DEGREE OF INSTITUTIONALIZATION

Before establishing new institutions, metropolitan areas need to overcome political inconsistencies and the lack of political will to work together. In most cases, the right balance must be found between the pragmatic, formalized approach of city administrations and informal, co-creative forms of cooperation. While positively perceived issues such as the development of recreational areas can serve as an impulse or "low hanging fruit" to informally start joint projects, tackling cross-border projects is more difficult when it comes to more unpopular topics such as settlement development. While informal, small-scale institutionalized networks often increase credibility and trust among stakeholders, much also depends on the commitment of individuals, such as individual mayors or parties. Increasingly, voices are being raised calling not only for smooth and discreet forms of metropolitan cooperation to avoid conflict, but also to let people participate in strategic issues. "Form follows function" is becoming an important principle when it comes to finding the right degree of institutionalization.

5. INCENTIVES AT NATIONAL LEVEL CAN PROMOTE COMMON VISIONS AND STRATEGIES

Even if it is difficult to realize real co-creative vision building processes, through which users actually develop strategies and projects together with planners or politicians on a national scale, it is this scale level that should be given more attention. Countries such as France or Poland show that incentives, such as tax benefits, can be provided at the national level to motivate spatially separated entities such as municipalities to cooperate with each other. EU funding initiatives are also increasingly helpful in this regard. Only if the lack of metropolitan governance is addressed in ongoing discussions can persistent political structures be loosened, and systemic obstacles overcome to pursue shared visions and strategies. This benefits not only the integration of different spatial areas (cooperation among neighbouring municipalities, urban and peri-urban areas), but also the integration of and dialogue between different government levels. ▪

PROJECTS

RiCONNECT
RETHINKING INFRASTRUCTURE

TirolCITY

ZERO CARBON CITY REGION

SUPERWIEN METROPOLE

PLACECITY FLORIDSDORF VIENNA

URBAN DESIGN LAB

PRODUKTIVE STADTLANDSCHAFTEN
BERLIN BRANDENBURG 2070

REVITALISATION DU CENTRE BOURG

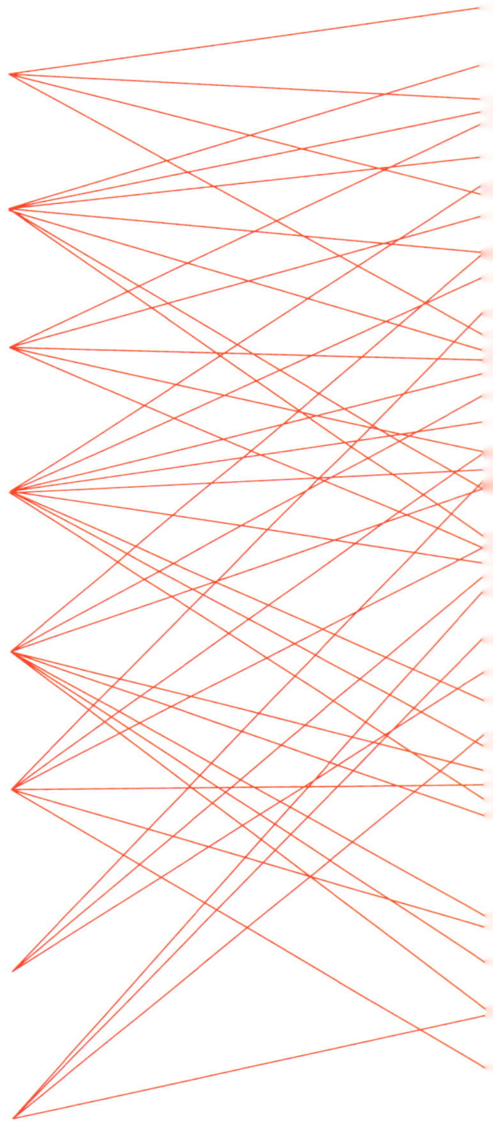

TOOLS FOR METROPOLITAN PLANNING

DATA MINING

FILMING

MAPPING

EXPLORATIVE WALKS

PHOTOGRAPHING

STAKEHOLDER MAPPING

VISIONARY MAPS

EXPERT INTERVIEWS

ONLINE EXHIBITION

TRAVELING EXHIBITION

ART INSTALLATIONS

MOVIE NIGHT

FORUM DISCUSSION

DESIGN STUDIO

OPEN CALL

URBAN LIVING LAB

WALKSHOP

LOCAL ACTION

PROGRAMMING THE LOCAL SCALE

To bring the metropolitan vision to a realistic and feasible level and initiate joint action, the local level is of particular relevance. Integrated local action is needed for specific sites, bringing together different stakeholders. Following an integrated and multisectoral planning approach, integrated action plans enable new developments and create place-based solutions. Through the temporary intervention of a Travelling Exhibition in public space, the local community is engaged in the discourse on metropolitan planning and design. In the frame of Regional Dialogues, planning officials and political decision makers are co-creatively developing new ideas on future development paths and organizational forms, according to their specific spatial context. Dialogue-oriented workshops stimulate local empowerment and capacity building. In Design Studios, the spatial, ecological, and economic situation of individual focus areas within the metropolitan region is addressed and different development scenarios and design solutions are put up for discussion by students.

CONVEY NEW IDEAS AND INITIATE DISCUSSION

Travelling Exhibition

The *SuperWien Metropole* envisions the city region Vienna-Bratislava-Wiener Neustadt as a new capital of Europe. In the European context, it acts as an instrument for the creation of a strong metropolitan region and at the same time addresses the global status of the region, manages its growth and defines its image and social concept.
The travelling exhibition *SuperWien Metropole* conveys new ideas for this city region, guiding further spatial planning. The visionary images focus primarily on the need for stronger regional governance and consider the region's history and location at the center of Europe. They highlight new possibilities that will allow the *SuperWien Metropole* to regain the international status it lost in the 20th century and define its new role in the future. The site-specific intervention provides interesting insights into the morphological and functional development of the Vienna metropolitan region and poses provocative questions about its future development. With formative conceptual graphics, the travelling exhibition generates new images of the Vienna - Bratislava - Wiener Neustadt city region. By travelling to various locations in the metropolitan area, where it was on display in different public spaces, the exhibition encouraged interaction and initiated a joint discussion with the interested public.

Travelling Exhibition in Liesing

SuperWien
phenomena

about MetroLab
The MetroLab is a metropolitan Think Tank and consulting service for the integrated urban development of metropolitan areas and city regions. It introduces participative, integrative and creative-artistic elements and develops innovative metropolitan strategies as well as place-based solutions. Based on a co-creative and dialogue-oriented planning and design approach it fosters not only placemaking interventions, but also the transfer of cutting-edge knowledge in creative urban planning and bureaucracy.
Between October 2020 and June 2021, the MetroLab is organizing four International Forums to stimulate a discourse on specific topics of metropolitan planning.
Das MetroLab ist ein Think Tank und Consulting Service für die Entwicklung von Metropolen und Stadtregionen. Mit partizipativen, integrativen und kreativ-künstlerischen Elementen werden innovative metropolitane Strategien sowie ortsbezogene Lösungen entwickelt. Basierend auf einem co-kreativen und dialogorientierten Planungs- und Gestaltungsansatz fördert das MetroLab nicht nur Placemaking- Interventionen, sondern auch den Transfer von neuestem Wissen in kreativer Stadtplanung und Verwaltung.
Zwischen Oktober 2020 und Juni 2021 veranstaltet das MetroLab vier internationale Dialogforen, die den Diskurs zu spezifisch
Themen der Metropolenplanung anregen.
METROLAB
FORUM
International Dialogue on Metropolitan Planning
OCT 12 & 13 2020
#1 METRO
What is the future of metropolitan mobility?
NOV 02 & 03 2020
#2 GROWTH
How to manage urban growth?
OCT 04 & 05 2021
#3 DELTA
Can metropolitan landscapes become resilient?
NOV 08 & 09 2021
#4 PROGRAMME
What is the new role of metropolitan areas?
METROLAB
SUPERWIEN
COCO
SUPERWIEN
METROPOLE

Impressions of the Travelling Exhibition in Liesing and Mödling

The Travelling Exhibition contains a QR code leading to an online survey

SuperWien
phenomena
metropolitan
vision
Male

STRENGTHENING INTER-MUNICIPAL PLANNING INSTRUMENTS AND COOPERATION

Regional Dialogues

To stimulate local planning processes in the Vienna metropolitan area, regional dialogues were held in cooperation with relevant planning officials and political decision-makers at different levels, from municipal to district level. These expert dialogues, held in the municipality of Gerasdorf, the district of Mödling and the Römerland Carnuntum region aimed to discuss the potentials and development opportunities of the respective focus area within the metropolitan region. The following questions were addressed: From which development impulses of these focus areas can the city region benefit and how can they help shape the future of the metropolis? What are the opportunities and challenges of spatial development across municipal boundaries? And what steering instruments for the sustainable development of the city region can be derived from this?
Learning from these three examples, the regional dialogue serves as a valuable exchange of experience and knowledge and is an essential element in strengthening inter-municipal planning instruments and cooperation. The key findings resulting from the workshops were finally fed into the forum discussion on the new role of metropolitan regions.

Even though all three focus areas differ in size and in their thematic objectives, they have one fundamental aspect in common: They are all part of Vienna's functional area and therefore face similar challenges, which do not stop at administrative borders. The sooner inter-municipal cooperation turns from an abstract idea into an active joint development of cross-border solutions, the sooner we will be able to tackle far-reaching problems like the climate crisis. Even though most of the stakeholders involved agreed on this, the individual views differed on the exact path to be taken to make the metropolitan region fit for the future. How should the metropolitan region best be organized and who should steer it and in what precise way? What concrete projects and actions should be pursued to realize a common vision for the future of the city region?

To motivate municipalities to take long-term actions with concrete measures at the local level, without losing sight of the broader spatial context, the respective focus area was contextualized as part of the metropolitan region at the beginning of each workshop. After a brainstorming session on the definition of the terms "city region" and "metropolis", the specific identity and regional self-image of the respective space was discussed commonly. It was found that the term "metropolis" is often associated with suspicion and that the metropolis as a major international city with all its advantages of social and cultural density only seems to be meaningful

when the surrounding area also can benefit from its function as a centre, including economic interdependencies. “City region”, on the other hand, was understood as a softer term that foregrounds the functional interdependencies and advantages of polycentric structures and potential uses.
While the local identities and mentalities of the focus areas are quite diverse and the thematic priorities and challenges also differ from one another, the mapping session showed that they all represent a dynamic part of the metropolitan region with which they are strongly interlinked. Thus, common tasks for future intra-regional cooperation and possible forms of their organization and governance could be defined. The municipality of Gerasdorf, which has already gained versatile experience in cross-municipality cooperation in the implementation of the *Regionalpark DreiAnger*, for example, spoke in favour of further qualification of green spaces and coordinated qualitative settlement development. The development of densification zones along public transport axes and the strengthening of active and sustainable forms of mobility also resonated in the region of Römerland Carnuntum, where a focus is also placed on the preservation of important green and leisure spaces. In addition, in the Mödling district, which is characterized by large-scale business locations, major importance was attached to the joint reorganization of resources and logistics.

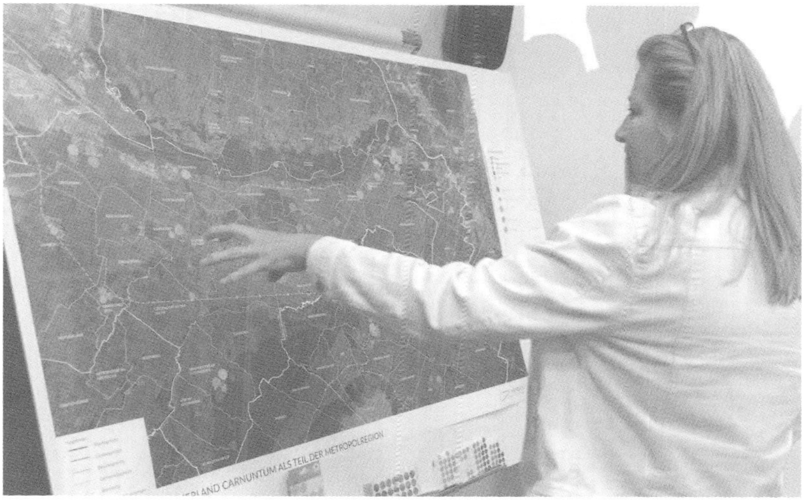

Regional Dialogues in Römerland Carnuntum, Gerasdorf and Mödling

Green incentives for cross-regional collaboration

Gerasdorf bei Wien

Gerasdorf bei Wien, which borders Vienna to the north is a municipality in the district of Korneuburg in Lower Austria and has 10.862 inhabitants in an area of 35.26 sq km. Today it consists of 5 historically grown villages (Angerdörfer), which on the one hand are characterized by old building fabric and on the other hand by newer single-family housing estates with trade and commercial enterprises. The municipality of Gerasdorf is mainly a residential area, whereby its good location and connection to Vienna make it a commuter town. Local recreation also play a significant role, as Gerasdorf is one of the three anchor points for the 3.000 ha *Regionalpark DreiAnger*, which stretches from the 21st district via Gerasdorf to the 22nd district and connects the landscape area Bisamberg with the future Norbert-Scheed-Forest. Thus, the regionalpark is a unique recreational area that extends across several municipalities and federal states and serves as best-practice example of successful supra-regional cooperation.

The Regional Dialogue, which took place in September 2021 in Gerasdorf bei Wien, started off by exploring the question of what makes Geasdorf unique compared to other areas in the Vienna metropolitan area. The participating local actors from politics, planning and administration described it as an "in-between town" that wants to become a city on the one hand and remain a village on the other, and as a place where the recreational areas of the *Regionalpark DreiAnger* are highly valued. It was also mentioned that the loss of the original identity of the area is a major challenge, that is accelerated by the influx of new residents and the departure of existing residents.

When asked about concrete ideas for a sustainable urban region, above all supra-regional mobility offers such as last mile concepts, expansions of the bike path network and bike rental systems were discussed. Furthermore, the preservation and mobilization of extensive green space structures as well as the coordination of settlement development and infrastructure for example through building land mobilization were debated.

As far as the future tasks of the city region are concerned, the mediation function between planning and administration as well as the task of persuasion and awareness building among the population and political actors were highlighted. Other important tasks such as the assurance of long-term stability, the development of the legal frameworks, identity building and sharpening, process and information management, and sustainable knowledge transfer were mainly discussed.

In the final debate on the question of how the city region can be organized in the future and which institutions are needed to manage it tall stakeholders agreed that the regionalpark can serve as a model and starting point for further cross-border cooperation processes, and to drive them forward, regional development structures with a joint management are necessary.

Reorganizing competencies with supra-regional significance

Concerns with supra-local and supra-regional appeal (e.g. in the area of local recreation, strategic land purchases) must increasingly be elevated to a higher level, which means re-negotiating responsibilities and competencies.

Strengthening awareness through intermediaries

In order to be able to accompany the city region into a sustainable future, regional driving forces in the form of committed persons or "caretakers" must be strengthened. They allow to mobilize concentrated forces within informal networks.

Setting up funding at EU or federal level

Long-term stability of regional development is to be ensured by platforms through which projects with a prospect of funding can be submitted.

Redefining responsibilities with the help of new institutions

Managing cross-border regional development must play a central role in the governance of the city-region. Which institution is best suited to do this remains to be negotiated: While a development agency could enable joint administration and stable management through municipal associations, a regional parliament with political responsibility would have the legitimacy to drive regional development agendas.

Organizing a metropolitan conference

A platform following the example of the metropolitan conference in Zurich should ensure exchange of information that represents the concerns of the metropolitan area at the federal level and promotes cooperation between municipalities, cities and even countries.

Rethinking metropolitan governance through cooperation

District of Mödling

The district of Mödling, which borders Vienna to the south, is an administrative district of the federal state of Lower Austria and has 119 240 inhabitants on an area of 277 sq km. The *Regional Master Plan of Mödling* (2016), structures the district into three functional sub-areas: the Wienerwald, the Southern Axis (Südachse) and the "Ebene". The more "rural" municipalities in Wienerwald in the west of the southern axis are characterized by high qualitive recreational areas and limited opportunities for expansion. The southern axis is dominated by more urban settlements, characterized by a high economic strength combined with a distinctive north-south infrastructural corridor, whose municipalities have largely reached their capacity limits. The again "rural" municipalities in the Ebene east of the southern axis stand out due to attractive housing, a lot of agricultural land as well as a strong population growth.

The Regional Dialogue took place in October 2021 in Mödling together with the *MetroLab* team and local stakeholders from local politics, planning and administration. When asked what makes the district of Mödling unique compared to other areas in the Vienna metropolitan area, the participants described it as a major link between the urban (Vienna) and the rural (Lower Austria) and as a place characterized by diversity. According to the stakeholders present, every place in Mödling is different in terms of demography, settlement pressure, infrastructural connectivity, and others, while in this diversity lie both challenges and potential. This diversity creates various areas of tension: on the one hand, there is a high quality of living and attractive local recreation areas, on the other hand, many municipalities are affected by heavy individual commuter traffic and high pollution levels. Many communities are also severely affected by high land consumption and rising housing prices due to the increased demand for peri-urban housing. In general, a lack of interaction in planning decisions between the different municipalities was highlighted.

With regard to concrete ideas for a sustainable urban region, above all supra-regional mobility concepts such as bicycle highways for commuters, recreation and freight traffic were discussed. Furthermore, the joint coordination of resources and logistics through the strengthening of regional agriculture and the implementation of a new regional market hall as well as ideas for joint a coordination of influx and redensification were debated.

The final discussion revolved around the question of how the city region can be organized in the future and which institutions are needed to manage it. The participants agreed that one focus must be on the development of supra-regional structures that address the various fields of action along a common vision and strategy. Finally, suggestions were collected on what such structures could look like in terms of good urban governance.

Creating an intra-regional platform for cooperation
The aim of the non-partisan organization must be to focus on the interests of the metropolitan region and the common identity of the individual municipalities to develop a comprehensive vision and strategy.

Strenghtening strategic programs at the federal level
The joint refinement of a common national vision and strategy would facilitate joint decision-making

Reconsidering existing supra-regional structures
Existing structures must be examined more closely for the best possible further development.

Introducing a regional multiplier
A (new) legitimized political actor who is well connected to the local communities would allow to bring together different mayors

Creating a regional parliament as superordinate "decision-making body"
It would strengthen the cooperation of the municipal bodies at a superordinate regional level. Common themes and responsibilities would result in lead cooperation projects that set a new benchmark for European metropolitan development.

Reinforcing joint funding at EU/ federal level
Long-term funding for metropolitan development is needed so that municipalities have an incentive to work together on a permanent basis.

A model region on its way to integrated spatial development

Römerland Carnuntum

The Region Römerland Carnuntum extends over the federal states of Lower Austria and Burgenland between the cities of Vienna and Bratislava reaching up to the Slovak border and consists of 30 municipalities. It is managed by the *Regional Development Association Römerland Carnuntum* and has set itself the task of jointly bringing the region forward in terms of sustainable regional development and promoting the preservation and improvement of living conditions. The region, which is considered a model project of regional development is characterized by a rather high quality of living, as well as a diversity of economic sectors. In addition, history and the landscape areas play an important role as they serve as important places for local recreation and tourism. The *Carnuntum Archaeological Park* stands for the long Roman history in the region, while the National Park Donau-Auen or the Carnuntum wine-growing region are popular destinations for local recreation.

The Regional Dialogue took place in September 2021, in Bruck an der Leitha. When the participants—actors from local politics, planning and administration—asked what are the distinguishing feature of the region Römerland Carnuntum in comparison to other areas in the Vienna metropolitan area, the participants mainly described two aspects: On the one hand, the rich historical heritage plays an important role and, on the other hand, and the region wants to become more future-oriented. In general, the region positions itself as a recreational area, with a lively culture of associations, a strong family cohesion and diverse landscapes. It describes itself as rural yet central (urban), thus combining the best of both worlds according to the participants.

Regarding the question of concrete ideas for a sustainable urban region, the participants primarily mentioned a reorientation of tourism through the prevention of the sealing and protection of fertile soils and by rethinking nature and bike infrastructure. Additionally, the expansion of public transport by implementing new carpooling and sharing concepts as well as the restructuring, clustering and coordination of logistics for more efficiency and sustainability were discussed. Asking how such projects can be realized, the participants mentioned, among other things, the bundling of competencies and the realignment of competency and decision-making powers for regional master planning.

In the following discussion, which explored the question of how the city region can be organized in the future and which institutions are needed for this, the participants agreed that, on the one hand, existing structures for regional planning need to be reviewed and developed further, on the other hand, new supra-regional structures should be created. Ideas were then collected on what such governance might look like.

Creation of a metropolitan office for the networking of competences

The creation of a metropolitan office with an informal character and financial resources, consisting of representatives from Bratislava and Austria, is intended to bundle competences.

Introducing regional think tanks

Regional think-tanks should take new paths of supra-regional cooperation on an informal level, whereby resources should also be made available to smaller municipalities, thus ensuring distributive justice.

Announcing model regions, prototypes

The activation of model regions, in which exemplary different approaches are tested and local networks are created is to be promoted.

Initiating future councils

As an informal instrument, the future council is to carry out scientifically accompanied citizen participation to give residents more of a say in city regional matters.

Creating a metropolis of strong regions: "regional conference"

Existing conferences (SUM, BAUM, etc.) and thus competences should be bundled into a common unit in order to tackle projects more efficiently and holistically.

FROM METROPOLITAN STRATEGIES TO DESIGN SOLUTIONS

Design Studios

Städtebau TU Wien

The two design studios *MetroLab Growth* and *MetroLab Program + Delta* were collaborations between MetroLab and the *Institute of Urban Design and Landscape Architecture* of *TU Wien*, taking place in autumn 2020 and 2021. In the two three- to five-week workshops, architecture students from the *TU Wien* worked on concrete design solutions by developing strategies for the metropolitan area of Vienna and defining concepts for programming cross-border urban and rural landscapes. The proposed concepts aim to integrate concrete design solutions at the local level into a large-scale vision of Vienna's urban region and not only propose built structures, but also contain reflections on transport, the linking of different spatial units, the creation of social infrastructure and production logistics.
The results make clear that innovation in the field of metropolitan planning always touches both the "hardware" and the "software" of our living spaces.

SUPERDONAU
pixel islands

Final presentations of the *MetroLab Design Studio Delta + Program* during *MetroLab Forum #4 PROGRAM*

Design Studio Metrolab Growth

Nela Kadic—Department of Urban Design TU Wien,
Stefan Mayr & Cédric Ramière—MetroLab

In the first design studio *MetroLab Growth* architecture students from *TU Wien* defined strategies for growth of the "Zwischenstadt" on the border between Liesing in Vienna and Vösendorf in Lower Austria during a three-week workshop.

In form of mapping analysis at different scales, students developed concepts for growth, including aspects of mobility, agriculture and recreation. The methodology was to design in parallel at different scales, namely the metropolitan and urban scale. The analysis of the phenomena of the overall region allowed existing correlations and flows to be understood in order to define a strategy that could be implemented at the specific location of the urban fringe. The interventions at the local scale reacted to the context and immediate surroundings.

What is growth regarding the landscape, mobility or climate change? What is a resilient typology for growth? What kind of infrastructure supports this regional densification? The result of the workshop were six ambitious projects, addressing the task in a unique, yet comparable manner. Each proposal dealt with its own interpretation of the regional infrastructural flows, especially to enable better public transport systems and transportation of goods, integrating the agricultural sector, and showing concurrent scenarios for densifying with new mixed-use typologies.

One project was a framework for new multifunctional types, which stacked new built structures upon existing monofunctional ones. Another approach was to enable cooperative growth at different central-locations levels, applicable from the metropolitan to the architectural scale. All of the proposals enabled car-free areas, that varied in size, by upgrading Vienna's public transport system and integrating it into the metropolitan region. What the projects also had in common was the intended neglect of the administrative border of Vienna and Lower Austria, as the cooperation between administrations plays a key role in planning in such locations.

Even though the workshop lasted only three weeks, the ambitious results deserve to be shown to a broader public and should be integrated into the discussion on coping with growth, both at the metropolitan and urban scale. ▪

Scan to watch the final presentations of the students design proposals!

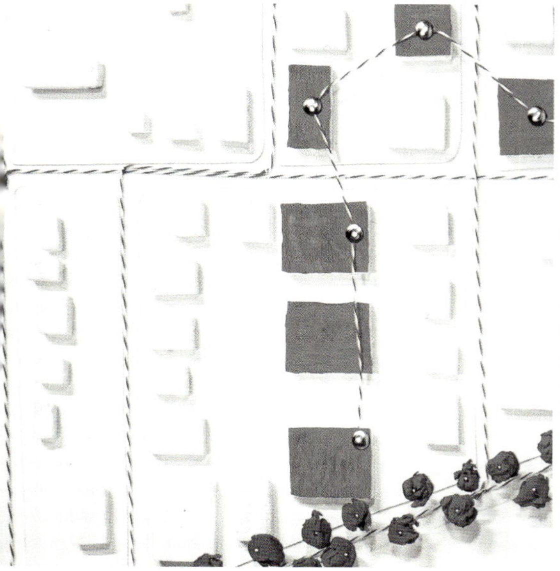

Design proposals of the students of *MetroLab Design Studio Growth*

SUSTAINABLE STACKING ON THE SUPERRING

Stefan Mayrhofer, Lea Storz & Markus Zorn

SUSTAINABILITY, LINKAGE, COMPACTNESS

This vision for growth of the Marktviertel consists of three main aspects: green public spaces, sustainable mobility and new building typologies.

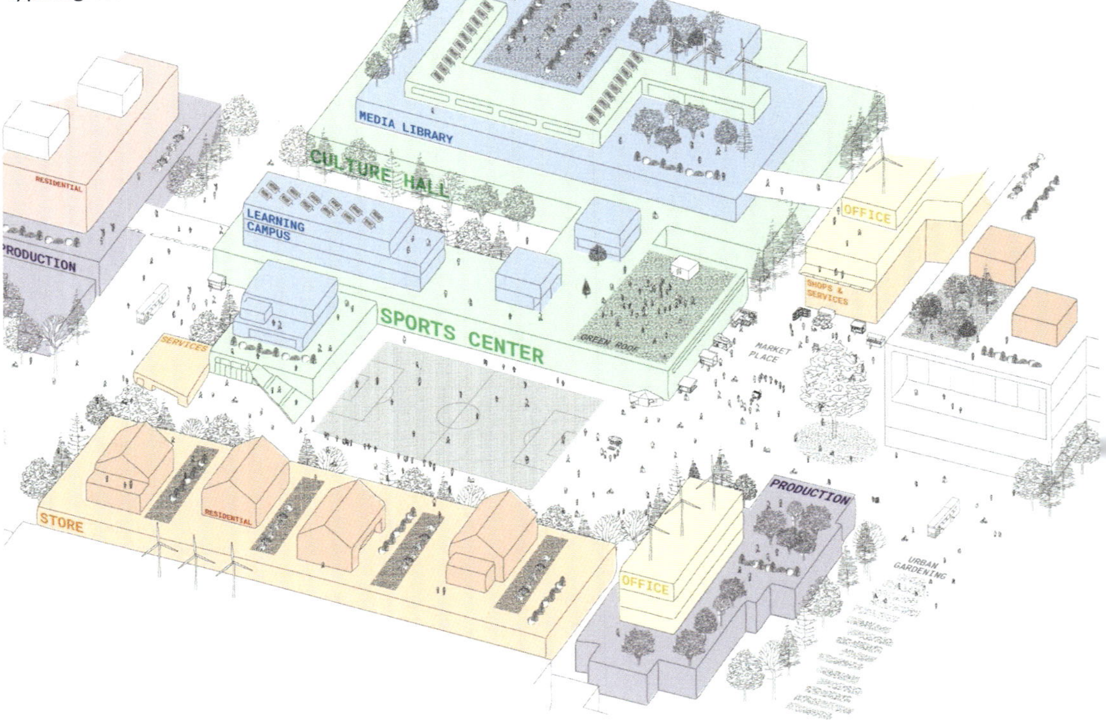

NEW CONNECTIONS

To ensure accessible and sustainable mobility, the underground line U6 will be extended to the new market area and the mobility hub. A new form of transportation, the **"Hyperloop"** will connect Wien, Wiener Neustadt and Bratislava.

SUSTAINABLE SPACES

Existing parking lots will be transformed into Green Public Spaces. The whole market-area will be converted into a car-free, pedestrian & cycling zone. Additional green areas will be provided on rooftops, which can be used for urban gardening and local food production.

COMPACTNESS

New building typologies which will be built upon existing structures to handle growth. Buildings around the market will be accessible by bridges and walkable rooftops. Such bridges can also be used to break urban barriers and link different parts of Vösendorf.

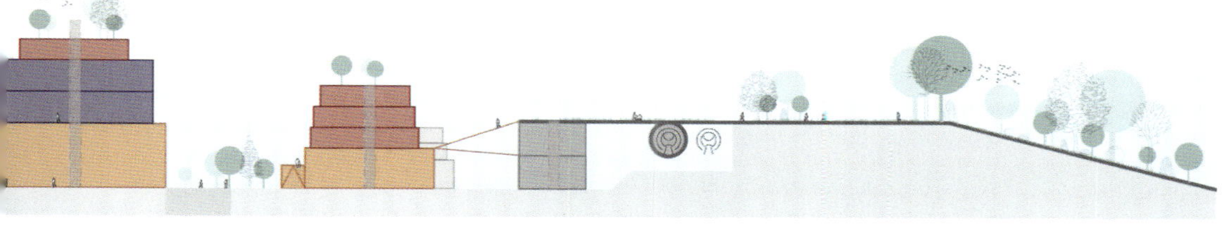

SUPERGRID

Alper Öztürk, Clemens Ferdinand Köstlbauer & Dominik Hütter

NEW AXES FOR BETTER CONNECTIONS
The concept is based on the SuperRing of the SuperWien Vision and was additionally supplemented by new axes to connect the surrounding villages and nearby cities to it. The goal is to make the SuperRing more accessible for everyone living in the metropolitan area. Also, these connecting axes should make it possible to distribute industrial, handcrafted and agricultural goods without trucks.

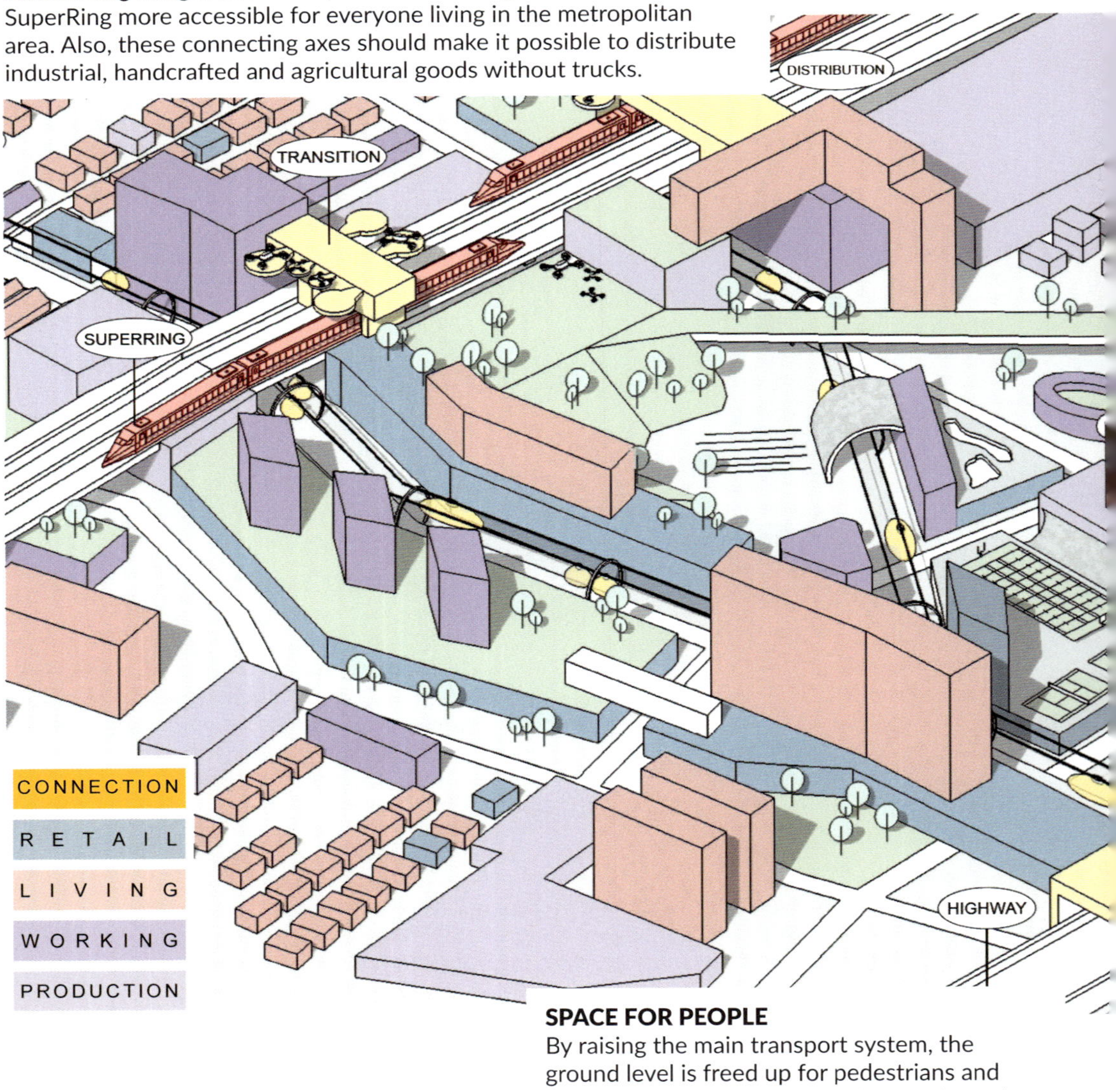

SPACE FOR PEOPLE
By raising the main transport system, the ground level is freed up for pedestrians and cyclists. The design removes the cars from the streets and gives the space back to the people.

MOBILITY GRID

The old highway route will be transformed into a climate axis where residential, office and retail projects can be located. The new system provides a grid of different mobility systems which also leads to growth of the surrounding areas because they are better integrated and connected.

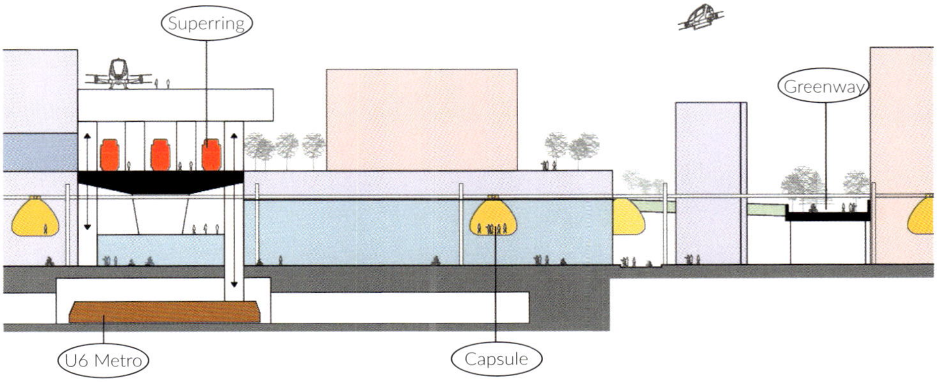

NEW URBANITY

The different layers of mobility meet each other at the Marktviertel, where a big mobile hub creates a mix of uses. It is a new kind of urbanity with highly concentrated nodes. It has a lot of potential for urban growth and and quality spaces for leisure.

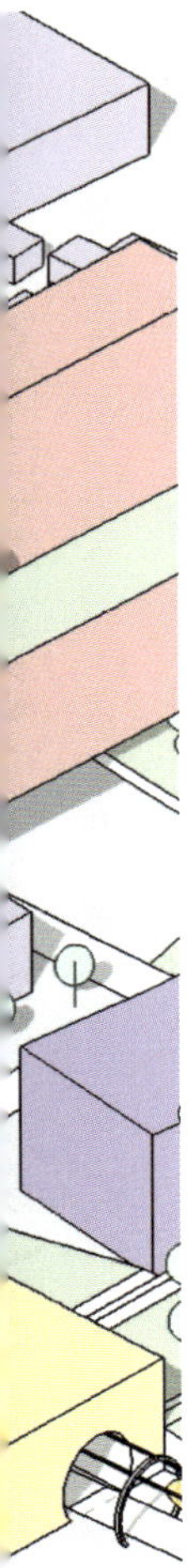

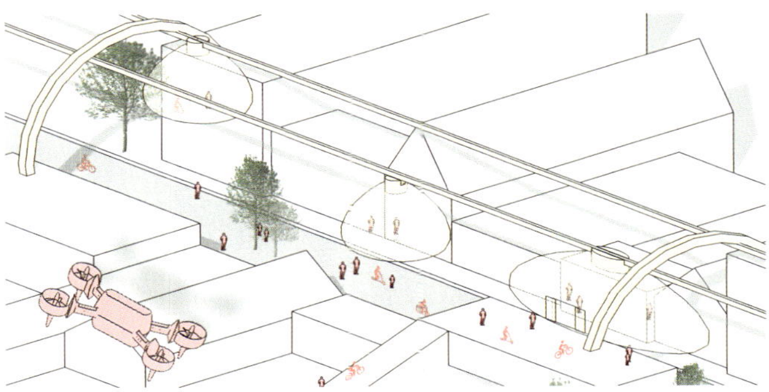

REDUCING MOTORIZED INDIVIDUAL TRAFFIC

The aim of the mobility layers is to reduce the individual motorized transport that occupies a lot of space. In the case of the fringe between Vösendorf and Siebenhirten there is a unique crossing of the A23 highway and the *SuperRing*. Since it is very close to the dense Viennese urban area the design cuts the highway transport at the mobile hub and establishes a new good connection to the *SuperRing* so that cars cannot go further.

PRODUCT OF TRANSITION

Katja Gadziak, Pamela Maldonado & Jelena Perkovic

MAINTAINING IDENTITY

The identity of Vösendorf is based on transit, production and distribution. Different central-urban levels have been examined to see how they can relate to each other while maintaining their own identity, in order to create a system for cooperative growth that is applicable from the metropolitan to the architectural level.

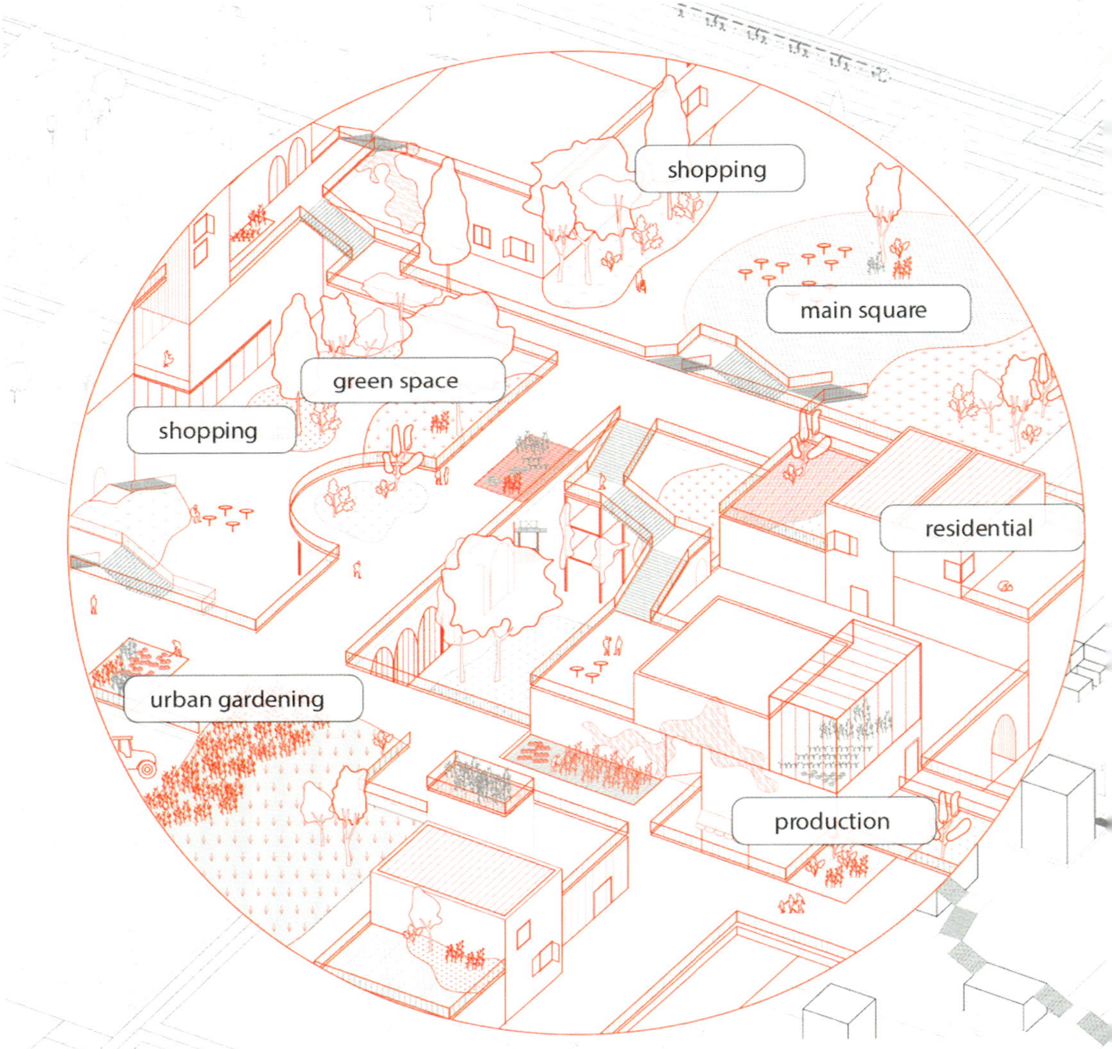

MIXED USE

This system of cooperative growth is intended to help distribute the oversaturation of equal living and working conditions throughout the SuperRing.

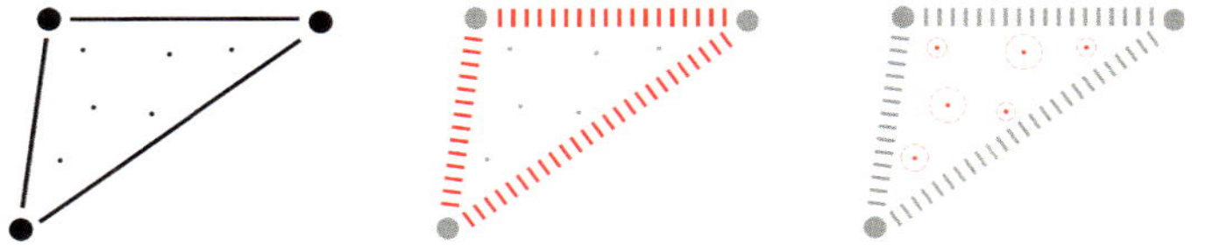

OVERCOMING BARRIERS

The (non-)physical barriers between the various designated centers in the Marktviertel with predominantly shopping and residential functions are overcome by spaces of production and green spaces.

GROWTH AS A QUALITY

Growth is understood in terms of quality. Growth and density are seen as opportunities and potential to bring new quality and well connected functions to the area.

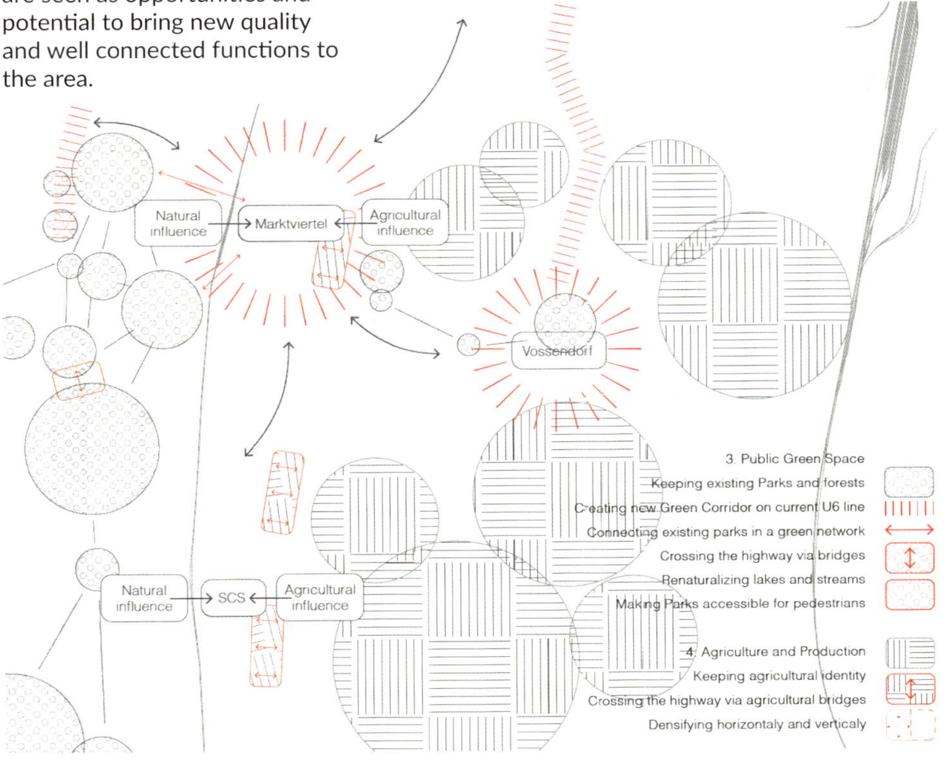

CONNECTING THE URBAN AND THE RURAL

The Marktviertel has the potential to break the barrier between urban and rural areas and create new relationships between them. It becomes a new transition area with many different functions and therefore with a high importance for the whole metropolitan area.

LAKE LEISURE LIVING

Martina Gentile & Iman Hirschman

STRENGTHENING MIXED QUALITIES
The design intends to wake Vösendorf from its deep sleep after many decades and give it new life by strengthening its qualities and making them usable again starting with the three L's: LIVING, LEISURE, LAKE. The idea is to truly reinvent Vösendorf by taking care to combine urban life with mixed use, support tourism, improve local mobility, create a new way of shopping and strengthen the community.

NEW LAKE PERSPECTIVES
The Wienerbergteich is a mountain ridge at the southern edge of Vienna. Since an urban planning competition idea in the 1980s, the Wienerberg recreation area has been located here with a total area of 117 hectares. This natural lake should now become a common place for all the residents of the area. The new development by the lake creates a "lake community living space" where mixed usages of shopping and leisure are all possible in the same area. By building a pedestrian bridge over the water, new routes open up new perspectives in the area.

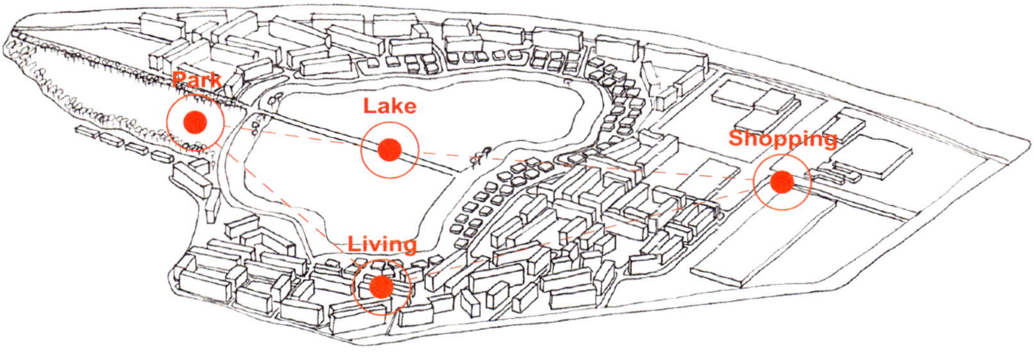

MORE SPACE FOR LEISURE

To make the entire area more accessible and user-friendly, the design creates a passageway through the highway. This will not affect car traffic and Vösendorf residents will have more opportunities to reach different areas within our urban development. Pedestrians and cyclists with their own paths around the lake will have a positive impact on residents. The beach strip leading to the lake, combined with a park, will provide many opportunities for all ages.

TERRACE HOUSES

The design combines apartments with large terrace buildings. All residential units face the now redesignated lake, at least doubling the density that now exists. The new buildings offer a diverse mix of modern housing for families, couples and people of all ages.

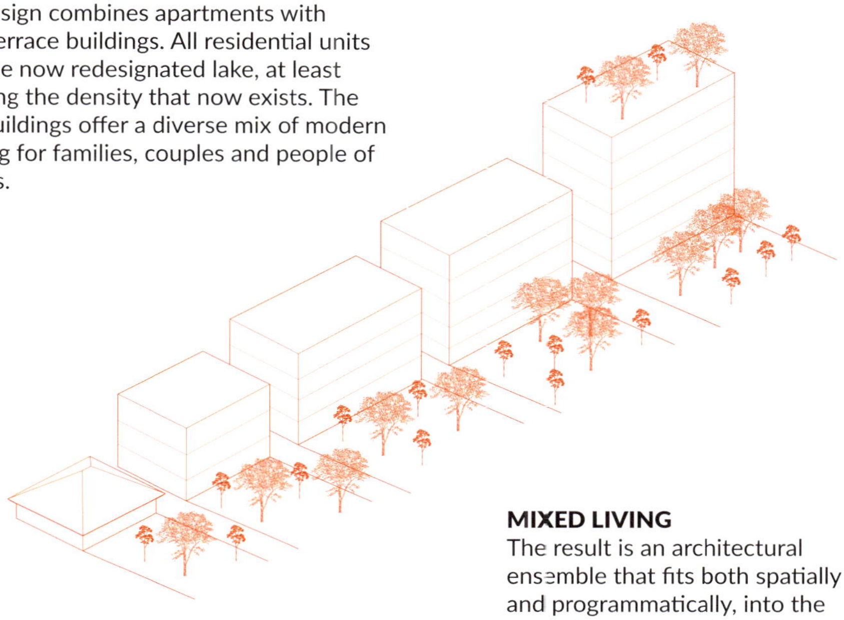

MIXED LIVING

The result is an architectural ensemble that fits both spatially and programmatically, into the new leisure concept and the lake as Vösendorf's new hotspot.

URBAN GREEN

Giorgia Bonet & Máté Milán Kresz

LIVING AND WORKING IN THE SAME PLACE

Vösendorf is a suburban area without well thought-out combination of housing and infrastructure. On the one hand, many people reside here and commute to the city for work. On the other hand, this area offers job opportunities compared to other suburban cities. This is a potential that needs to be exploited. The idea of the concept is to provide employment opportunities for the residents of the area and create a more livable city based on the human scale.

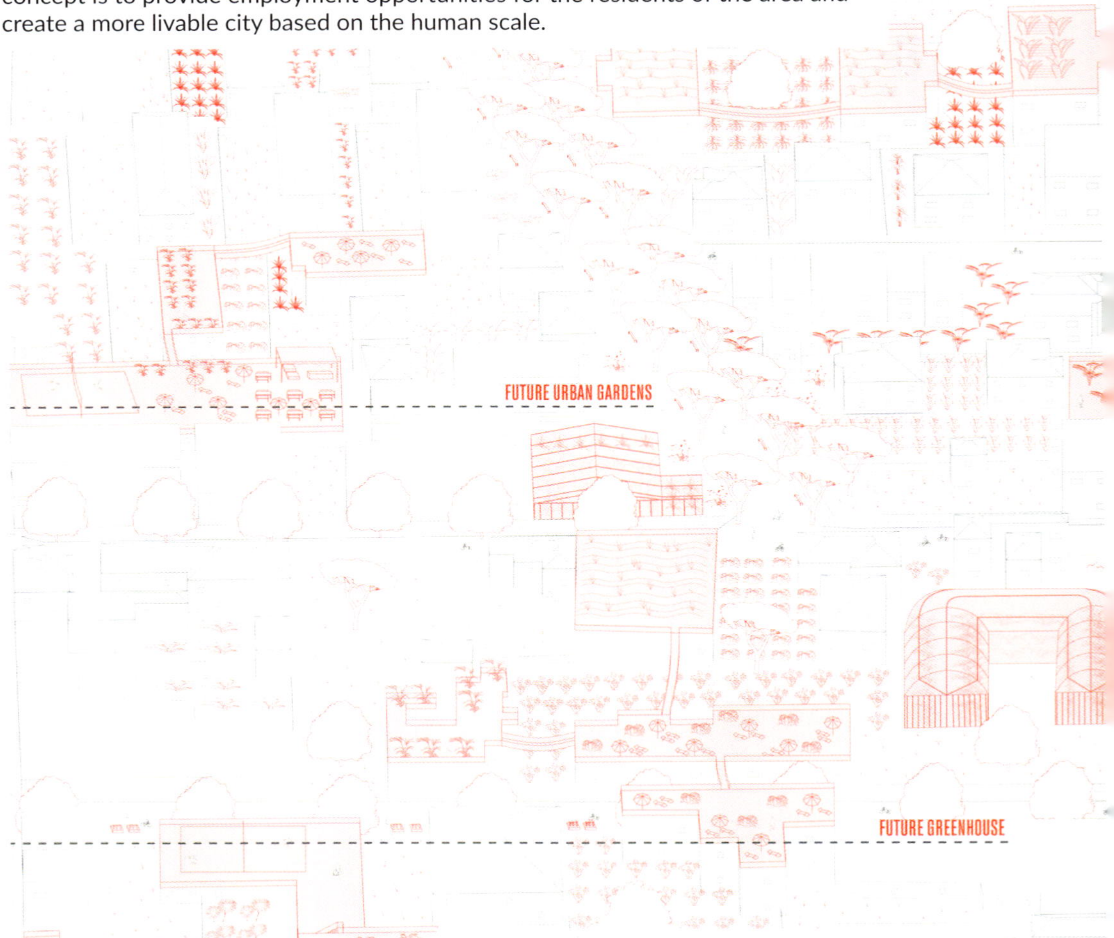

URBAN FOOD PRODUCTION

The streets are equipped with new trees and more green spaces, fundamental for this design is the creation of new urban gardens for growing own food This type of urban food production also takes place on rooftops and unused fields, where it also plays an important role for the microclimate. New skate parks and playgrounds are being created.

Current situation

Future situation

LESS CARS, MORE MOBILITY

New car-free spaces are to be created in Vösendorf, with the SuperRing linking up with the existing transport system. Cars will be stopped outside the ring with a P+R facility, and at the same time new transport connections to the ring will be connected. The idea is that the most livable stop of the whole SuperRing will be based on the multi-modal connection between the subway, the local railroad and the new train system.

MORE SPACE FOR CYCLISTS

With new cycling infrastructure and pedestrian areas, people are invited to use Vösendorf in as many ways as possible. The *SuperRing* will also connect all the cycle paths around the ring. New bike-share docks near stations are intended for daily use, such as commuting to work or grocery shopping.

A LOCAL NETWORK

Alessandro Zanin, Nikos Kouklakis & Rick Rütten

LINKING THE RURAL AND THE URBAN

The space between the cities Vienna, Bratislava and Wiener Neustadt and its old industrial and agricultural heritage could be connected with the cities and create a strong network to transport products around the whole metropolitan area. This would then create a stronger link between rural and urban production.

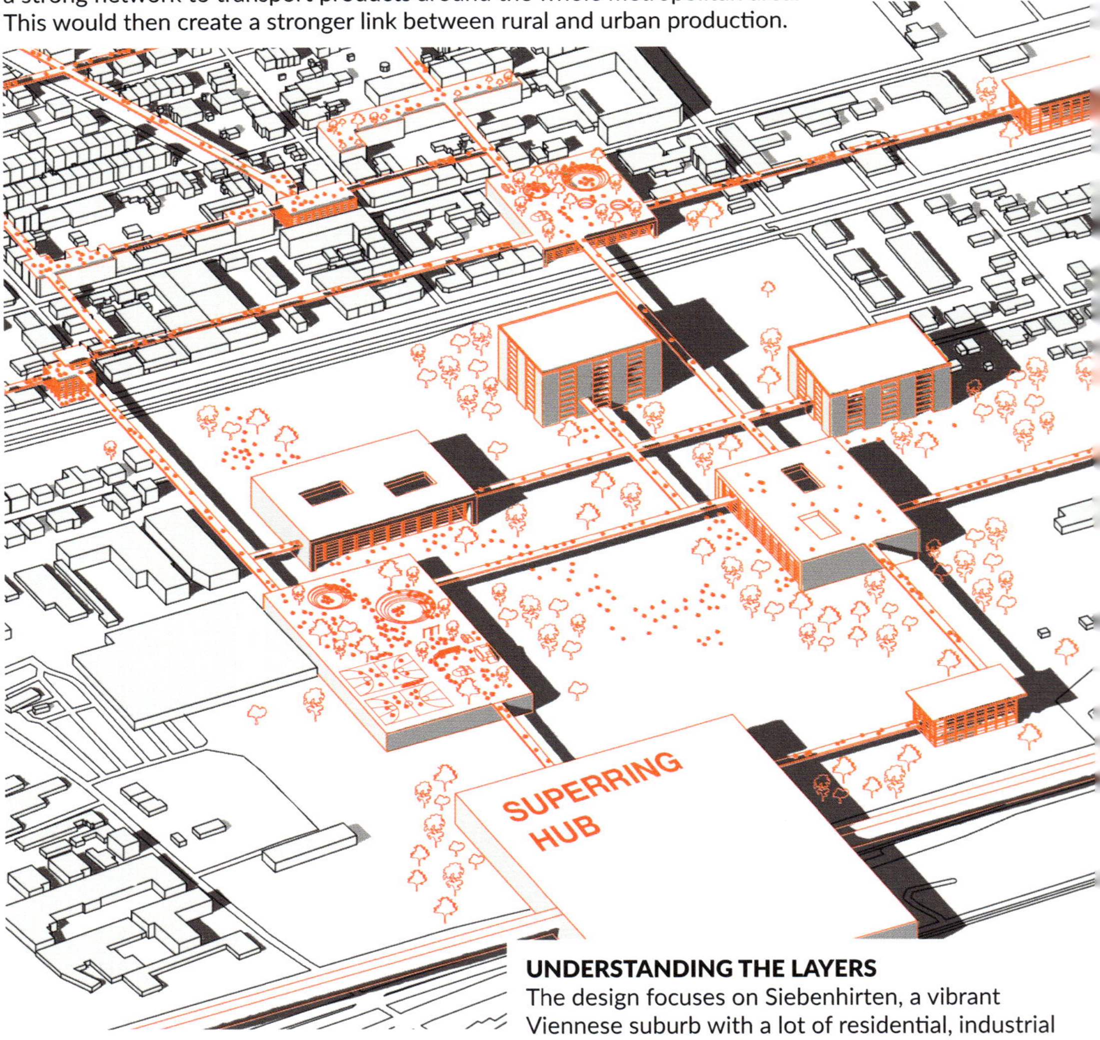

UNDERSTANDING THE LAYERS

The design focuses on Siebenhirten, a vibrant Viennese suburb with a lot of residential, industrial and agricultural zones which are strictly divided by the dominant mobility system south of Vienna. It is key to understand these layers to create a system that brings all these areas together.

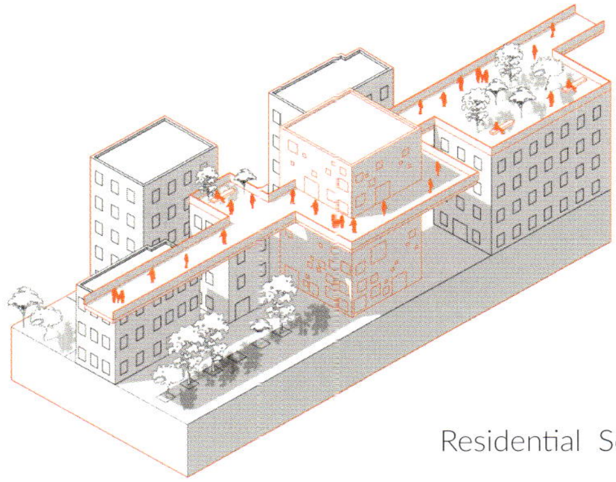

MIXED-USE

Adjacent to the SuperRing hub is the new town center with a mixed-use concept where residential, manufacturing and recreational areas interact and are connected to the existing public transportation network.

Residential Scenario

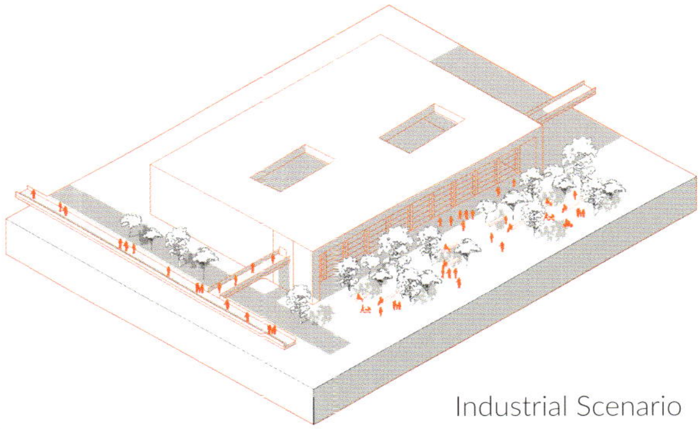

Industrial Scenario

WALKABLE CITY - "SKYWALK" SYSTEM

Our main goal is to develop a walkable city of the future, where a better flow and transition time for residents can be achieved. Our proposal is based on a network that is raised from the ground and creates a "skywalk" system for pedestrians and bicycles that is closely connected to the new SuperRing station.

Design Studio Metrolab Delta + Program

Nela Kadic—Department of Urban Design TU Wien
Stefan Mayr & Cédric Ramière—MetroLab

The second Design Studio *MetroLab Program +Delta* was looking for concepts for programming the urban and rural landscapes in the metropolitan area of Vienna. During a workshop of five weeks, the students explored strategies for the *SuperWien Metropole*, followed by spatial answers on the local scale. The focus area was defined vaguely along the administrative border between Simmering in Vienna (Simmeringer Hauptstraße, Dreherstraße) and Schwechat in Lower Austria.

After an initial site visit, students individually created visions in the form of collages. The collages were the first approach to the place and the reaction to a subjective analysis of scales, atmospheres, programs and landscapes. They described the character and context, some would be utopian, others dystopian. They transfigured, romanticized, criticized or exaggerated the phenomena of the focus area and therefore set first steps for radical concepts, that were later an important basis for the design projects. The five further developed projects were questioning increasing land consumption, mono-functionality or motorized mobility, they were implementing new programs, new forms of mobility and at the same time preserving existing qualities of the territory.

Welcome to Superdonau develops from the waterfront, tying leisure and production within the growing city between Vienna and Bratislava. A canal system enables the expansion of the delta, forming new centers, and enabling agriculture and industry next to residential areas. The project *Pixel Islands* questions the hierarchy of connections and the mono-functionality of the urban-rural fringe. The car-friendly city is transformed into an "human-oriented city" with direct connections for non-motorized transportation. At the same time, it provides space for mixed use by introducing a second layer, that is programmed with reference to the immediate context. *Re.Live* cartographically identifies the existing built and social infrastructure and different scales, preserves existing qualities, and improves the area by programming in a sustainable and subtle manner. Finally, *Delta Hub* initiates cross-border cooperation, by placing subcentres along administrative borders and *Ring Ring Ring* introduces food forests, permaculture and agroforestry to the Zwischenstadt. Working on different scales allowed us to identify the dynamics and phenomena of the territory. It revealed existing practices, flows and patterns, contradictions and challenges. The design-based approach, both on the metropolitan and local scale, enabled place-based strategies, coming from experimental concepts, yet reacting sensitively to the context, and, thus, creating innovative visions for a resilient future perspective. ▪

Final presentations of the *MetroLab Design Studio Delta + Program* during the *MetroLab Forum #4 Program*

Scan to watch the final presentations of the students design proposals!

Collages

As a warm-up task and first approach to the design area for the subsequent designs, the students were asked to present their future vision of the metropolitan region in the area of Dreherstrasse between Simmering and Schwechat in collages.

Wien
30 ZONE

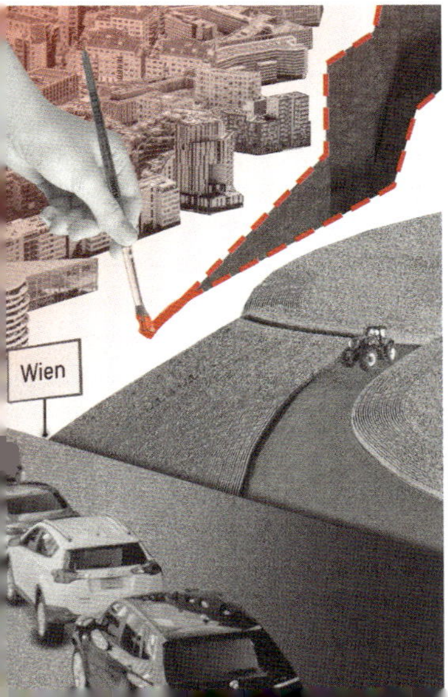
Wien

SUPERWiEN
Where does our food come from?

RING, RING, RING

Marcel Catalin Bumb, Vanessa Minhuey Espinoza and Felix Alexander Neudeck

ANALYSIS OF THE EXISTING

The border area of Simmering and Schwechat was identified as bleak, lifeless and disconnected from the rest of Vienna. Although the area is characterized by many dense residential buildings on the Viennese side, there is little to no activity in public spaces. We propose the following four interlinked measures to counteract these issues and thereby seek to create more lively and sustainable public spaces.

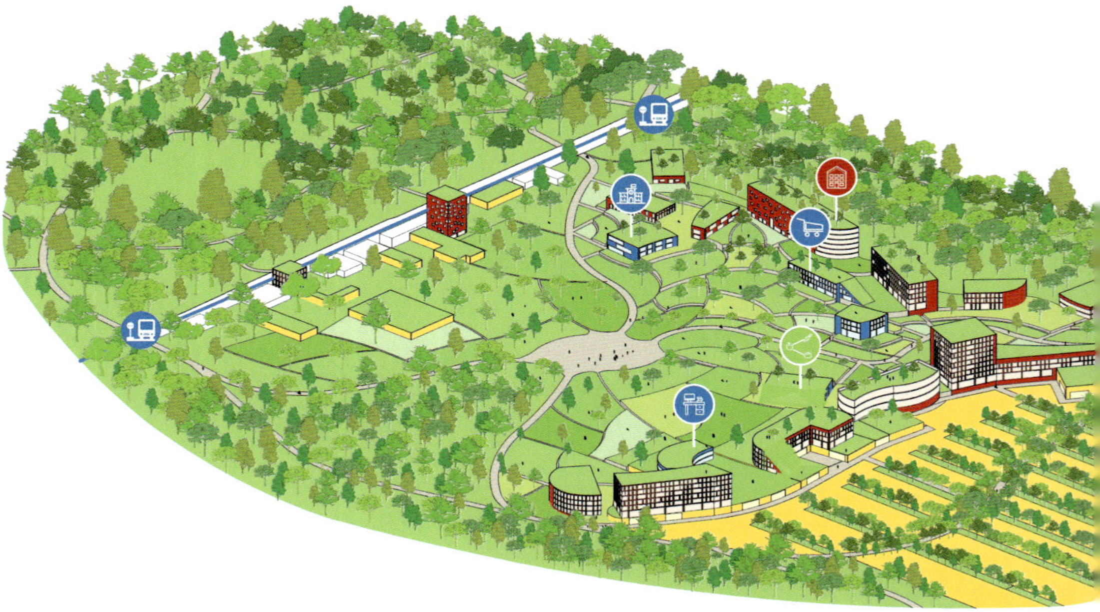

CONNECTING THE GREEN

Even though there are green open spaces in the form of urban agriculture on the side of Lower Austria, they appear lifeless due to monocultures and conventional agriculture principles. Linking existing and reclaimed green areas in accordance with the STEP 2025.

CONNECTING THE PEOPLE
Create new centers in form of rings, including existing structures and linking them with each other and the city through green corridors. People are being attracted to nature with food forests and recreation areas.

A GREEN RING AROUND VIENNA - STEP 2025

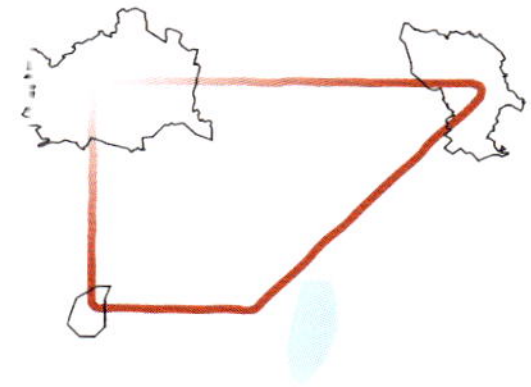
THE SUPERWIEN RING: VIENNA - BRATISLAVA - NEUSIEDLERSEE WR. NEUSTADT

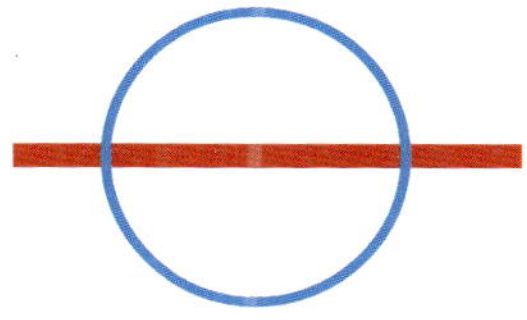
NEW URBAN CENTERS ALONG THE SUPERWIEN RING

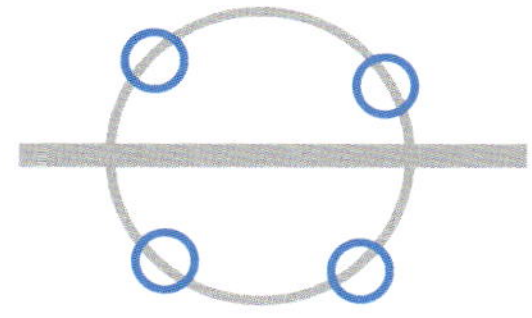
RINGS OF BUILDINGS MAKE UP THE CENTERS

CHANGING AGRICULTURE
Conventional agriculture practices are inefficient in their use of space and have negative effects on ecosystems. We propose to make agriculture more diverse, sustainable and space efficient with new innovative agriculture principles which are: Food Forestes, Permaculture and Agroforestry

FOOD FORESTS: high density food, low maintenance, public

PERMACULTURE: high density food, high maintenance, private

AGROFORESTRY: medium density food, medium maintenance, semi public

EXPLODING CONCRETE
Reclaim unused and unattractive spaces as well as spaces that will become obsolete in the future, recreate fertile soils and make them green. Instead of concrete there will be space for blue and green infrastructure, nature, food production and leisure.

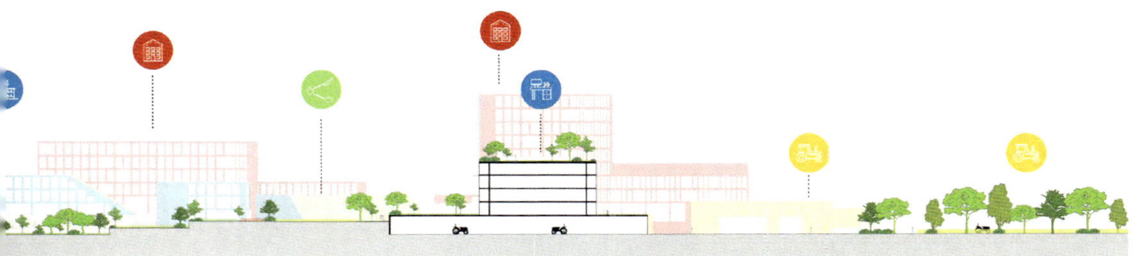

RE·LIVE

Sara Borjanovic, Angelica Pedrotti and Ilia Verzakov

STRENGTHENING CONNECTIONS, CREATING ATTRACTIVE ACTIVITIES
The metropolitan scale strategy of this design aims to control the growth of the cities, improving and preserving the existing and designing the new in a sustainable way. The strategy is based on three main points: the creation of new nodes, the improvement of the connections between cities and villages and the creation of new attractive activities

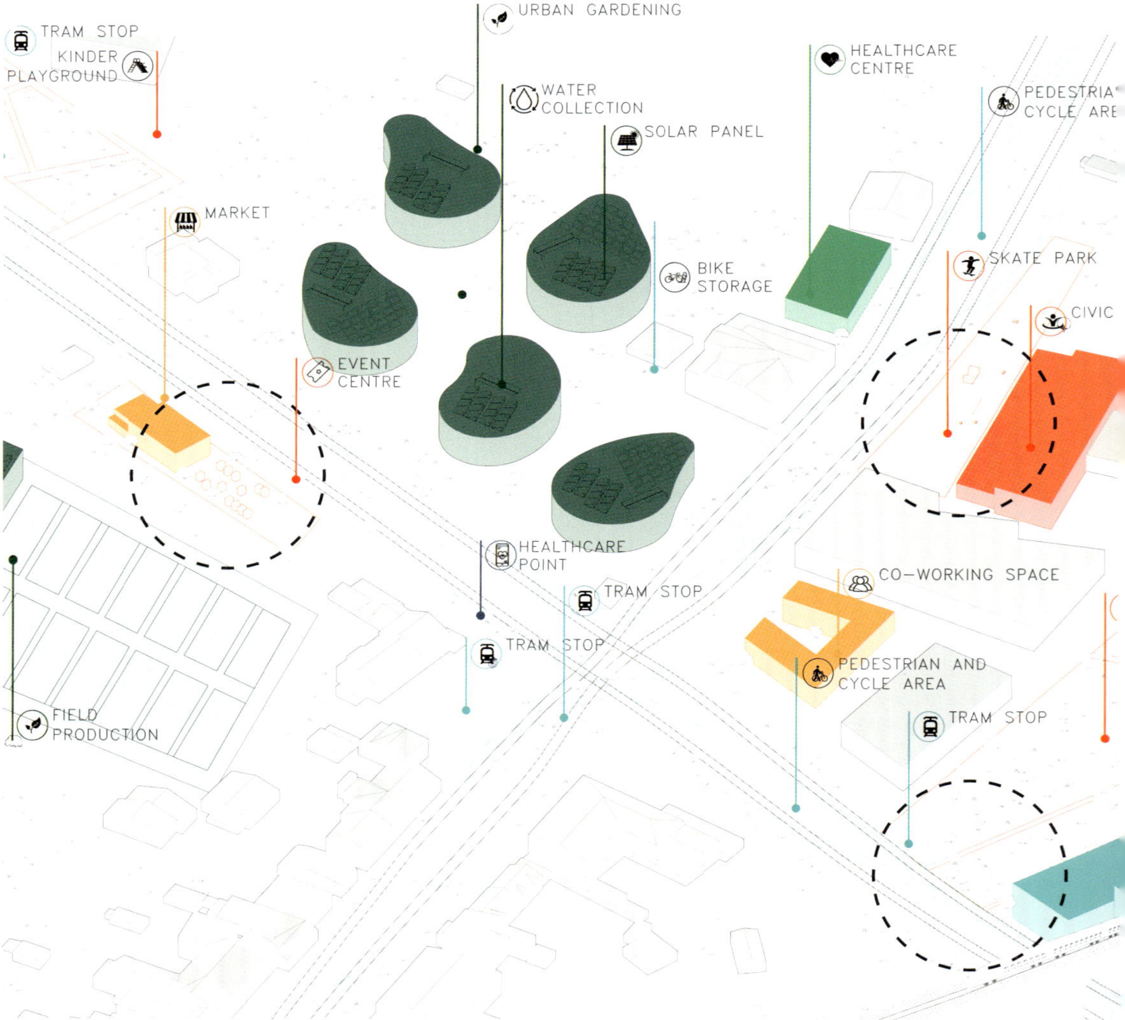

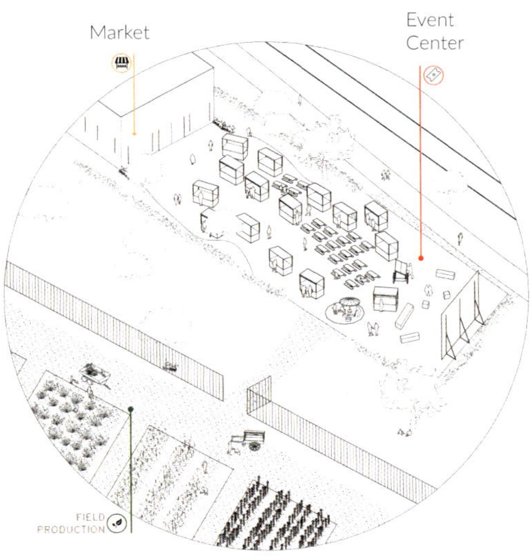

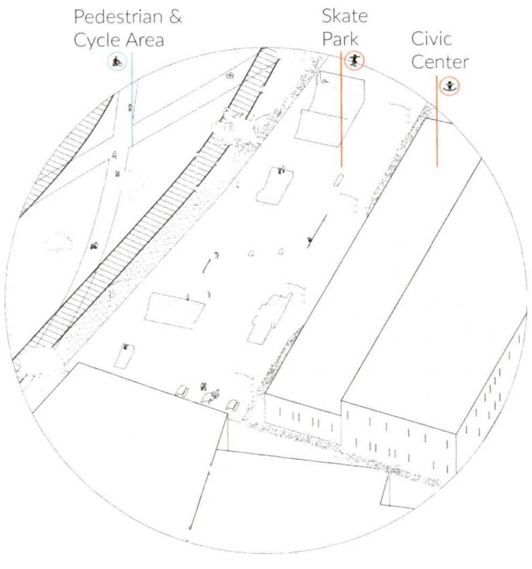

NEW ACTIVITIES, NEW NODES

Different radiuses were established for each of the major activities identified, such as work, leisure, health, education, and production, to determine where they should be present and then to add new activities in spaces where they are not. Based on these criteria, the new nodes could be created.

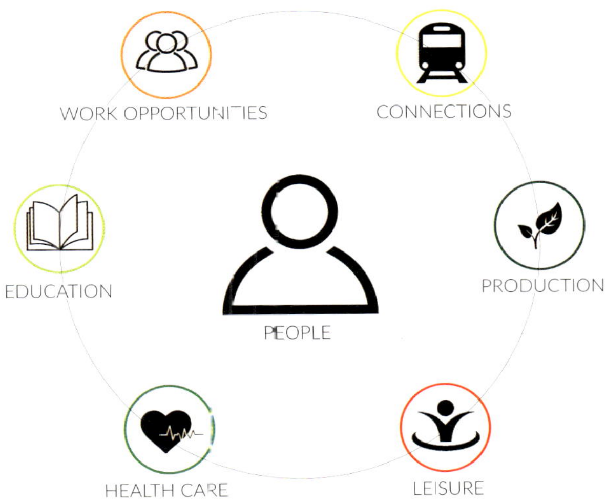

NEW NETWORKS

All the new nodes are being connected with new green infrastructure and public transportation routes. By this way, new networks between towns and villages, as well as between the villages themselves are created which helps to control the growth of towns in rural areas. Additionally, new pedestrian and cycling lanes as new car-free connections routes are created.

THE LOCAL SCALE

Bringing the strategy back to the local scale, a new attractive node along Dreherstraße is created. New activities and infrastructures are added such as productive areas, healthcare buildings, co-working spaces, educational centers and new public spaces as well as new green infrastructure connections.

SUPERDONAU

Amanda Immler, Paulína Slivková and Katharina Stell

CONNECTING NATURE AND THE CITY

The concept of SuperDonau focuses on what was once set outside the cities: Nature on the one side, because it has not been seen as part of the city, and industry on the other side, because it has been seen as dirty, loud and ugly. The process of connecting Vienna and Bratislava opens new opportunities to reconnect natural and human productivity and re-think the growing city.

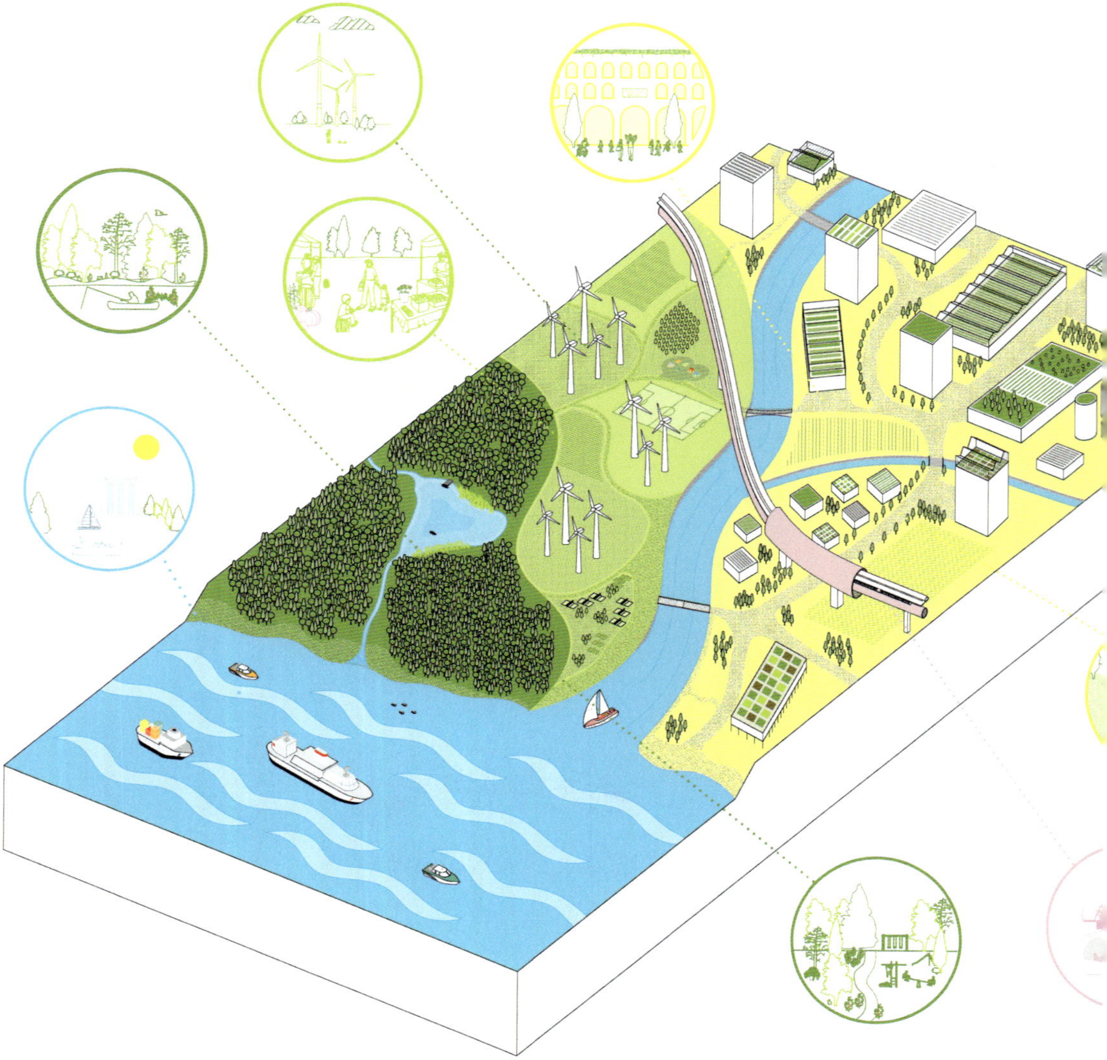

AGRICULTURE, INDUSTRY AND HOUSING

The main idea is the inclusion of productivity. Unlike Vienna, Superdonau focuses on mixing agriculture, industry and housing. The Danube is not only used as a place for recreation and natural cooling but is instead set back in the city center and reintegrated as a traffic route.

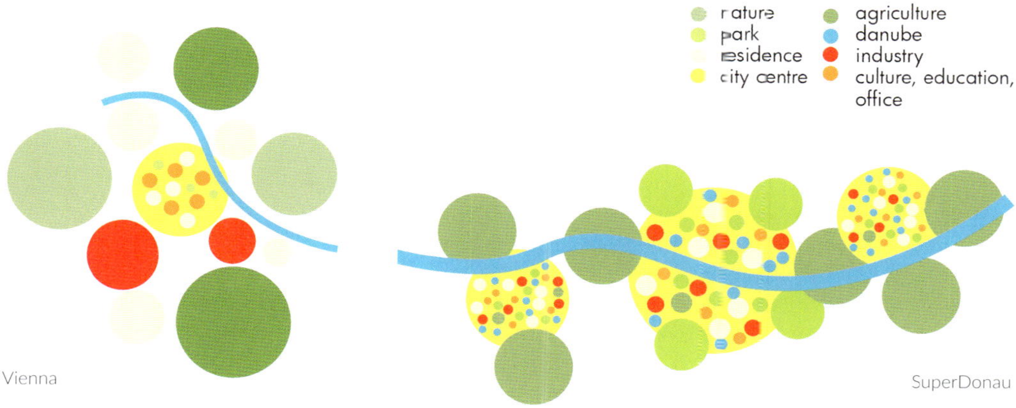

NEW NETWORKS

The network develops from the existing natural situation, widening given side rivers and opening up new canals and paths and therefore create a super delta. The new centers evolve from the Danube and spread through all layers, always being connected through the supply network and the Danube.

THE DANUBE AS A CONNECTOR

Evolving from the Danube, like historically grown city structures, Superdonau develops from the waterfront, mixing wild nature, parks and a new supply network to the growing, more dense and mixed-programmed city centers. The Danube spreads as a connector over the whole region and reinforces its quality for the city.

LOCAL AND SUSTAINABLE PRODUCTION

The different layers bring back local and sustainable productivity to the inhabitants of the metropolis. Agriculture and manufacturing are visible in every layer of the city, in different forms and scales, from hands-on self-farming to big industries. The supply system and the Danube break through the layers and connect the centers, the water and nature.

PIXEL ISLANDS

Julius Bartz, Jumi Radde and Theresa Steiner

CITIES OF THE PAST

There were two fundamental factors driving the design: first, over the past 70 years, cities have been planned primarily for cars rather than pedestrians or cyclists. Second, mono-functional urban areas have formed in the cities of our time, making space available primarily to a single type of use. The opportunity for a healthy mixture of our living environment in the sense of the city of short distances has been missed.

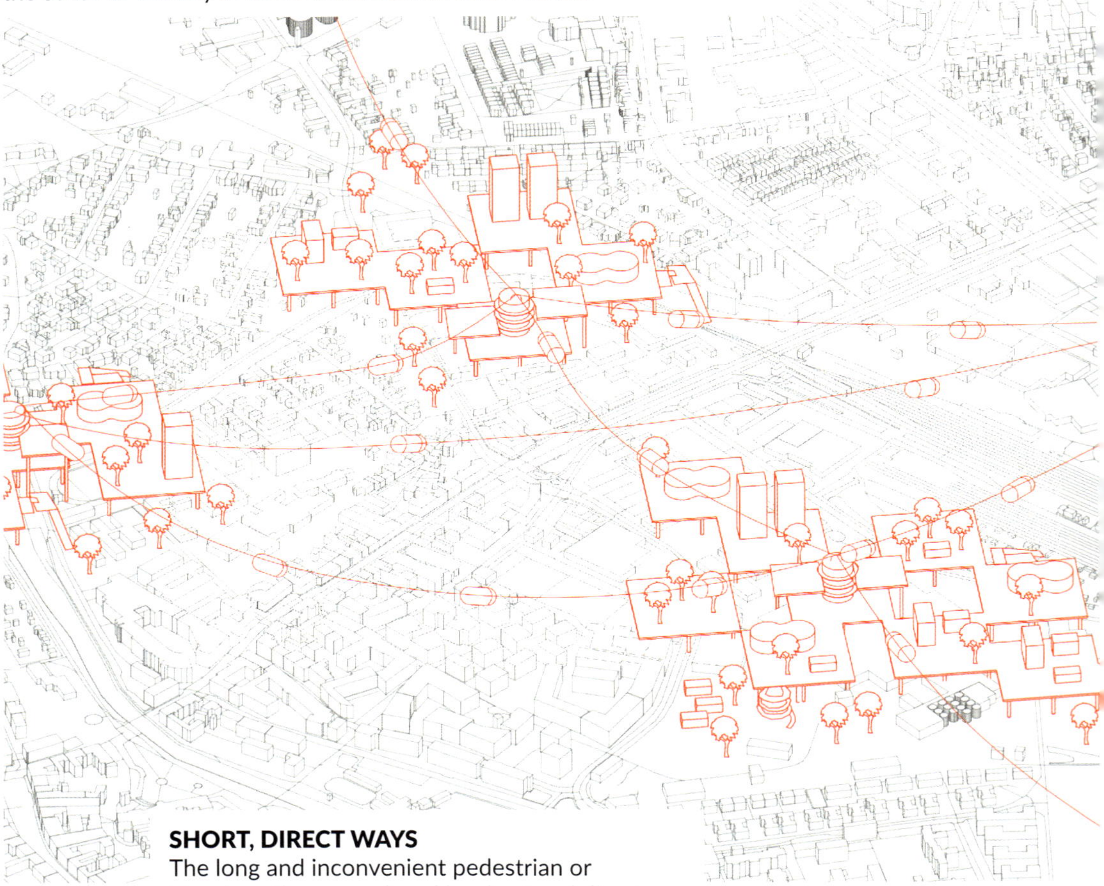

SHORT, DIRECT WAYS

The long and inconvenient pedestrian or bicycle paths are replaced by short and direct connections to the required functions. This leads to a drastic reduction of car traffic and the recovery of a lively urban space.

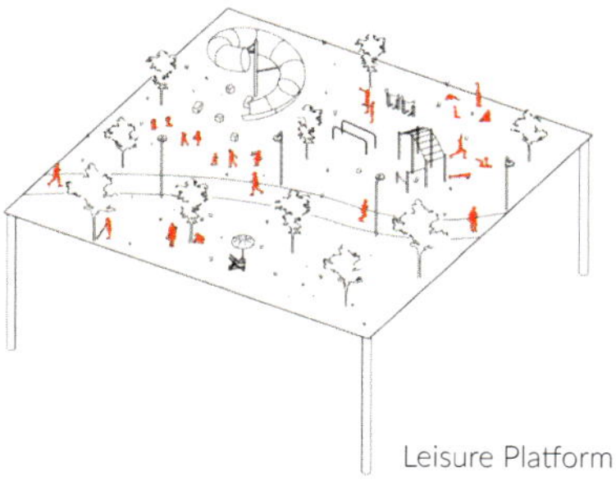

Leisure Platform

BETTER CONNECTIONS

In order to achieve better connectivity within the district and to improve the interregional connection of the residents, all "Pixel Islands" will be connected to each other by means of a cable car, which will subsequently also be linked to the "Superring".

THE SECOND LAYER OF PIXEL ISLAND

The concept of "Pixel Island" is to create an urban area with mixed functions and to connect them in a new way. The focus is on non-motorized transport systems. As a potential building site for these interventions, we see the possibility to implement a second layer above the current street level.

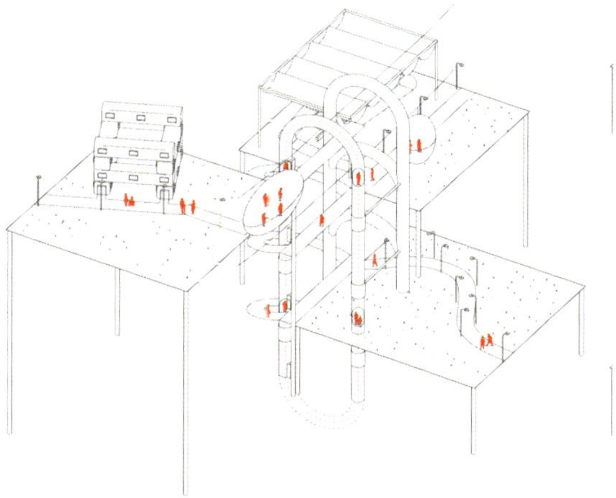

Transport Platform

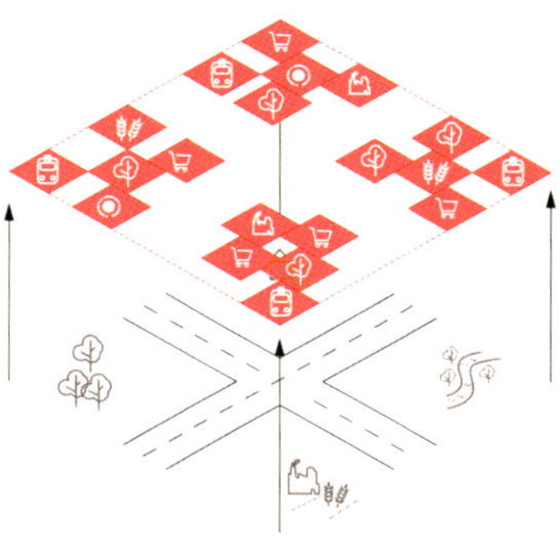

MIXED USE

This second layer will be programmed with reference to the context in which it is located. By docking meaningful functions directly to the evolved monostructural neighborhoods, a mix of uses is created in conjunction with high quality public spaces for all equally considered user groups.

DELTA HUB

Ekaterina Mihaylova and Michal Vitcovic

GREEN INFRASTRUCTURE AND RENEWABLE ENERGY

Considering the increasing consumption of land and the challenges related to the climate crisis, the project aims to preserve and create green infrastructure and at the same time create a new urban center with mixed use. In this way, the project addresses sustainability, climate change, uncontrolled growth and new demands for mobility in the outskirts of city.

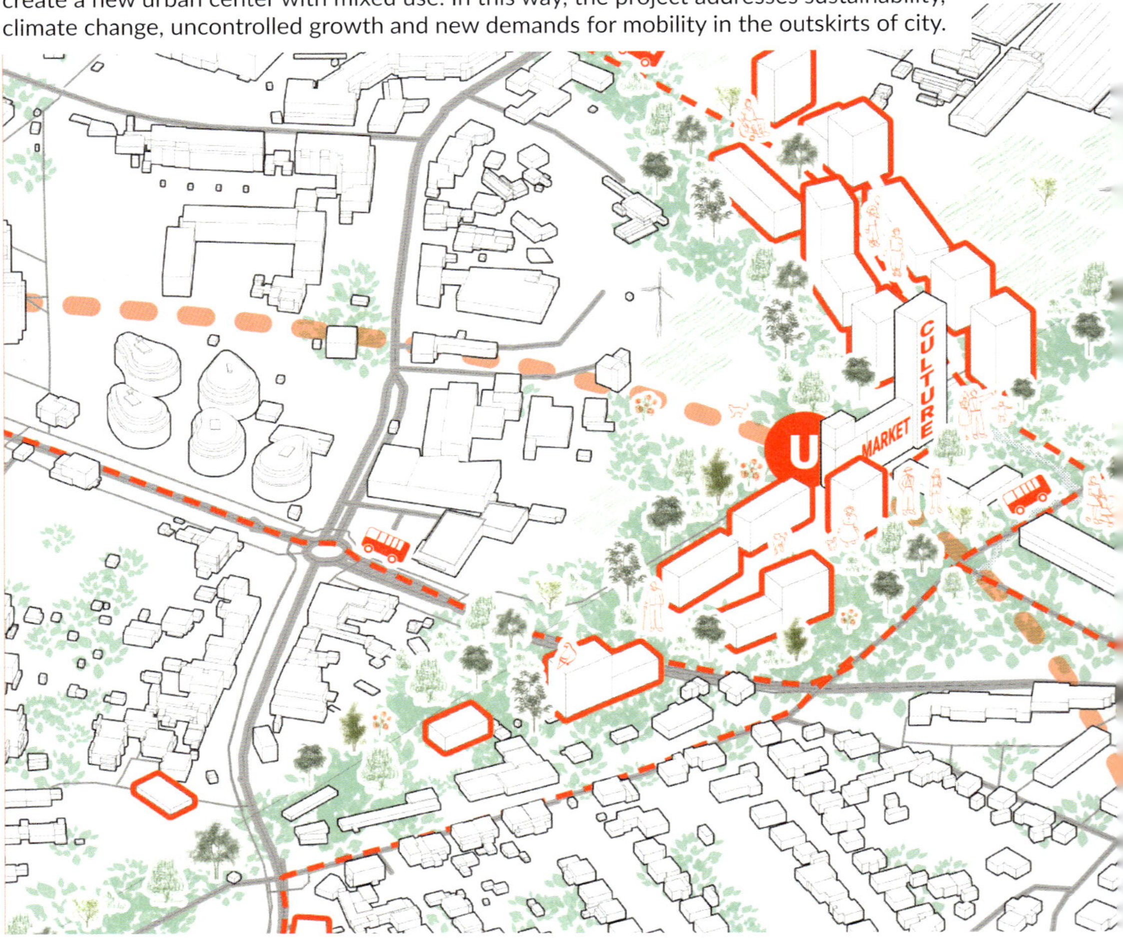

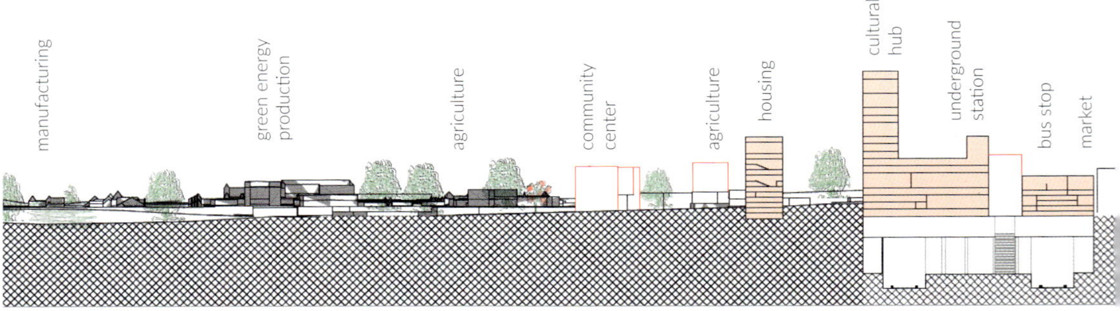

A NEW LIVELY URBAN CENTER

The missing functions on site are integrated in so-called downtown of Dreherstraße. The proposal transforms the void between two administrative units into a local urban center. There are many new functions that make the place a lively metropolitan area: Cultural sites, organic markets, playgrounds, green gas stations, rooftop gardens, vertical agricultural facilities. It contrasts with the defoliated neighborhood and in such manner boosts the development of the surroundings.

NEW CONNECTIONS AND NETWORKS

A connection to the main subway line to the airport is provided near the old loaves' factory while at the same time the local public transport network is reconnected.

SUSTAINABLE ENERGY PRODUCTION

Additionally, renewable resources—biomass-, solar-, geothermal-, wind- and hydro energy—are implemented to create a resilient metropolitan area. Additional facilities for the production of renewable energy will be added to the existing ones.

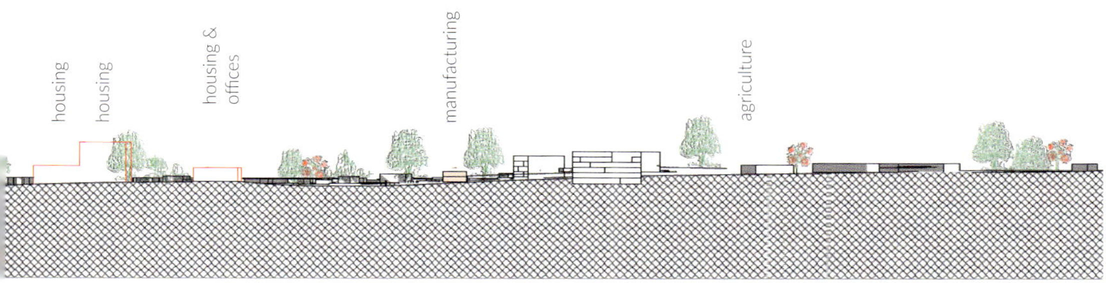

COMMUNITY

Contributors

Wolfgang Andexlinger
Head of the Office for Urban Planning, Urban Development and Integration, City of Innsbruck

Alina Bärnthaler
Junior Urban Planner & Socioeconomist, MetroLab

Herbert Bartik
Head of Department Quarters & Real Estate Urban Innovation Vienna

Joan Caba
Senior Urban Planner at the Urban Planning Department of Àrea Metropolitana de Barcelona (AMB)

Antonella Contin
MSLab Coordinator, Department of Architecture and Urban Studies (DAStU), Politecnico di Milano

Hélène Coussedière
Architect and Landscape Designer at the Landscape Agency BASE

Eva Czernohorszky
Director of Technology Services, Vienna Business Agency

Anna Detzlhofer
Managing Director, DnD Landschaftsplanung

Floridea Di Ciommo
Transport Analyst, Co-Director cambiaMO|changing Mobility, Madrid

Alexandre Di Cocco
Project Manager in the Strategy and Innovation Department of the Société du Grand Paris

Lena Diete
Junior Urban Designer, MetroLab

Marek Dinka
Division of Spatial Planning, Bratislava City Administration

Melanie Dobernigg-Lutz
Austrian Association of Cities and Towns

Michel Duchène
Former vice-president of Bordeaux Métropole, Author

Flora Fessler
Urban Designer, Research Engineer at AIT Austrian Institute of Technology, former MetroLab

Christoph Fink
Metropolitan Cooking, Vienna

Yvonne Franz
University Assistant, Department of Geography and Regional Research, University of Vienna

Gerald Franz
Urban Development & Mobility, Urban Innovation Vienna

Siri Frech
Landscape Architect, Raum+Strategie - Office for Coproductive Urban & Rural Development; Neuland gewinnen e.V.

Paul Gerretsen
Architect, Urban and Regional Planner, Director of Deltametropolis Association, Rotterdam

Vanessa Giolai
Architect, Urban Foot Atlas Vienna

Peter Görgl
Post-doc at the Institute for Geography and Regional Research at Universität Wien, Modul5 GmbH

Jérôme Goze
Chief Executive Officer, SPL La Fabrique de Bordeaux Métropole (La Fab)

Raphaela Graf
Managing Director of VIENNA REGION Marketing GmbH, Location Marketing at the Business Agency Burgenland

Andreas Gugumuck
Farmer & Entrepreneur, Future Farm

Mara Haas
Urban Planner, future.lab Research Center TU Wien, former MetroLab

Andreas Hacker
Manager SUM South, Metropolitan Area Management Vienna/Lower Austria

Kurt Hofstetter
Senior Coordinator, International Building Exhibition Vienna (IBA_Wien 2022)

Nela Kadic
Senior Lecturer, Institute for Urban Design, TU Wien

Helga Kromp-Kolb
Chairwoman of the Climate Change Centre Austria, University of Natural Resources and Applied Life Sciences Vienna

Michaël Leymarie
Urban Planning Expert in Mobility and Transportation Infrastructure, ADP Ingénierie, Paris

Roland Krebs
Urban and Regional Planner ZT, Co-managing Partner superwien urbanism, co-founder of MetroLab

Pia Kronberger-Nabielek
Spatial Planner and Analyst, PBL Netherlands Environmental Assessment Agency

Kersten Nabielek
PBL Netherlands Environmental Assessment Agency, Department of Spatial Planning and Quality of the Local Environment

Philipp Loidolt-Shen
Azolla Ecosystems, Vienna

Vincent Neumayer
Project Manager, Multi-modal Mobility Management, Wiener Linien GmbH

Daniel Löschenbrand
Architect, Urban Foot Atlas Vienna

Markus Nollert
Co-owner of urbanista.ch and co-director of the Spatial Transformation Laboratories at ETH Zurich

Thomas Madreiter
Planning Director of the City of Vienna Planning Department

Javier Ortigosa
Mobility-Urban Planner & Transport Researcher at Àrea Metropolitana de Barcelona (AMB)

Anna Mayerthaler
Team Coordinator ÖBB 360° - Mobility & More Program

Volkmar Pamer
Architect and Urban Planner, MA 21 A – City of Vienna

Stefan Mayr
Architect ZT, Co-managing Partner superwien urbanism, co-founder of MetroLab

Daniela Patti
Architect and Urban Planner, Co-founder of Eutropian Research & Action

Mathias Mitteregger
Project Manager AVENUE21 future.lab Research Center, TU Wien

Gilles Pinson
Professor of Political Science at Science Po Bordeaux

Elke Mittmann
Lecturer École nationale supérieure d'architecture de Strasbourg, director Maison de l'architecture Centre-Val de Loire

Cédric Ramière
Architect DPLG, Co-managing Partner coco architecture, co-founder of MetroLab

Judith Recio Heredia
Architect and Urban Planner, URBACT-RiConnect, Àrea Metropolitana de Barcelona (AMB)

Johannes Suitner
University Assistant at the Urban and Regional Research Department of TU Wien

Christa Reicher
Professor and Chair of Urban Planning and Design at RWTH Aachen University

Paraskevi Tarani
Architect and Urban Planner, RiConnect, Major Development Agency Thessaloniki

Michael Rosenberger
Urban Development and Urban Planning, Urban and Regional Development Unit - City of Vienna

Gregory Telepak
Speaker Mobility, MA 18 - City of Vienna

Claudia Staubmann
Architect DETSV, Co-managing Partner coco architecture, co-founder of MetroLab

Iván Tosics
Urban Sociologist, Metropolitan Research Institute, Budapest

Bernhard Steger
Head of Department for District Planning and Land Use, MA 21 A – City of Vienna

Janin Walter
Spatial strategist and freelance artist, Technical University of Berlin

Christina Stockinger
Project Manager Regionalpark DreiAnger, MA 18 - City of Vienna

Renate Zuckerstätter
Manager SUM South, Metropolitan Area Management Vienna/Lower Austria

Many thanks also to: Viktoria Bayer, Irene Bittner, Eliette Felkel, Martin Heintel, Andrés Kilstein, Florian Lorenz, Karoline Mayer, Anna Majoral, Ramon Munoz-Raskin, Levente Polyak, Michael Reindel, Oliver Ressler, Marlene Rutzendorfer, Manuel Torresan, Viktor Vogler and to all the students of the Design Studios Growth and Delta+Program as well as to all contributors to the Regional Dialogues! Thank you for your valuable input!

BIBLIOGRAPHY

Adam, Hubertus (2011): Glattalstudie—Die Gruppe Krokodil plant eine neue Stadt neben Zürich, In: Archithese, 3, pp. 64-67.

Appleyard, B. (1981): Livable Streets. Berkeley: University of California Press.

APUR (2015): Les boulevards de la métropole, une transformation engagée. Note N°96. APUR Atelier Parisien d'Urbanisme.

ARM—Azienda Romana Mercati. Sistema Agricolo Roma (2013): l'agricoltura ed il sistema agroalimentare romano verso una nuova PAC.

Barbier, E.B. (1994): "Valuing environmental functions: Tropical wetlands". Land Economics 70(2), pp. 155-173.

Choay F. (1992): L 'orizzonte del posturbano , E. d ' Alfonso (a cura ci) , tr.it., Officina, Roma.

City Planning Department of Helsinki (2013): Helsinki City Plan 2050.

Contin, A., Galiulo, A., Sánchez Fuentes, D. (2020): Tellme metrodology: Cartografía Metropolitana como herramienta metodológica de la sostenibilidad, 3er Congreso Internacional sobre Sustentabilidad en los Hábitats, ITESO – Guadalajara, Mexico.

Corominas, M. (2017): Dels carrers a la modalitat o dels escacs al parxís. Quaderns de Recerca en Urbanisme, 7, pp. 18-35.

Crang, M. & S. Graham (2007): Sentient cities: ambient intelligence and the politics of urban space. Information, Communication & Society 10(6), pp. 789–817.

D'Alfonso, E. (2000): Architettura, Milano: Mondadori.

Daily, G.C. (1997): Introduction: What are ecosystem services? In "Nature's Services: Societal Dependence on Natural Ecosystems". G.C. Daily (ed.). Washington, D.C.: Island Press.

EC, OECD (2019): The EU-OECD definition of a functional urban area. By Lewis Dijkstra, Hugo Poelman, Paolo Veneri. OECD: Regional Development Working Papers.

EPRS | European Parliamentary Research Service, Vasilis Margaras (2019): Metropolitan regions in EU cohesion policy.

ESPON (2007): Study on Urban Functions. ESPON Study 1.4.3 IGEAT, Brussels. Final Report March 2007. (Data represent 2004.)

ESPON EU (2016-17): SPIMA—Spatial Dynamics and Strategic Planning in Metropolitan Areas.

ESPON (2018): SPIMA—Spatial dynamics and strategic planningin metropolitan areas

ESPON, (2019-20): MISTA—Metropolitan Industrial Strategies & Economic Sprawl.

Eurocities (2013): Metropolitan Areas in Action - Concluding Report.

Europe1 (2016): L'équivalent d'un département français disparaît—il tous les sept ans?

European Commission (2020): Handbook of Sustainable Urban Development Strategies. European Commission, Joint Research Centre, Seville.

European Parliamentary Research Service (EPRS) (2019): Metropolitan regions in EU cohesion policy.

European Union (2011): Cities of tomorrow. Challenges, visions, ways forward. European Commission, Directorate General for Regional Policy.

Frampton, K. (eds.) (1999): Megaform as Urban Landscape. Raoul Wallenberg Lecture. Ann Arbor: University of Michigan.

Fenton, J. (1985): Hybrid Buildings in Pamphlet Architecture 11. Princeton: Princeton Architectural Pr.

Freisitzer, K. & Maurer, J. (eds.) (1987): Das Wiener Modell. Erfahrungen mit innovativer Stadtplanung—Empirische Befunde aus einem Grossprojekt. Wien.

Gerőházi, É. & Tosics, I. (2013): Metropolitan Areas In Action. Analysis of European cities. Background study for the Eurocities publication Metropolitan Areas In Action Summary Report.

Gerőházi, É. & Tosics, I. (2018): Addressing Metropolitan Challenges for the Barcelona Metropolitan Area. Lessons from five European metropolitan areas: Amsterdam, Copenhagen, Greater Manchester, Stuttgart and Zurich.

Harrison, P.A.; Berry, P.M., Simpson, G.; Haslett, J.R.; Blicharsk, M.; Bucur, M., Dunford, R.; Egoh, B.; Garcia -Llorent, M.; Geamănă, N.; Geertsema, W.; Lommelen, E.; Meiresonne, L. & Turkelboom, F. (2014): Linkages between biodiversity attributes and ecosystem services: a systematic review. In Ecosystem Services, 9, pp. 191–203.

Hastaoglou-Martinidis V. (1997): A Mediterranean City in Transition: Thessaloniki between the Two World Wars. In "Facta Universitatis", Series: Architecture and Civil Engineering. Vol.1, No 4, pp. 493 – 507. University of Niš

Herce, M. (2009): Sobre la movilidad en la Ciudad. Barcelona: Editorial Reverté.

IEA (2018): World Energy Outlook. Paris: International Energy Agency.

IPCC (2022): Climate Change 2022—Impacts, Adaptation and Vulnerability. Summary for Policymakers.

Koolhaas, R., (1995): The Generic City, Rotterdam: Sikkens Foundation.

Kunc, J et al, (2021): Size matters: Development and cooperation of municipalities in the Brno metropolitan area.

Lefèvre, C. (1998): Metropolitan government and governance in western countries: a critical review. International journal of urban and regional research, 22(1), pp. 9-25.

Lyons, G. (2015): The future of transport. Initial Perspective, Future Agenda.

Maki, F., (1964): Investigations in collective form, Washington: The School of Architecture-Washington University.

Machon, N. (2021): Urban Wastelands Can Be Amazing Reservoirs of Biodiversity for Cities. In Di Pietro, F., Robert, A. (eds) "Urban Wastelands. A Form of Urban Nature?" Switzerland: Springer Nature.

Mayr, S.; Ramière, C. (2018): SuperWien Metropole. A new Capital for Europe. Folio Verlag, Wien.

Mumford, L. (1963): The Highway and the City. Greenwood Press.

NRC—National Research Council (2004): Valuing ecosystem services: toward better environmental decision-making. Washington, DC: National Academies Press.

OECD (2013): OECD Metropolitan database.

OECD (2014): The OECD Metropolitan Governance Survey - A Quantitative Description of Governance Structures in large Urban Agglomerations.

Ortiz, P. (2014): The Art of Shaping the Metropolis, McGraw-Hill Education.

PBL (2019a): Oefenen met de toekomst. Scenario's voor stedelijke ontwikkeling, infrastructuur en mobiliteit in Nederland voor 2049. Ruimtelijke verkenningen 2019. The Hague: PBL Netherlands Environmental Assessment Agency.

PBL (2019b): Scenario's voor stedelijke ontwikkeling, infrastructuur en mobiliteit. Verdieping bij Oefenen met de Toekomst. Ruimtelijke Verkenning 2019. The Hague: PBL Netherlands Environmental Assessment Agency.
PBL (2019c): Oefenen met de toekomst.

PBL (2020): Rehearsing the future. Scenarios for urban development, infrastructure and mobility in the Netherlands in 2049. The Hague: PBL Netherlands Environmental Assessment Agency.

PDU (2019): Metropolitan Urban Master Plan (PDU) strategic proposal.

Pickett, S. T. A.; Cadenasso, M. L.; Grove, J. M.; Nilon, C. H.; Pouyat, P. V; Zipperer, W. C.; & Costanza, R. (2001): Urban ecological systems: Linking terrestrial ecological, physical, and socioeconomic components of metropolitan areas. Annual Review of Ecology and Systematics, 32, pp.127–157.

Pinson, G. (2010). "France", dans Michael Goldsmith, Edward Page (dir.), Changing Government Relations in Europe. From Localism to Intergovernmentalism, London, Routledge, pp. 68-87.

PMMU (2016): Diagnosi del Pla Metropolità de Mobilitat Urbana, Àrea Metropolitana de Barcleona.

PTPG (2010): Piano Territoriale Provinciale Generale della Provincia di Roma (PTPG).

Recio, J.; Pretel, L. & Ortigosa, J. (2018): Public Transport Accessibility Measures and Urban Planning Implications in Barcelona's Metropolitan Area. Transportation Research Board Conference, Washington D.C.

Region Köln/Bonn (2019): Agglomerationskonzept Köln Bonn 2019.

Rittel, H. & Webber, M. (1973): Dilemmas in a General Theory of Planning, Policy Sciences 4, no. 2, pp.155–169.

Rubbo, V. (2018): Looking at Metropolitan Areas as Laboratories of Metropolitan Governance. Metrex Bernd Steinacher Fellowship 2016-2018.

Rull, R.; Caba, J. et al. (2019): RiConnect Baseline study. Available from: https://urbact.eu/riconnect-baseline-study.

Schilthuizen, M. (2019): Darwin Comes to Town. London: Picador

Sennett, R. (2018): Building and Dwelling. Ehitcs for the City. Penguin Random House UK.

Shane, D.G. (2005): Recombinant urbanism. Conceptual Modeling in Architecure, Urban Design and city Theory. West Sussex, England: Wiley-Academy.

Taylor, P. W. (1986): Respect for nature: a theory of environmental ethics. Princeton NJ: Princeton University Press

Terra! Onlus (2018): Magna Roma, perchè nel Comune agricolo più grande d'Italia i mercati rionali stanno morendo. Roma: Terra!Onlus.

Torresan, M. (2019): Il bacino d'utenza dei mercati giornalieri di Roma. Quanti romani hanno un mercato sotto casa?. In Il rilancio dei mercati. Spazio pubblico, servizi comunitari ed economia circolare, edited by D. Patti, L. Polyak, and M. Torresan. Vienna: Cooperative City Books.

Tosics, I. (2013). Sustainable land use in peri-urban areas: government, planning and financial instruments. In: Nillson, K., Pauleit, S., Bell, S., Aalbers, C. and Nielsen, T.S. (eds.) Peri-urban futures: Scenarios and models for land use change in Europe. Springer. pp. 373-404.

Townsend, A. (2014): Re-programming mobility. The digital transformation of transportation in the United States. New York: Rudin Center.

UNEP (2018): Emissions Gap Report 2018. Nairobi: UNEP.

United Nations (2020): Urban Climate Action Is Crucial to Bend the Emissions Curve. UN Climate Change News, Article / 05 Oct, 2020.

Van Dijck, J.; Poell, T. & De Waal, M. (2016): De platformsamenleving. Strijd om publieke waarden in een online wereld. Amsterdam: Amsterdam University Press.

Vougias, S. (2010): The myth Thessaloniki: The Myth of the linear City.

Watts et al. (2018): The 2018 report of the Lancet Countdown on health and climate change: shaping the health of nations for centuries to come, The Lancet, 392 (10163), pp. 2479–2514.

Zammataro, A. (2020): Transactive building types for territories in transition, PhD Thesis, Politecnico di Milano. Doctoral Programme in Architecture, Built Environment and Construction Engineering, Supervisor: A.Contin, 32nd Cycle

Zukunftsagentur Rheinisches Revier (2022): Raumstrategie Rheinisches Revier 2028+:

METROLAB

RESEARCH | DEVELOPMENT | SERVICE

The *MetroLab* is a metropolitan Think Tank and consulting service for the integrated urban development of metropolitan areas and city regions. It introduces participative, integrative and creative-artistic elements and develops innovative metropolitan strategies as well as place-based solutions. Based on a co-creative and dialogue-oriented planning and design approach, it fosters not only placemaking interventions, but also the transfer of cutting-edge knowledge in creative urban planning and bureaucracy. Facing the immensity of contemporary urban challenges, the *MetroLab* works with an elaborated toolbox of metropolitan planning.

The *MetroLab* team consists of the partnering offices Superwien urbanism, based in Austria, and CoCo architecture, based in France and Austria. The joint MetroLab office in Vienna was founded in 2020.

SUPERWIEN
architecture urbanism

superwien is a studio for architecture and urbanism based in Vienna, Austria. The office supports public and private institutions in order to achieve sustainable urban change. Besides developing strategic plans, masterplans and public space projects, Superwien specialises in participatory and dialogue-oriented planning techniques from the national to the global scale.

COCO
architecture, urbanisme, *etc.*

CoCo architecture was founded in the Dordogne by French-Austrian architects in 2005. The architecture and urban design office employs new methods of practicing architecture through ambitious and varied projects all around the globe. CoCo architecture aims to be a catalyst for social change, putting environmental and lifestyle values at the heart of human endeavour. Its architecture reflects local thinking and traditional attitudes as well as modern approaches.

Imprint

© 2023 by jovis Verlag GmbH
Texts by kind permission of the authors.
Pictures by kind permission of the photographers/holders of the picture rights.

All rights reserved.

Cover: Wolfgang Lehrner & MetroLab

Editors and Co-Authors: Roland Krebs, Stefan Mayr, Cédric Ramière, Claudia Staubmann
Editorial Team: Alina Bärnthaler, Lena Diete, Flora Fessler, Mara Haas
Guest Authors: Hélène Coussedière, Floridea Di Ciommo & Andrés Kilstein, Alexandre Di Cocco, Antonella Contin, Siri Frech, Paul Gerretsen, Jérôme Goze, Pia Kronberger-Nabielek, Michaël Leymarie, Kersten Nabielek, Markus Nollert, Javier Ortigosa, Daniela Patti & Levente Polyak & Manuel Torresan, Gilles Pinson, Judith Recio Heredia, Christa Reicher, Paraskevi Tarani, Iván Tosics

Copy-Editing and Proofreading: Celene Kay-Russell
Research: MetroLab
Design and Setting: MetroLab
Photographs: MetroLab
Illustrations: MetroLab

Printed in the European Union.

Bibliographic information published by the Deutsche Nationalbibliothek.
The Deutsche Nationalbibliothek lists this publication in the Deutsche Nationalbibliografie.
Detailed bibliographic data are available on the Internet at http://dnb.d-nb.de.

jovis Verlag GmbH
Lützowstraße 33
10785 Berlin

www.jovis.de

jovis books are available worldwide in select bookstores. Please contact your nearest bookseller or visit www.jovis.de for information concerning your local distribution.

vienna business agency

MetroLab is supported by the
Vienna Business Agency

www.metrolab.design
www.superwien.com
www.cocoarchitecture.fr

ISBN 978-3-98612-011-5